FAMOUS ENGAGEMENTS
Volume II

By the same author, and distributed by Leo Cooper Ltd

FAMOUS ENGAGEMENTS (Volume I)

Famous Engagements

Volume II
MARATHON TO PASSCHENDAELE

---

by

LIEUTENANT-COLONEL
HOWARD GREEN

LEO COOPER · LONDON

*For Rudolf and Bluebell
with my love*

*First published in Great Britain, 1971, by
Leo Cooper Ltd., 196 Shaftesbury Avenue, London W.C.2
Copyright © 1971 by Leo Cooper Ltd*

ISBN 0 85052 040 1

Printed in Great Britain by Western Printing Services Ltd, Bristol

CONTENTS

ACKNOWLEDGMENTS

The author wishes to thank:

Mr. Benjamin Christopher of Ladysmith, Natal, for help in providing the photographs of the Town Hall.

The Vicars of Bosworth and Naseby, the Reverends E. R. Boston and J. W. S. Mansell respectively, for much help in the two chapters on these battlefields.

Lastly, perhaps it should be firstly, Mrs. Betty Greenwood whose typing of the manuscript has been so willing, speedy and efficient. It is impossible to exaggerate the material help she has given me.

ILLUSTRATIONS

PREFACE

This book is intended primarily for the keen amateur historian who is fond of travel. It is for those who want to see for themselves those places, so well described in history books, which seem so far away.

The amateur wants in his history not only scholarly accounts of events, trends, developments. He can find out for himself names of kings, statesmen, and generals. Records of marches, sieges, retreats, invasions are all available in public libraries. He wants more.

He wants to visit and walk over the actual site where a battle took place—the place where men such as he experienced hardship, danger, victory or defeat. He wants to see what they saw.

He wants to extract impressions of Regiments, their Commanding Officers, the men, the ground, the climate, the physical features that influenced the action.

To stand on the Timvos at Marathon, by Richard's Well at Bosworth, behind Sulby Hedge at Naseby, at Colonel Long's gun sites at Colenso, on the Canal Bank at Mons, by the big tree at Le Cateau, to look into the great crater at La Boisselle is to induct reality into those famous engagements. This book may bring life into the events of yesterday.

If the reading of this book brings half the pleasure it has been to visit the sites and write about them, the author will indeed be rewarded.

HOWARD GREEN

Craigwell Manor,
Aldwick,
West Sussex.
July 1970.

ix

Marathon

490 B.C.

THE history of Greece falls into three broad periods. Firstly, its rise from the Minoan exodus from out of the North in about 1600 B.C. which crystallised around Athens, its expansion into the city-states, and then their fusion into one state, Greece. Colonisation of Sicily, Southern Italy, the lands bordering the Black Sea, the Mediterranean, the Aegean Islands and parts of the northern coasts of Africa followed, and by about 800 B.C. the Empire of Greece stretched tenuously from Barcelona to the Black Sea, from Cairo to the Crimea.

In these eight hundred years Greece was to impose her culture on this vast territory which she had opened up. Trade always follows the flag, and by 500 B.C. an amazing expansion of sea-borne commerce within the Mediterranean and the Near East had occurred. For the convenience of her merchant adventurers, she invented coinage in 700 B.C., which gradually took the place of barter and was to become the symbol of wealth. She needed ships, men and national character to discover, invade, conquer and then colonise these territories and by her financial and material strength she ruled the world. These eight hundred years were the great years of Greece.

The second period of her history was to last for five hundred years and was to consist of several wars, large and small, to repel or punish aggressors or to deal harshly with her own city-states within her borders. Like most young things, her 'children' were finding their feet and although not demanding independence were wondering why they could not participate in the government of themselves and the Empire.

Offensive, punitive, or defensive operations against Sparta, who demanded 'recognition' of Peloponnese, Corinth, Thessaly, Ionia and Aegina were necessary, in some cases to be repeated, and the news spread round the world that the monolithic state of Greece was not entirely master in its own house, and although considered previously to be supreme, might in fact be vulnerable.

By about 600 B.C. Persia had become a great power, largely through the brilliance of her king, Cyrus. She expanded westward and occupied Asia Minor, Syria and the coast towns of Phoenicia, now Lebanon, absorbing the outposts of Greece in her stride, Several of these colonies, feeling that the strong arm in Athens was not so effective as previously, readily threw in their lot with their new masters, and Persia advanced again. Cyrus was succeeded by Darius, another great man, and under his personal leadership, Egypt, Cyprus and Thessaly were all occupied by Persia, whose Empire now stretched eastward to the Indies, westward to Cyrenaica, and from the Caucasus to the Persian Gulf. With the complete subjugation of Asia Minor in the centre of this vast semicircle, Greece, across the water, known to have troubles of her own as well as great colonies and wealth, was an obvious next step.

The Phoenicians had come out of the wilds of Asia, several centuries before the Persians, and settled in what is now Lebanon around the ports of Arvad (north of Tripoli), Byblos, Tyre and Sidon where they quickly became a sea-faring nation. They were the first great metal-workers, and building themselves ocean-going ships in these four ports, sailed far and wide in search of iron and tin. Some reached Cornwall and several of the tin mines there today owe their origin to the Phoenician adventurers. They were the first people to sail straight out to sea, out of sight of land, rather than hug the coasts, or jump from island to island as all previous sea-going people had done. The Persians found in these wonderful ships in the Phoenician ports a ready instrument to their hand for the sea-borne invasion of Greece.

In Greece there was considerable internal unrest. Athens was tired and weakened by the previous ten years of self-defence against her recalcitrant 'children'. In particular Sparta was indifferent to what Athens felt—and she was consistently resisting authority, making trouble and being awkward. Across the Aegean, Aegina, in sight of Athens, was openly hostile. Although there was no actual war, the atmosphere teemed with hatred and dislike all round, and it might burst into flame at any moment. Nevertheless, the menace of Persia, word of whose ship-building and commandeering in Phoenicia was reaching Athens, encouraged a *rapprochement* between her and Sparta, a menace that rose above the local petty differences and squabbling.

The third period of Greece's history, which does not concern this chapter, ran from after the death of Alexander the Great in 321 and witnessed the decline of her military and material strength. But the remaining three hundred years of the millenium saw the Hellenistic era, the great development of her culture, architecture, philosophy, drama, oratory and literature—the glory that was Greece.

In early summer, 490 B.C., the Persian fleet in its Phoenician ships, probably manned by Phoenician crews, sailed along the Cilician coast, and round the south-west corner of Asia Minor to the island of Samos. About 500 ships carried an élite force of cavalry and infantry. Mostly the men were Persians from the inland areas of their country, hard, seasoned, experienced, a long way from home but under an able leader, with the great adventure of crossing the water against a reputedly weakening and wealthy enemy. There were about 20,000 of them, and few had ever seen the sea before.

Darius intended to capture an island or two on his way across, and in particular, to halt, re-victual, and fill up with water at the island of Euboea.

Considerable resistance to this operation on the island was offered by the inhabitants and a force of infantry had to be landed to subdue the resisting islanders and to commandeer what was wanted. Ten days were spent in the disembarkation, operations and re-embarkation. This unexpected resistance infuriated the Persians, and after finally achieving their objective, and before sailing for the mainland, they plundered and burnt the Temples and drove inland all the inhabitants still left alive. Many of the women they took with them.

This delay enabled word to be taken to the mainland, and so to Athens, that a Persian invasion was imminent. At once the Athenians sought the aid of the virile and war-like Spartans, trusting that in the face of common danger the latter would not only rally round them but could be trusted neither to desert to the enemy nor to be faint-hearted in the presence of a great force.

Immediately the Assembly in Athens heard of the imminent landing, and without knowing where it would take place, it ordered the army of 10,000 men to march out at once to Marathon, a forced march of sixteen miles. It chose the right spot and as it passed through the mountains and descended the foothills on to the Plain of Marathon it saw the Persian fleet lying close inshore, with its troops encamped just above the beach.

The Plain of Marathon stretches along a crescent-shaped line of sea-shore, with the pronounced promontory of Cynasura at its northern end. An almost continuous chain of five low mountains girdle the Plain forming a mountain barrier and backcloth. The Plain is about six miles from north-east to south-west—and is about three miles from the foothills of the mountains to the shore. At the top end of the Plain and just short of Cynasura was a large marsh, impenetrable to cavalry and probably to infantry. Across the Plain from the foothills runs a sizable stream at right angles to the shore, the Charadra. It bisects the Plain into roughly equal halves.

The Persian fleet beached its ships and landed the infantry and cavalry between the Cynasura Cape and the mouth of the Charadra on a frontage of one mile. Moving inland for only a quarter of a mile, the force then encountered the marsh. Swinging into a gigantic left-wheel its right outer flank cleared the marsh and came up against the Charadra. This stream bed, almost dry in mid-September, is about forty yards wide, its bottom is strewn with large boulders, stones and scrub. Its left bank is about six feet high, the right bank about three feet. It forms little more than a delaying hindrance to infantry. To cavalry, however, it would form a serious obstacle and as the cavalry of the Persians formed a very considerable part of their army this obstacle became a very serious tactical consideration. The infantry then crossed the stream-bed, and took up a position with their backs to the sea, the right flank resting on the Charadra three hundred yards up from its mouth. The left flank, almost a mile away, found another small marsh on its left forming a protective feature. To complete the new picture, the Persian fleet moved down the coast and re-anchored offshore behind the new position. Altogether a nice tactical position for the 20,000 men.

Meanwhile the Greeks were sitting in the foothills around the present village of Vrana, where the track which they had followed from Athens debouched into the plain. Here, owing to the broken nature of the ground and the numberless ridges and stream-beds, they were safe from the enemy cavalry which they could see ranging over the plain. They could also see that the Persian line, re-forming in its final position, was twice their own strength of 10,000 heavily armed infantrymen, but with no horsemen. Clearly they must wait for a possible false move by their enemy. This curious position of waiting and inactivity, wherein an invading force landing on a hostile shore, and a patriotic army defending its homeland, both did nothing, seems to have lasted for several days.

The Greek army of 10,000 men consisted of ten tribal regiments, each under its own general. There was no Commander-in-Chief and each 'tribal' general took his turn—for a day at a time—to decide on a course of action. On reaching Marathon and seeing the Persians, five of these generals favoured doing nothing. Among the more aggressive five was one, Miltiades, who by great experience, and by force of personality, persuaded his four supporters to 'lend' him their day of command so that he would be Commander-in-Chief for five days—a striking example of the application of two essential qualities necessary in a leader—dominance and acceptability.

Each day the Persian Army 'stood-to', expecting an attack, while the Greeks almost imperceptibly advanced each night until they were within a mile of the still stationary Persians. To protect themselves from cavalry attacks on their left flank each night they cut down trees from the thickly wooded country around them and erected rough stockades. One night some deserters from the Persian Army approached the stockade, and passed a message—'The cavalry are away'.

Miltiades, still in his five-day period of command, acted at once. The Greek Army was deployed into line of battle and three great wings were formed, the outer ones being much stronger than the centre, the intention being to overlap the Persian flanks. At dawn the Greek line advanced rapidly across the gently sloping plain, and when within arrow-range charged at the double. On the two wings the heavily armed Greek infantrymen, with their longer spears, routed their opponents and very soon had almost surrounded their wings. In the centre, however, this thin Greek line was attacked by the strong Persian centre which advanced a considerable distance. Thus both sides had their rear seriously threatened.

The two Greek wing attacks now turned inwards and attacked the Persian rear elements, a movement that so greatly embarrassed the Persians that they recalled their advanced middle wing into the centre of the conflict. A mêlée ensued.

All ideas of formation or cohesion or plan were given up by both sides and an interminable series of little individual fights developed all over the field.

The move of the Persian/Phoenician fleet from its first anchorage near the Cynasura to the second one behind the new infantry position across the Charadra was, prima facie, an obvious one. It preserved the principle of concentration. But it showed the Persian infantry, formed up for battle only 300 yards inland, an easy way out. It suggested that there might be an alternative to victory—defeat, retreat, and re-embarkation. Instead of 'burning their boats' they could see them there, 'just in case'. It was psychologically unsound to post them so near and in full view.

The battle raged for long but at last the ferocious ardour and patriotism of the Greeks triumphed and the Persians fled to the beach, closely pursued by the triumphant Greeks, almost drunk with success.

Many Persians, wading out to the ships, were caught and killed from behind. Seven ships were captured (a rare case of infantry on land capturing armed war-ships afloat), although the vast majority got away, with the remaining unwounded soldiers.

9,600 Persians were killed at Marathon—one man in two—while the Greeks lost only 192 of their 10,000.

In the centre of the battlefield the Greek dead were buried in a mass-grave and many years later a great mound was erected over the site forty feet high and a hundred yards in circumference, the Timvos. On the top are some seats and a plaque inscribed with a quotation extolling the famous victory and the patriotism of the Greek soldiers.

In 1880 a plough turned up the remains of some human bones about a hundred yards away from the Timvos—doubtless a body overlooked during the main collection of bodies and when their burial was being carried out.

The view from the top of the mound is, of course, extensive and the whole field of the battle clearly and easily seen. It appears to be entirely level, and the very slight slope down which the Greeks charged is almost imperceptible. The land is now under cultivation, as it probably was in 490 B.C., and the few scattered individual trees, in no way obscuring the view, show what a task it must have been to fell their predecessors to make the nightly stockade on the Greek left flank.

The beach itself is of perfect sand, and in the summer is a favourite picnic and bathing spot for the 20th Century Athenians. What little tide there is goes out a long way and it is easy to see how the Persian ships must, in many cases, have been stranded a long way out when disembarking the invaders. The chaos after the defeat, with terror-stricken Persian soldiers being chased and frequently struck down while trying to re-embark must have been acute. The Phoenician oarsmen and crews must indeed have nearly panicked when seeing the way the battle was going and then the mad rush for the boats. It is surprising that so many ships did manage to escape.

The marsh into which the Persians blundered on first landing four miles up the beach, has been drained and is now the landing-field of a civilian flying club in Athens, with its control tower, club room, workshops and car-park. But driving along the road skirting the aerodrome on the way to the club the ground is seen to be today very marshy, covered in reeds and coarse grass between the landing-strips. Apparently incapable of agriculture, it is used only for the grazing of a few sheep.

The promontory of Cynasura is bigger and higher than had been expected. To have landed where the Persians first got ashore was a sound spot to choose as the Cynasura would have provided a considerable sheltered anchorage for the ships had a northern, or north-eastern, wind got up.

The great battles in history so often supply some unanswerable problems, and Marathon is no exception. The greatest is where were the Persian cavalry during the battle, the cavalry which the deserters said 'Are away'. Not only were the Greeks, so vulnerable to hostile mounted action, entirely unmolested in their advance, but these horsemen disappear from history. There is little doubt that they were left behind on the beach, the ships in the general panic not waiting for them.

In the heat and excitement of the re-embarkation after the defeat no horses could possibly have got on board, yet there is no evidence of these 5,000 mounted men, left behind on the beach, being captured, pursued, or even reported to be anywhere, either in large parties—or as individual fugitives; they simply were 'missing'. Presumably when left behind they rode off into the hills, but we don't know.

Wherever they were—and in any circumstances—they would need food for themselves and forage for their horses. They would speak only the Persian language and would thus be immediately conspicuous, even if they had discarded their military dress and assumed that of the local peasants. This disappearance of 5,000 men and horses is so inexplicable that there must be a common-sense explanation.

It is probable that while a few of the more expert riders got over the Charadra, and entered the battle (albeit with little effect), the vast majority were unable to descend the bank and cross the stream and seeing the defeat, rode off into the hills, where despite marauding tactics they were finally surrounded and starved out. The mystery lies in the fact that these 'operations' were either never recorded by an historian or more likely were recorded in some way and the record lost. It is not impossible, therefore, that some day some account is found that will tell us what happened.

Several speculations have been made to account for their absence. None of them stand up to elementary military tactical argument.

One speculator suggests that the cavalry embarked before the action. Why should they? The Persians knew and could see their numerical superiority, firmly believing, and with good reason, in a great victory. To re-embark the cavalry after only a few days ashore must jeopardise the otherwise certain victory. To land, inevitably with difficulty, a force and then re-embark it without opposition and with a probable success in sight seems pointless. It had neither achieved anything nor had it been threatened.

The same speculator then argues that the cavalry were never intended to be anything more than a protective screen in a landing and subsequent advance—or as a rearguard to cover a possible re-embarkation. But the role of mounted troops is not to cover a fighting re-embarkation. This is the task of light mobile infantry which having withdrawn to the beach by successive bounds, finally discharges its last arrows and then scrambles aboard the probably already moving ships. No mounted men could possibly fire a last salvo of arrows and then re-embark their horses—already in a highly excited state. Utter chaos would ensue and more horses and men would be lost than embarked.

Another suggestion has been put forward that the cavalry had gone ahead of the infantry when the latter had crossed the Charadra. But no explanation is offered as to what these horsemen were doing or where they were during the days that elapsed between disembarkation and the day of the battle, or during the battle itself. There is no evidence of them harassing the Greeks in their nightly moves forward or of any action by them during the engagement. There is no evidence as to how they crossed the great obstacle of Charadra—if they did, which is highly unlikely.

Another possibility has been put forward that the Persian horses were grazing and watering in the marsh—so far away that they knew nothing of the battle. This says little for even the most primitive system of command or communications at Persian headquarters. It is inconceivable that the invading commander, immediately he saw the Greek advance, did not at once send for his cavalry to come to his assistance in some way or another. Even if the Charadra was impassable to horsemen, the mounted men could easily have walked into the shallow water on the beach, and passing outside the mouth of the little stream, come up on the right flank or on the rear of the main Persian position.

The question of the casualties at Marathon has always been debatable. Herodotus says that 9,600 of the Persians fell. All would be killed as the triumphant and fanatical Greeks would take no prisoners and would kill every wounded enemy they found. But this figure of 9,600, about 45% of the total invading force seems, prima facie, suspect.

It is probable that far fewer than this were killed in the actual battle. The majority of the 9,600 were caught, and killed, as they waded out to their boats. Some probably were drowned if they fell, heavily encumbered with arms and equipment, in four or five feet of water.

The Phoenician sailors resting on their oars and watching the battle from only a few hundred yards away, saw the disaster to their masters, saw them streaming down the beach to the boats, saw the Greeks hotly pursuing them, killing those whom they caught. Doubtless the Phoenician oarsmen, thinking discretion the better part of valour, pulled into deeper water in self-protection so preventing many hundreds of Persians from reaching safety. The latter were caught in deepening water, their boats out of reach, and their triumphant enemy close behind.

The sight must have been extraordinary. Thousands of heavily armed and accoutred soldiers up to their waists, perhaps to their shoulders, in the sea, fighting individual battles. Half of them panic-stricken, only concerned with 'sauve qui peut'—while the others, bloodthirsty, victorious, were determined to have their pound of flesh. This pulling into deeper water explains why so few Persian ships were lost.

The Greek casualties are more understandable. Herodotus puts them at 196 killed, say 2% of the whole, not an unusual figure in those days for a victorious army when no small-arms fire existed. The number of wounded would probably amount to another 500, but they would not be killed off by their enemy as the Persian wounded were, though few would recover from serious wounds. In those days medical knowledge or treatment was almost non-existent. But these 500 were not 'killed in action'—a fact that explains the tremendous difference in the casualty figures of each side.

Marathon is one of the fifteen decisive battles of the world. Why is it so classified? It did not usher in or see the end of an era of military dominance by one great power over its neighbours. It did not bring about the end of a dynasty. It did not see the introduction of any new weapons or tactics. It was but a victory which did not avert the Persian invasion of Greece ten years later, an occupation that was to last until 447 B.C. Wherein lies its notoriety?

Marathon was fought when the morale of the Greeks was at a low ebb. She had been leading the world for 1,100 years—an exhausting process that throughout history has invariably lowered the vitality of any race. She had passed her peak of material, military and physical, greatness. She was beset with troubles at home, troubles in her colonies, and threats from overseas. She dreaded the anticipated invasion by Persia. Subconsciously she was on the downward path from world greatness.

Then came Marathon—and the dreaded invader with an army twice the size of the defender was utterly defeated and driven back into the sea. Immediately Greek morale rose and Greece remained a great power for another 200 years. Suddenly to know that the tired little army of a tired nation was better than the best had the most enormous tonic effect.

It is comparable to the effect on the morale of France by the battle of Valmy in 1792, which became a 'decisive battle' for the same reason. The French Revolution was petering out; the French felt, rightly, that the world was against them. There were threats from across their eastern frontier and all they had was an ill-armed, barely organised, rag, tag and bob-tail army, many of the men being armed with pitch-forks. But they had the wild, burning enthusiasm of revolution, a revolution that had released them from tyranny—they thought—and they would fight to the death to pre-serve their new-found liberty.

At Waterloo many old soldiers in Napoleon's Imperial Guard, The Old Guard, had fought at Valmy as boys. There they had helped to light a torch. That torch lit a flame of confidence, of 'superiority', that was to last for twenty-three years. Neither France nor the world could see that from the victorious army of Valmy would emerge Napoleon's Army of France, which would win Jena and Austerlitz, Wagram and Friedland, would invade Russia and capture Moscow, occupy Spain and Portugal, encamp at Boulogne and threaten England.

In exactly the same way the barely hoped for, certainly totally unexpected, victory for the Greeks at Marathon raised their morale too. In the next twenty years the successes at Thermopylae, Salamis and Plataeae were made possible because of the moral and psycho-logical effect of Marathon. The military recovery started there was to last until the end of Alexander the Great's career, in 323 B.C.—one hundred and sixty-three years after Marathon. It becomes one of the decisive battles of the world because of this rejuvenation only and not for any material or strategic result.

Bannockburn

1314

THROUGHOUT their long history the Scots have been the most independent race in the world. They have not fused with other races, excepting by individual marriages, they have not willingly given up their sovereignty. Today they regard everyone born out of Scotland not as an Englishman or a Frenchman, not as an Italian or American, but simply as not a Scot. Everywhere in the world they are found, in every walk of life, business, professional, services, mixing willingly, acceptably, happily with the local society. In addition they keep intact their little national set, a little Highland enclave, which meets on St. Andrew's Night for an annual gathering, to toast the Haggis, to talk of Bonnie Scotland—once a year an evening when Sassenachs, born south of the border, are welcome but are definitely visitors.

This strict and far reaching nationalism, far exceeding that of the Irish, the Welsh, the French, is difficult to explain. As might well have been expected, it is not occasioned by a geographical feature, features which elsewhere in the world have separated two races. Between Scotland and England there is no Irish Sea, no Straits of Dover, no Pyrenees, no Rhine, no Himalayas, there is little more than a line drawn on the map.

This outstanding and extreme nationalism, perhaps better described as national insularity, if such a term can be applied to a country that is not an island, was born about A.D. 100. About this year the Roman invasion of the British Isles reached its far limit along what became the border from Carlisle to Newcastle. Beyond this limit they found a mountainous country, far less productive than England, already being colonised. Its inhabitants resisted the Romans valiantly and with such success that the Romans felt the game was not worth the candle—the price was too high, the prize too meagre.

Accordingly they discontinued probing raids, and withdrew to the narrowest, and therefore the most easily defensible, neck of land between the two larger areas—the border. Knowing the warlike and almost savage qualities of the Scots, the Romans built a great wall to keep the Scots out of England and to deter them from raiding. The wall, a great military fortification, sixty miles long, was garrisoned by Roman troops at full strength.

As the Romans gradually colonised England, Englishmen were recruited into the Roman legions. By 415, when the Roman Government and Administration left England, it was Englishmen who thus manned the Wall against the Scotsmen.

The Wall fenced the Scots in, they thought, and was held in strength to keep them out of England. It infuriated them and determined them to remain independent, an entirely separate nation.

Their resentment was made stronger in 1088. King William II on one of his defensive sorties beyond the Wall was struck by the tactical position of the old Roman settlement at Carlisle, and had its castle rebuilt, fortified and garrisoned. Situated at the western end of the Roman Wall it matched Newcastle at the other end, and thus closed the two doors out of Scotland. The raids into Durham and Cumberland became markedly less frequent after the completion of the fortress, and the Scots felt they were now even more excluded from England, knowing they were not wanted there.

Psychologically the existence of the Wall and the reason for its building were by far the greatest factor in creating, and indeed maintaining, the tremendous national independence of the Scottish nation.

About the time the Romans left England there were seventeen great clans of Scotsmen north of the border. Practically everyone belonged to one or other of these clans, and those who did not were regarded as outsiders, a very small minority.

No country has ever had such vast congregations of families knitted into clans. In each clan many men had the same surname, although coming from all grades of society. The Laird in his castle and the crofter at his gate often had the same name, were of the clan and each owed a rigid loyalty to each other and to the 'family'. The MacDonalds, the Campbells, the MacKays, the Crawfords, the Douglases and others jointly made up the whole fabric of the nation. Surprisingly each clan did not come from one particular district, and although individuals intermingled easily, it was not common for them to marry out of their clan. Each clan retained for many centuries its complete individual identity and often mutual dislike, distrust, and active enmity towards some other clan.

This fragmentation of a patriotic race into large groups pointed to an inevitable fusion into one nation sooner or later.

By 840 the gradual, almost imperceptible, merging of the clans into four great 'families' was complete and the fusion became geographical. In 843 the 'King' of one group, became 'King' of another through a legal but disavowed marriage and the second step towards one nation was taken. This double 'group' ruled Scotland by fear and intimidation for one hundred and seventy-five years, until in 1018, it conquered the two lesser, and separate, groups. The new king, Malcolm, became King of the four groups of clans, the first King of Scotland.

All became 'Scotsmen' though retaining rigidly and jealously their clan identity and *esprit-de-corps*. A similar federation of three races in South Africa, the Dutch, the British and the French, into 'Afrikaaners' is happening today.

For the next three hundred years the history of Scotland is largely that of the warring clans trying to put their own nominee on the throne. In less than three hundred years, Scotland had eighteen kings, an average reign of only eighteen years. In this period four of its monarchs died by murder or in battle while two others were deposed.

In 1272 Edward I succeeded to the throne of England. He had prudence, energy, and most important, foresight. He was one of the great English kings. His statesmanship was far beyond his era and he saw the futility and danger of a hostile, virile, nation on his northern border, a nation that largely spoke English. He also saw the desirability of the four countries, England, Ireland, Scotland and Wales making up the British Isles, being one country with one central government, although made up of four races. There was no geographical frontier or obstacle between England and Scotland, or between England and Wales, and he rightly regarded the seventy miles of the Irish Sea as of far less importance than the twenty-one miles of the Straits of Dover.

(The latter had already made a barrier between England and France to cross which William of Normandy had to mount a full-scale invasion. History was to show the vital part it played in the Armada, Napoleon's intention to invade England, the unmolested

passage of the British Army to France in 1914—and Hitler's frus-
trated invasion in 1940.) Edward believed that the four countries,
united, had a better chance of repelling an invasion from the Continent than otherwise. Union was strength, and his far-sighted
strategy was the right one.

Towards the end of the chaotic period of Scottish strife for the
Crown, in 1286 the King, Alexander III, died. Although only
forty-four years of age all his children had predeceased him and the
next heir was his granddaughter Margaret, the Maid of Norway,
the child of Eric, King of Norway.

Edward I saw his first chance of uniting the two kingdoms by
arranging a marriage between this girl, soon to be crowned Queen
of Scotland, and his own son, Edward, Prince of Wales. The off-
spring of this marriage would be the first and lawful Monarch of
both England and Scotland. But, tragically, Margaret died on her
way over from Norway, Edward's scheme fell to pieces and, worst
of all, Scotland was left without an heir to the throne.

Surprisingly the Scottish barons invited Edward to act as umpire
between the nine claimants to the throne. He agreed to do so, on
condition that he went as 'Overlord of Britain'—and that whoever
he chose would be his subordinate. The 'trial' was held at Berwick.
John Balliol was the successful candidate but immediately after
his coronation showed clearly that he had no intention of admitting
Edward's paramountcy and the Scottish nation at once lined up
behind him to secure their continued independence. For the next
twenty years strife again raged in Scotland.

Edward, determined on the union of the two countries, led several
successful expeditions across the border against Scottish leaders of
armies who were intent on defending their district and their country.
These he regarded as rebels, and his forces showed scant mercy to
captured towns or prisoners. He deposed Balliol by force, putting a
pair of puppet nobles in as regents, and occupied many castles of
the great barons (several of whom openly sided with him). Sir
William Wallace, one of Scotland's great national heroes, led expeditions to besiege them, but was captured and murdered. Another
patriot came on the stage, Robert the Bruce, 'King' of Scotland.

Bruce, too, had a considerable force of soldiers under his hand
and marched south to the Wall. Edward marched to meet him, but
died suddenly. He might have defeated Bruce but he could not have
conquered the Scottish nation and kept it down by force of arms,

no matter what form of occupation he was to enforce. His successor, his son, now Edward II, was never the man to face successfully the strong, warlike, dedicated Scottish people, and the lack of strong leadership and military skill on the English side became at once apparent.

Step by step Bruce won his way. All the bigger towns were re-occupied by his forces, with one exception the great castles were re-occupied, and the scattered English forces were often isolated and in great danger. Stirling Castle alone held out, though closely invested by Bruce.

In 1314 Edward II led a huge army across the border to relieve Stirling. His intention was to recapture it on Midsummer Day, the 24th June, while Bruce with a far smaller army determined to give battle to the 'invader', to prevent the last English stronghold being relieved. Bruce, outnumbered two to one, had two very strong cards in his pack—the burning enthusiasm of patriots fighting for their native soil to defend it—and the inadequacy of the military skill and determination of Edward II.

Early on 23rd June, Bruce having left barely a sufficient force to continue the siege of Stirling and to prevent a sortie, had mustered some seven thousand men to resist the English army advancing to relieve Stirling Castle. He had, he knew, several hours to select and prepare a good defensive position. Both luck in finding one and skill in exploiting it were on his side.

Three miles south of the Castle a stream flowed roughly east and west, the Bannockburn. After a mile or so it veered away to the north-east and enclosed a large marsh, some three-quarters of a mile wide, and half a mile from south to north—the Carse. Almost impassable, it formed an excellent natural defensive obstacle and Bruce rested his left flank on it. A mile north of the burn lay a wood —New Park—another helpful feature for defence and Bruce took up his main position between it and the burn, knowing that if retirement became necessary his infantry—by far the greater position of his army—could slip away to its shelter close behind them. Edward II's cavalry, the majority of his army, would be at a great disadvantage, and very foolish, if it tried to pursue infantry in a wood. The apparent superiority of the English army was not so considerable as its numbers implied.

Away to Bruce's right flank lay Gillies Hill, a sharp, easily seen feature, with sides of considerable declivity, dominating the battlefield. Prima facie it was a most desirable objective for the attackers, a tactical prize—outflanking the defence—but it was covered with trees.

His two flanks resting on natural obstacles, his rear protected, and a stream in front of him, Bruce had done well to find the site and to recognise its value. However, he was not satisfied and utilised his few hours by digging large pits in the ground between the burn and the wood. In them pointed stakes were erected and above them, just covering their points, the turf was relaid. Beyond the pits ran the Bannockburn, forty feet wide and its banks twelve feet high. Not a formidable obstacle in itself but sufficient to delay and obstruct advancing infantry. The Scottish army took up position between the stream to their front and the wood to their rear.

About 4 o'clock on the 23rd, Bruce and his men saw the English army approaching. One of the largest armies that a king of England had ever led and with a majority of mounted men, it must have made an awe-inspiring sight to the Scottish soldiers now resting behind their pits. They could see how vastly it outnumbered them, and many must have wondered what chance they had. The defenders on the walls of Stirling Castle, two miles away, must have seen their English comrades arriving to relieve them and have been greatly heartened by the magnificent sight.

By the time the English army had come up and concentrated for the attack it was too late to fight that day, and so both armies lay down in full view of each other to rest and await tomorrow's battle. But two unexpected incidents occurred before dusk.

An English Lord, named Clifford, rode off at the head of a large body of horsemen on a roundabout way to Stirling Castle to carry assistance to it and bid it be of good cheer. Bruce seeing this move told one of his subordinate 'generals', Randolph, to cut Clifford off. But Randolph only had foot-soldiers and although catching Clifford and clashing with him, was in trouble and it seemed likely that not only would he be beaten but that the English horsemen would reach the Castle and so come behind the main Scottish position. Another Scots 'general', Douglas, then went to support Randolph but the English horsemen, seeing the reinforcement coming up, turned and rejoined their main army.

Shortly after this minor skirmish another small party of English cavalry crossed the burn and approached the Scots, somehow missing the pits. Bruce out in front of his lines and carrying out an inspection, was seen by the English commander, de Bohun, of this patrol who, recognising him personally, charged him on his great war-horse, weighed down with armour and the lance. Bruce on his much handier pony side-stepped from the Englishman's path and as he passed dealt his assailant one blow with his battleaxe, a blow that split his skull in two. When remonstrated with by his subordinate leaders for risking his life in this way Bruce replied how sorry he was that the blow had broken the wooden handle of his battleaxe.

Next day, 24th June, the greatest day in Scottish history, the Scots 'stood-to' at sunrise. About 8 a.m. the English archers advanced across the Bannockburn—vulnerable by themselves and unescorted by cavalry. Bruce immediately sent his small but efficient cavalry force against them, and although the archers turned their fire on the horsemen, doing great execution, the cavalry triumphed. The English bows were of no use at close quarters, and the Scottish horsemen getting in among the enemy were soon able to kill many and put the remainder to flight.

Edward II then tried to retrieve this disaster by ordering the whole of his force to charge against the Scottish front. The majority, being mounted, galloped forward on a wide front and rode into the unseen pits. The greatest chaos ensued. The front lines of horsemen went down into the pits, following lines were unseated, their horses trampling the survivors of the front lines. The Scots advanced and found the now dismounted cavalry an easy prey. The foot-soldiers armed with their pikes were able to kill every Englishman found; the latter could not in many cases rise from the pits, or disentangle themselves from their plunging horses or even if free, rise quickly because of the weight of their armour.

The English infantry were able to negotiate the pits and advanced towards the main Scottish position, but with little dash or impetus and they were held by their enemy, determined not only to defeat the hated English but to drive them out of Scotland for ever.

The fighting now was around the pits out in front—and along the Scottish front line. Both armies were locked in a death struggle; honours were even so far.

Suddenly the fortunes of the Scots changed. The English saw coming down the slopes of Gillies Hill a body of men carrying flying banners. It was only the servants, gillies, and camp followers from Bruce's camp, who had occupied Gillies Hill as a grandstand to see the fight. Carried away by the tension of the situation in which both armies were locked together, they could no longer resist joining in, although virtually unarmed. But the English troops seeing this, apparently new, army advancing down hill on to their open left flank lost heart and started to give way. The Scots were naturally much heartened by this wavering of their enemy, and were fighting more fiercely than ever. Quickly the English army turned and fled in all directions. Sensibly Bruce kept his victorious army in hand, and did not venture out of his position until quite certain that he would not be attacked again.

Many English soldiers, fleeing towards the town of Stirling to seek shelter with their besieged brothers, were drowned in the treacherous Carse. Others went towards the Firth of Forth, where, pursued by Bruce's now released horsemen, they were driven into the river and there drowned. Many tried a direct flight to the rear but in recrossing the Bannockburn were caught by other small parties of Scottish cavalry.

Edward seeing the battle lost found a way round to Stirling Castle, thinking he would be safe there, in a fortress with undefeated English troops. But the Governor, an Englishman, refused him entry, saying that if he did admit him he must be surrendered next day, by a private agreement he had made with Bruce. Edward rode away and, by luck, at Dunbar found a boat to carry him to Berwick where he was safe.

This was the greatest victory the Scots ever gained. They felt their twelve hundred-year opposition to the Wall was now justified. As it had kept them out of England they had, with Bruce's pits, turned the English out of Scotland.

Scotland was once again free; their overwhelming victory at Bannockburn had once again proved that they were one people, one nation which intended to remain so.

Bannockburn is an outstanding example of a people fighting on their own soil to resist an invader—determined to win or die. A nation in such circumstances has an additional quality beyond the normal military ones of efficiency, training, tactics, stamina, weapons. Patriotism in the defence of the homeland is the most powerful of all weapons, the most enduring of all qualities, as Hitler would have discovered in 1940.

Today the battlefield of Bannockburn is easy to find. It can be seen from one view-point and has several physical features still existing which influenced the action.

The imaginative National Trust for Scotland owns some fifty acres around the 'Borestone' on the top of the Bannock Brae where Bruce set up his standard. About twelve of these acres have been turned into a vast well-kept lawn. A large car park just off the main road from Stirling to Falkirk leads into a new building where photos of the area, wonderfully graphic plans of the battle, and clearly written brief accounts of the major points of the action are mounted on great notice boards. In front of these boards is an excellent model of the battlefield as in 1314. There is a well-equipped bookstall.

From this excellent exhibition the visitor walks up a well-kept path to the 'Rotunda'—a large circular wall enclosing a monument built over the remains of the 'Borestone'. A large flagstaff marks the highest point of the rise from where a superb view must have been, and can still be, obtained of the whole field. A few yards back from the 'Rotunda' is a gigantic equestrian statue of Bruce, unveiled by the Queen in 1964.

Looking around into the distance there is much to be seen. New Park, quite an eminence, is now entirely denuded of trees, and a housing estate completely covers the area of the wood that might have been so useful to Bruce had he been compelled to retire. These houses come right up to the northern edge of the National Trust property, where they abruptly stop, and it is nice to see and realise that the Trust's beautifully cut and rolled 'lawn' is safe from modern encroachments.

Off to the north-west is Gillies Hill, still largely covered with trees. It makes an excellent 'grandstand' and the camp followers there could see the whole of the battlefield. Their excitement, mounting as the battle progressed, must have been unendurable, eventually becoming uncontrollable.

Just to the front of Bruce's right flank was a considerable bog— there were in 1314 many in the area—'Halberts Bog'. Its existence was probably not known to Edward II and had he advanced in that area he must have got into grave difficulties. Bruce doubtless found it and avoiding it, used it as yet another natural obstacle in his favour. This very low-lying piece of ground, though still damp and heavy has been drained for farm-land. The Bannockburn passing through it has been canalised and the few cottages on its bank today lie directly in the middle of the old bog.

The Burn meanders across the low-lying fields until it reaches the main Stirling–Falkirk road, where today it passes under a large bridge carrying the main road. Hereabouts its banks are ten feet deep and at their summit thirty feet apart.

Doubtless the ravine was not so deep or wide six hundred years ago, and the present dimensions have been caused by the erosion of the winters of these six centuries. In 1314 this road, one of the most important in Scotland, probably did not need a bridge to carry it over the then shallow water-way and a ford was almost certainly all that was necessary. Nevertheless the burn generally created a considerable obstacle to mounted troops, and some dislocation, 'bunching', and probable minor losses of direction must have occurred during its passage. To advance again after this 'annoyance' and then to encounter the pits must have indeed shaken the English morale.

The site of these historically notorious pits can only be very approximately conjectured. To the west of the road is open farmland, gently rising back to the Borestone Brae, and the pits could have been anywhere within four hundred yards back from the burn. To the east of the road, and on a more probable site, a large housing estate has been built, almost down to the stream and it is impossible to express any opinion as to where the pits might have been dug.

Close to the exhibition hall is the 'King Robert' Hotel, adjacent is a Scottish crafts and souvenir shop of high quality selling many varied and ingenious souvenirs. Half-way down the main road to the Bannockburn is the '1314 Inn', while farther up the road is the 'Borestone Bar'.

The whole area is a Mecca for Scotsmen. The atmosphere of their great victory is everywhere. Some 80,000 visitors, mostly Scots, come yearly to see it during its open season.

Bosworth

1485

THE battle of Bosworth brought to an end the Wars of The Roses. It brought to an end not only a civil war, lasting thirty years, and in which twelve battles were fought, but also eighty-five years of violence. A period when numberless people of importance and of influence were killed, or whose murder was arranged, by similar people on the other side. Men, and women, lost their lives for their political loyalties, for adhering to the leaders of their factions, for following the king, or his rival. In these eighty-five years intrigue, treachery, murder and beheading without trial were commonplace. At no time in England's history has violence been so widespread or so calmly accepted as one of the hazards of birth or position. In this period, commencing with the murder of Richard II in 1400, a year after he had been deposed, until Bosworth, eighteen persons of royal blood, the blood of Edward III, or their spouses were killed in battle, executed openly, or murdered secretly.

Indeed, to be a descendant of Edward III was to be not far away from a death-sentence throughout the fifteenth century and well into the Tudor Age. Even as late as 1553, and on the death of Edward VI, Lady Jane Grey, a harmless, gentle, studious girl, a granddaughter of Henry VII and only seven generations from Edward III, was placed on the throne much against her wishes and abilities. She reigned for nine days. The rightful heir, Mary I, threw her into the Tower where, of course, she too was executed.

Richard II was deposed on account of his violence to his great nobles, his intractability to his ministers and advisers, and possibly because of his lowered sanity occasioned by his grief at the death of his wife. He died childless, and immediately the competition to be his successor became intense, the throne wide open. The Duke of Lancaster became King Henry IV—he was the son of John of Gaunt and the eldest brother of the Black Prince. But the next

22

brother, Edmund, Duke of York, had left a son on his death, Richard. He was a lusty, capable, man with designs upon the throne. He carried the House of York forward against the House of Lancaster and thereby staged the York and Lancastrian struggle to last 85 years. His claim clearly was second to that of Henry IV but it mattered little. Ambition, intrigue and force were what counted. For the next fifty years these two men and their descendants, ably abetted and indeed violently spurred on by the immensely powerful nobles, caused unrest, fear among the people and national disruption of the country. There was no open conflict, but a smouldering fire was aglow.

The accession of Henry IV to Richard II's throne is usually accepted as a landmark in England's constitutional and monarchical history. It is held to show that the throne of England is not entirely hereditary but to a certain extent elective. If the king could not rule or would not, if he did not measure up to his responsibilities or was found wanting or unwilling he had to go, either by force or persuasion. England did not want him. Edward II was murdered, Richard II deposed, Henry VI deposed and probably murdered, Edward V (the little prince in the Tower) murdered, Richard III killed at Bosworth (he would almost certainly have been murdered sooner or later), Charles I executed, James II ran away, all for incapacity, or worse, for not listening to the people's wants, aspirations or rights. Many will remember in this century a tragic abdication and the reasons thereof.

Henry IV reigned for only fourteen years, and never was it more true to say 'Uneasy lies the head that wears the Crown'. Constantly he had to counter the intrigues of his opponents, the supporters of the now dead Richard II. Shortage of money forced him to treat the House of Commons with respect. The only real power the Commons had was to control taxation and it was during this century and for this reason that the Commons increased their prestige and indirect power, power which was eventually to grow so vastly.

Henry was in his later years troubled by his conscience. Had he been right in seizing the throne from his cousin, Richard II—was he a usurper? He suffered pain, both physical and mental, and died in 1413 at the early age of forty-six.

He was succeeded by his son, Henry V, one of England's most romantic monarchs. He succeeded smoothly to the throne, the dynasty of Lancaster being now firmly established. He renewed the

war with France which had started long before in his great-grand-
father Edward III's reign, and won fame in 1415 at the battle of
Agincourt. Five years later he married the daughter of the King of
France. Shakespeare has made him a gallant knight in shining
armour, the hero in two of his plays, 'Henry V' and 'The Taming
of the Shrew'.

A son was born of the marriage, Henry VI—to reign for thirty-
nine years. A humble, pious, ineffective man, who, while he was
young, spent some time in a monastery. Towards the end of his
stormy life he would frequently wear a monk's habit. More than
once during his reign he was insane. No wonder there was another
upsurge of plots, intrigues and scheming to dethrone the king—or
at least set up a regency for a while during his recurring incapacities.
Struggles for the regency turned into struggles for the Crown itself,
and soon fighting started between the Lancastrians, the King's
family, his supporters who chose a red rose as a badge, while the
Yorkists, led by the King's cousin Richard, to be killed at Wakefield
in 1460, chose a white rose.

The Wars of the Roses had begun.

It is not intended to tell the story of the Wars of the Roses here.
Fourteen battles were fought during its course, and such famous
names as Tewkesbury, Barnet, Shrewsbury, St. Albans (twice) and
Wakefield, appeared in history, each to see bloody fighting between
Englishmen. The great peers, Warwick (the Kingmaker), Salisbury,
Somerset, Neville, Beaufort, led armies through the country, ravag-
ing each other's territory, Englishmen capturing, torturing and
killing Englishmen. But Henry VI, sheltering from the storm at
Windsor, took no part. A gentle, pious, upright man, he had not the
capacity or the stomach to fight for his undoubted right, but his wife
Margaret of Anjou was made of sterner stuff.

She was the mainspring behind the Lancastrians and was as
fierce as her husband was meek. In spirit, courage, resolution, ambition and mercilessness she was a match for any of the English
barons. There was nothing of the softer sex about her—and her son
Edward was as bloodthirsty and cruel as his mother. He too was
killed at Tewkesbury and so ended the Lancastrian line, but not the
Wars of the Roses. Henry now became quite insane and was confined while Margaret became virtually Commander-in-Chief of the
Lancastrians, defeating the Yorkists at the second battle of St.
Albans. Margaret should have marched on London and seen Henry

on to his throne again, but she dawdled fatally. The son of Richard of York, Edward, now the leader of the Yorkists, an abler man than his father, reached London, and was now acclaimed King Edward IV. Again he led his Yorkists, although defeated at St. Albans, against the Lancastrians and at Towton in 1461—finally defeated them.

The White Rose had won. Henry was again confined in the Tower after a temporary freedom, Edward of York, Edward IV, re-entered London and claimed his capital. The following night, Henry VI, meek and humble to the end, was stabbed to death. The truth will never be known but many people at the time believed his assassin to be Richard, Duke of Gloucester, younger brother of the new king. His name has also always been connected with the murder of the new king's young sons, the future Edward V and his brother, Richard, the 'Princes in the Tower'.

Edward IV had won the war for the White Rose of York. His reign of twenty-nine years was largely occupied in keeping the great families of Warwick, Somerset, Neville, Woodville and his brother Clarence from uniting against him and he succeeded in doing so by arranging marriages which prevented coalitions or ensured political alliances, in either case in his favour. His reign is largely noteworthy for the calming of the passions aroused in the Wars of the Roses, and ensuring the survival of the York dynasty. He was an active and energetic monarch, but cruel and vain. Handsome, and with charming manners he was very popular, but a vicious and licentious private life brought him to an early grave.

He had two sons, Edward V, who never reigned, and Richard. His brother Richard, Duke of Gloucester, tricked these two little boys, aged 12 and 10, on the death of their father, to leave their mother and seek safety in the Tower. The Great Council appointed Richard to be Protector of the Realm and at once Richard had all power in his hands.

Three months after his appointment as Protector, the Peers offered Richard the Crown. On accepting it and to protect himself against opposition he beheaded the two strongest men in the country who were against him. To make himself even more secure, he procured the murder of the young King, the lawful King of England, and his brother, in the Tower, and so became himself the lawful King. In two years he too would be killed, at the Battle of Bosworth, and so end the life of perhaps the bloodiest of our monarchs. He instigated directly the murder of not less than ten people whom he thought might be his rival for the throne—or merely get in his way.

The vile murder of the two little princes in the Tower turned most people against him. His popularity was never great and had it not been for his strength of character, which the people believed would maintain the peace fostered by his brother Edward IV—he would never have been offered the Crown by the Great Council. But now even the upholders of the cause of York resolved that a Lancastrian on the throne would be better than this bloodthirsty Richard. And one was available.

Henry Tudor, grandson of Queen Catherine by her second marriage (her first husband had been Henry V), had this left-handed claim but his mother—Margaret Beaufort—was the great granddaughter of John of Gaunt, and he was thus indeed a Lancastrian.

When Henry Tudor was fourteen years of age, during Edward IV's reign, his mother was advised to get him out of the kingdom. He was clearly the nearest Lancastrian to the throne and with the Yorkists in full power he was in grave danger. He lived in Brittany until, aged 23, he heard of the death of Edward IV, and that little Edward V was King but in the Tower.

Margaret Beaufort remained in England, ever watchful for a chance to bring her son home. Although openly supporting Richard III—she carried the Queen's train at the Coronation—she also intrigued with the disgraced Duke of Buckingham against the King. Buckingham had been Richard's chief and favourite minister, but left his master, his post, and the court, angrily when he heard of the fate of the two little boys in the tower. His action symbolises the feelings of most decent people then and today, whose sympathies will usually be with children, especially when they are ill-treated. He was captured and of course beheaded for merely demonstrating a criticism of the King. His murder—he had committed no crime—only served to turn yet more Yorkists into Lancastrians.

Buckingham, before his capture and murder, aided by Margaret Beaufort and several of the great families in the west of England, invited Henry over from Brittany. The invitation came from both parties, all being sick of the present bloodthirsty regime. It reminds one of a similar invitation, representative of both Whigs and Tories,

sent two hundred years later in 1688 to William of Orange to come
and deliver England from yet another tyrant.

Leaving Brittany, his home for many years, Henry landed at
Milford Haven with 2,000 French mercenaries, many Welshmen
joining him because of his Welsh name. He picked up more supporters from the great Lancastrian families in the west, and not a
few Yorkists in Wales. He moved due north to Aberystwyth (there
is a tradition that he spent a night at the Manor House of Wern on
on the way, his men doubtless in the farm buildings around the
house, and in the fields). This northern route enabled him to pick
up reinforcements from North Wales, always a Tudor stronghold,
and turning east met more help in the Stanley country. Somewhere
along the route Henry picked up a youth, David Cecil, a younger
son of a minor manor house, and carried him on to Bosworth Field
and so on to the Tudor Court. This boy was the origin of the fortunes of that Cecil family which was to serve England's two great
Queens, Elizabeth and Victoria, so brilliantly in centuries to come,
and which has been a power in the land politically ever since 1485.

Seven days after leaving Milford Haven he reached Shrewsbury,
where he halted for a few days.

His thoughts must have been troubled indeed. Here he was,
almost in the heart of England, leading an army of not more than
5,000, and barely an army at that; composed of three nationalities,
French, Welsh, and English, it was quite unorganised, untrained,
poorly led, for Henry had little or no military experience. But it had
enthusiasm, a mission to relieve an oppressed people, and for
Henry, two prizes, the Crown of England to which he had a lawful
claim and the daughter of Edward IV as a wife. If he could succeed
he would go down in history not only as the vanquisher of a bloody
tyrant but, by his marriage, uniting the Houses of York and Lancaster and so bringing to an end eighty-five years of fighting about
this very question.

On the other hand, failure could mean for him only one thing—
his beheading in the Tower. He knew many of his subordinates
would suffer the same fate and worst of all Richard, by a victory
over the invader, would be more firmly on his throne than ever. He
would doubtless tighten the screw and Henry would have done
more harm to the people of England than if he had stayed away.

He passed through Newport, Stafford, Lichfield, Tamworth and
Atherstone, where he met the two brothers Stanley, whose actions

on the battlefield of Bosworth were so greatly to influence the coming engagement.

The story of the Stanleys is complicated. Margaret Beaufort, mother of Henry VII, had married as her second husband Thomas, Lord Stanley, who thus became Henry's step-father. But Stanley was a Yorkist, a supporter of Richard III, the leader of a considerable body of his own troops, and, in Derbyshire, a most powerful baron. His son, Lord Strange, was on Richard's personal staff and Richard kept him there to make sure of the Father's loyalty (slightly suspect anyway) and to be used as a hostage in the event of his fathers' desertion. Thus Stanley, with his stepson Henry, the claimant to the throne, on one hand and his son in the power and custody of Richard on the other, was indeed in a delicate position.

The third Stanley, Sir William, younger brother of Lord Stanley was also a powerful man with a considerable following of troops. He had already been declared a traitor by Richard and so could and did openly throw his hand in with Henry. Lord Stanley had to be much more careful and could not show his hand until the last minute.

News of Henry's landing at Milford Haven did not reach Richard at Nottingham until four days after the event. Immediately he issued orders for what would today be called mobilisation. When Henry reached Shrewsbury Richard's army was assembling at Nottingham, and he ordered a general rendezvous at Leicester.

Sir William Stanley now joined Henry, and informed his brother Lord Stanley who was falling back, half-heartedly, to join the King at Leicester of what he had done, suggesting that the elder brother, too, should march to Henry's standard. Henry and the two Stanleys met secretly at Atherstone where the 'family' had three thousand men encamped. The next day a considerable number of deserters from Richard's army came in and Henry now had seven thousand men, all imbued with the spirit of liberation from a tyrant.

On 21st August, Henry marched on and camped that night at White Moors, three miles south-west of Market Bosworth. Richard marched forward from Leicester on hearing that Henry had left Lichfield, and camped on 21st August at the village of Sutton Cheney. The two armies were thus about two and a half miles apart.

The King felt supremely confident, and the odds certainly seemed to be on his side. He was much more experienced than his opponent, who had never been in action before. The royal army

was composed largely of Englishmen, while Henry had three nationalities under his command. Henry's seven thousand men were out-
numbered by Richard's eight thousand.

There was a big 'but'. Richard was by no means sure how much
he could trust his great barons. Sir William Stanley had already
shown definite signs of disaffection and been outlawed. Lord Stanley
refused to come in to the King's camp for orders, pleading sickness.
Other subordinate leaders, notably the Earl of Northumberland,
gave Richard much disquiet.

At dawn on the 22nd both armies made for Ambien Hill, a small
hillock standing at the end of the low ridge running to the south-
west of Sutton Cheney. It was to be the centre of the battlefield and
was equidistant from both camps.

Both leaders looked anxiously for the two uncertain Stanley
forces, Sir William to the north and Lord Stanley to the south. All
four forces were in sight of each other and an extraordinary situation emerged. The two main forces opposite and facing each other
were like two football teams, waiting for the referee's whistle to
kick off. On the two touch-lines stood two considerable groups of
spectators, each waiting to see which side was winning before it,
too, joined in—on the winning side, doubtless.

Below Ambien Hill and directly in any line of advance by Henry
towards the hillock lay a large marsh, unseen and undiscovered by
Henry's 'scurryers'.

The battle started in a race for Ambien Hill. The King's scurryers, more practised, more enterprising and more confident, got to
the ridge and moved along it, well before Henry, whose advance
lacked purpose and drive.

The King's vanguard under Lord Norfolk reached the hillock
and, facing south-west, took up a defensive position. The main body
under Richard came up soon afterwards, and took post among and
behind the units of the vanguard. The rearguard under Northumberland was ordered to join as soon as possible and when up, to face
due south.

As Henry neared Ambien Hill he saw that Richard was already
there in force. At the same time his leading units found the marsh
and found it to be a considerable obstacle. To prevent his main
body from piling up behind the marsh-bound vanguard, he ordered
a sharp left-wheel and thus moved due north, only five hundred
yards from the Royal vanguard now in its defensive position. His

right flank was badly exposed, and Richard's men opened fire. However, the range was extreme for the archery of those days and little damage was done to Henry's flank march.

Presently leading troops of the advance cleared the marsh, following almost exactly the line of the modern railway from Nuneaton to Derby. When its head reached where is now the little railway station of Shenton, Henry's force formed flank to its right and a fire-fight ensued. But the range although lowered was still too great for the fire to cause many casualties.

Norfolk and Richard now held six hundred yards of the ridge in strength and the King began to look behind him for his rear-guard and Northumberland to come up and take its place on the left of the south-west-facing line. Richard knew the basic principle of war-concentration.

But Northumberland did not come up and remained just west of Sutton Cheney—a mile back. From here he could see the two Stanley armies, and he did not intend to risk action and involvement until they showed their hands. He saw that if they intervened on the side of Henry's army—as he suspected they would—Richard could hardly avoid defeat. Northumberland thought discretion the better part of valour and remained a spectator for the whole battle.

Meanwhile down in the valley, ammunition as a result of the fire-fight was running short, and a pause in the operations occurred. Each side was closely watching the other and waiting for it to make the first move. Then, imperceptibly and with no command, or plan, or even intention, yet almost simultaneously, the two armies advanced against each other and the two lines met in a head-on collision on the slope of the hill. The present Glebe Farm today is approximately at the centre of the engagement.

It lasted rather more than an hour as each individual and supporting sub-unit on both sides came into action.

And then the Stanleys intervened. Coming hot foot from the north and from the south they attacked Richard's two wings. In vain he looked for Northumberland's help but when he realised that this powerful noble, too, had failed him he recognised that he was being surrounded, that he might lose the battle, his throne, and, in those days, his head.

As an undoubted hero, a capable, volatile soldier, brave to the last, Richard mounted his horse and, collecting his bodyguard, he rode into the enemy.

Whom did he seek? Prima facie it would be his chief opponent, Henry. But Henry with that lack of military experience and knowledge was, understandably, not up in front directing operations, but well behind where he could exert but little influence, and well he knew it. Anyway Richard's little party, now isolated in the Lancastrian army, could hardly be expected to find the commander-in-chief, doubtless well protected by his own bodyguard. It seems probable that Richard knew full well that his predicament was not due to Henry, whose tactics had not been of much account so far. Surely he realised that his peril was so largely due to the flank attacks of the Stanleys.

It seems likely that Lord Stanley coming up from the south was as unaware of the marsh as Henry had been an hour earlier. He almost certainly blundered into it, too. Richard, seeing the chaos into which Stanley's force had temporarily fallen saw his chance and galloped down the hill with his efficient, brave, but all too small escort. He, too, ran into the marsh, where his charger was hopelessly bogged and he unseated.

Surrounded by enemy infantrymen who could move slowly in the marsh when mounted men could not, he was captured, almost isolated and killed. Shakespeare's famous line: 'A horse, a horse, my kingdom for a horse,' was probably not only written as an outstanding line in one of the great dramas of the world but was founded on fact. What other cry would an unseated horseman, in the midst of dismounted enemies, make?

When Richard's death was known resistance ceased. His army knew that he was a childless widower and that they fought for him alone. To go on fighting and risking their lives was literally pointless. Why be killed for a dead monarch? The Royal army melted away as completely as did the English army when the only other English king to die in battle perished at Hastings.

There was little pursuit. Henry's enemy had been Richard III—not his army, who were now to become his subjects. A goodly number of Richard's men fled to the north-east—three hundred years later a large number of relics, arms, etc. were found to the north of Sutton Cheney.

Henry set up his headquarters on a hill two miles to the south of the battlefield. Here Lord Stanley was handed Richard's crown, picked up in the marsh, and in full view of the cheering soldiers he placed it on Henry's head, hailing him as King Henry VII.

So the Wars of the Roses ended and the Tudor monarchy, to last one hundred and eighteen years, commenced.

Lord Stanley, a traitor to his king and to his word, but a patriot who stood for his country, decency and humanity, was largely responsible for this epoch-making victory, and as such is an outstanding Englishman.

The only two physical features that affected the battle are, of course, the southward slope of the hill, and the marsh below it. The downward slope and the ridge itself are much less formidable than most accounts give their readers to imagine. The slope is barely one in twenty and the whole ridge cannot be called anything more than a rise in the ground. The hillock at the western end is noticeable but no more.

Richard's position along the ridge certainly gave him good observation all round, and a certain advantage of being on 'higher ground', but it didn't amount to much. Nevertheless any attack on him had to come uphill—such as it was—rather than over level ground. There is no evidence as to the weather or, more important, recent rain and so the condition of the ground cannot be assessed. It may have been dry. But even so it is heavy soil, perhaps clay and an advancing body of men on foot would not find it easy going up the slight slope. The armour they wore was another heavy burden. Henry's men had marched along almost non-existent roads, in mediaeval boots (which had only felt soles) for fifteen days—covering a hundred and seventy miles—and they must have been very tired. They lacked the discipline of experience and how to look after themselves, and the slope of Ambien Hill, meagre though it was, becomes more and more a factor in Richard's favour.

The marsh at the bottom of the slope, being directly in the way of Henry's advance, was a great feature vitally affecting the action. Lying as it did, covering a large section of Richard's front with its almost impenetrable terrain, it should have formed a great protective obstacle guarding a large part of the front and thus allowed Richard to concentrate farther west and in a greater density. As he, an experienced soldier, did not take advantage of this natural obstacle so greatly in his favour, and lined part of his army along the ridge overlooking the marsh, it seems probable that he, too, was not aware of its existence.

Today the marsh is covered by a wood of ninety acres, and prima facie the ground seems normal with trees growing as in any other wood.

But a walk into the wood will soon disclose large batches of coarse reedy grass, such as is often found in boggy ground, or on common land not well drained. The wood, or bog as it was in 1485, is on a slight, almost imperceptible slope, which is the end of Ambien Hill before it finally flattens out.

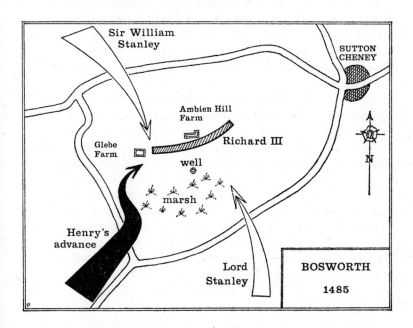

On the northern side of the marsh is a spring, now called Richard's Well, although it is not a well and nothing more than a permanent trickle out of the ground. It never stops and unquestionably caused the marsh to be constantly supplied with water which drained away on the far side. It is the cause of the heavy ground in the wood today and the farmer claims that in any weather the ground is damp all round.

In 1646 the land was enclosed, being cut up into fields, but the bog was useless for agriculture and so the wood was planted. But outside the wood and below the spring even today a horse might well get bogged, especially after heavy rain.

It is almost certain that when Richard saw the advance of the

Stanleys and decided as a last forlorn hope to charge into the enemy with his little escort, he galloped down the hill and was suddenly bogged very near the spring. It may have been right beside it. Richard would run into the marsh at full gallop, where his horse would immediately stumble. Almost certainly the horse, sinking suddenly into a foot of mud, would throw him and he might well have been killed before he could rise.

In 1813 a small stone pyramid was erected over the spring—or rather—over where the wet ground starts, and one can safely assume it is the site of his death, the last Yorkist King of England.

When Glebe Farm was being built in the eighteenth century, four cannon balls were dug up on the western end of Ambien Hill. Twenty-five years ago another cannon ball, made of stone and about four inches in diameter was found, while quite recently another was dug up one hundred and fifty yards due east of the spring. These three finds make a pattern, showing the royalist position along the hill, its crest and slopes. They were fired by Henry's army. There is no evidence that Richard had any guns.

The story of Richard's crown, which he was undoubtedly wearing, being found under a thorn bush is but a legend. Nevertheless someone found it much later in the day, probably in the mud, and brought it to Lord Stanley. There was no more suitable person to place it on Henry's helmet and proclaim him Henry VII than Lord Stanley, who, by his traitorous desertion of his king and intervention on the other side, changed completely the course of the English monarchy and made Bosworth a decisive battle in British history.

The battlefield is very easy to find and to walk over. It is best approached from the village of Sutton Cheney whence a drive of half a mile along the road to Shenton will bring the visitor to the northern slope of Ambien Hill. A walk along the cart-track to Glebe Farm is obvious and the farm is the centre of the battlefield.

The farmer reports that in the summer months a large number of visitors arrive to see the battlefield, mostly Americans and school parties. He advises bringing Wellington boots as the walk down the slope to Richard's Well is rarely dry and even after rain a week before is still very muddy.

Just west of Sutton Cheney and on the road to Shenton is the tumulus where Northumberland waited. It is five feet high, clearly defined and from its summit, mounted, he could easily see three-quarters of the battlefield in front of him, including the positions of the two Stanleys. The tumulus is still there, now enclosed in a delightful garden of a small country house. On it grow two sizeable trees and in April a mass of daffodils.

In Sutton Cheney church is a plaque on the north wall of the nave. It reads:

> 'Remember before God Richard III, King of
> England, and those who fell at Bosworth
> Field, having kept faith, 22nd August
> 1485. Loyaulte Me Lie.'

It was placed in the church, and is now maintained, by the Coventry branch of The King Richard III Society; this society aims to exonerate Richard's reputation, to prove he did not murder the little princes in the Tower and that he was a good and great king cruelly mishandled by history—surely the most difficult task any historian ever undertook.

Naseby

1645

THE outstanding event of the seventeenth century in England was the differences between King and Parliament. Twice within fifty years did the two clash, twice wars and battles about the succession of the Crown were fought on English soil, twice as a result of these differences did the throne become vacant.

Charles I was beheaded as a brave man who stuck to his principles, no matter how much Parliament and people disagreed with them. But James II ran away from his post unable to face opposition from Parliament and public opinion. He never set foot in England again.

In the first three years of the Civil War Charles I was to lead half his own people against the other half. With his half, in battle, he won victories and was defeated. He became a fugitive, was captured and executed. A Parliamentary dictatorship followed for fifteen years. The executed King's son was then restored to the throne and the Royal Succession resumed.

But in the seven years power passed from the monarch whose word and will had been paramount since 1066, and now was to be in the hands of the people—Parliament. The King was no longer to rule. He or she would, in the future, reign. In these fifteen years the whole government of the country was transformed from dictatorship into democracy.

The rift between King and Parliament started in the reign of James I. The King and his son were inclined to be tolerant to the Roman Catholics, the King because he was naturally of a tolerant disposition and Charles because he had married a Roman Catholic wife. There was a strong Puritan element in the House of Commons, which was in time to become supreme. It became as a result increasingly and fanatically anti-Catholic. It is this fact that largely accounts for the differences between the first two Stuart kings and their parliaments. In brief the country was divided between the

High Church monarchy and authority and the Low Church 'people'.

But there were other causes of friction. Englishmen were 'growing up', were becoming better educated, more thinking, more inclined to ask why. Still intensely loyal to their rulers, they gradually saw that they were governed by dictatorship, a system they had blindly accepted since the Norman Conquest and which had worked well. But now, they wondered, could not their own abilities be utilised in the affairs of their country—and for its benefit, Was the monarch the only capable man?

Another reason for the average man's opportunity to think, look, see, ponder was the absence of external danger. For the greater part of Elizabeth's long reign the Englishman's mind was filled with danger from abroad. His reliance on the Crown as the guiding and controlling authority to defend him was absolute, and his patriotism rose to great heights. The whole country was knit together by the fear of the Armada, as it was after Dunkirk, and he had no time or inclination to argue about authority or question its decrees.

The defeat of the Armada in 1588, however, slackened the bonds and obligations of instant and unquestioning obedience and in this relaxed state of mind he started to think.

James I had been harsh, arrogant and tactless. He told Parliament that as it was blasphemy to dispute what God may do, so it was sedition to dispute what God's lieutenant upon earth might do. From the day of that speech in 1611 parliament was arrayed against the King, resisted every one of his acts, hindered all he tried to do. On one occasion the Commons suggested a suitable line on a foreign affair. They were told by James that it was not their business. They entered a protest, passed in the House, in their Journal, adding that it was their freedom to discuss any topic. James sent for the Journal and tore out that page.

James I was an able and intelligent man, but it was a pity that he did not recognise the dawning conscience of Englishmen to their own rights, abilities and reasonable desire to participate in their own affairs. Had he done so, and passed on such modern ideas to his son, there might not have been a civil war, Charles I would not have been executed and there would have been no battle at Naseby.

But Charles, although a less able man than his father, was more stubborn, rigid and bigoted. In religious matters in particular, partly due to the influence of his Roman Catholic wife, he was quite immovable in his attitudes in support of everything Catholic and against anything giving encouragement to Protestants. The Queen was constantly striving to obtain concessions for her co-religionists, she actively intrigued with foreign powers, and worst of all held the most extreme political opinions as to the King's authority, the royal supremacy, and the wickedness of all who opposed it.

It was tragic that the reigns of these two bigoted, strong-minded, and intransigent monarchs should have coincided with the emerging consciousness of ordinary English people, with their desire for representation, participation and democracy. Such a coincidence could only result in a head-on clash, which might well, and did, end in civil war.

On Charles's accession he found the Treasury in low water. He needed money to repay a national debt to the King of Denmark, to equip a fleet to attack Spain and to prosecute the long-drawn-out war with Scotland. Parliament would not grant the funds, and Charles threatened to take taxation entirely into his own hands, and levy a forced loan. When it became necessary to enforce this loan, five titled men refused to pay and were imprisoned.

Charles had already dissolved two parliaments, but now called together a third one. Its first act was to pass the Petition of Right, the two most important clauses being that the taxation of the people except by consent of Parliament was illegal, and that arbitrary imprisonment without cause was also outside the law.

In the next fourteen years there was a succession of attempts by the King to force his will upon Parliament, mostly concerning money, taxation, and religious matters, their doctrines and formularies. Almost on principle the Commons resisted each and passed various acts confirming democracy and the rights of an elected Parliament.

Finally the King went down to the House of Commons with four hundred soldiers to arrest five leading members on a charge of treason. The five members having been warned of such action on the part of the King were deliberately absent. But the damage was done. The members greatly resented the personal intrusion of the monarch into their Chamber, regarding it as a scandalous breach of privilege, and on his departure he was hooted out of the building with cries of 'Privilege, privilege'.

Both sides made preparations for war in the next seven months.

Both sides tried to get control of the Militia, Parliament passing an Act to call them out. Charles, however, vetoed the Act—as he had the legal right so to do.

In April 1642 the Governor of Hull refused the King permission to enter the town. Civil War was not far off, and in August Charles raised his standard at Nottingham Castle.

The Great Civil War had begun, to last seven years.

The first three years saw an intensely active period of fighting, a period that ended with the battle of Naseby. To see not only the end of a war but also the end of centuries of monarchical dictator-ship and the weaning of Parliamentary democracy from its birth, places Naseby within the magic circle of decisive battles of British history.

The English people were split into two camps; one, patriotic, adhering to the King, loyal to the principle of monarchy, the divine right of kings; the other, also patriotic, loyal to their country and its welfare, believing in the sovereignty of the people, believing in the seventeenth century.

Broadly the supporters of Parliament, the Roundheads, were in the east of England and the Midlands, living to the east of a line from Portsmouth to Liverpool, and south of a line from Liverpool to Hull. The whole of the west of England, the Southern Midlands, Wales, and the counties north of Manchester were Kingsmen, Cavaliers. They drew their strength from the nobility, the landed gentry and their retainers, and the small townsmen. They were strong in cavalry, with an eye for the tactical use of ground; the men were easily led as the men in the county regiments have always been. They were tough, used to exposure, not over-intelligent and followed their King as their man, the man they loved. He was a gentleman.

The Roundheads were largely city men, narrow in outlook both political and physical, quick, intelligent and capable, easy to teach, quick to learn, and by their intelligence convinced of the righteous-ness of their cause, democracy and self-expression.

As an asset Parliament had possession of London, and, with the wealth in the City, was well able to prosecute a war. It was strong in infantry who were better trained than their fellows in the Royal-ist army. The latter, however, had better horses and were better riders. Thus as the opening months of the Civil War were to be largely occupied by cavalry manoeuvres and actions, the King's forces were at considerable advantage. Another great asset to the Cavaliers was Prince Rupert, a nephew of King Charles, not yet twenty-three. A born cavalry leader, he was also a capable general. Parliament's generals, Lord Essex and Lord Manchester were not so good, and lacked strength of purpose and dominance over their men in the early stages of the war.

Each side had about 13,000 men. Most were amateurs, except for a few of the Royalist officers. Both armies were really makeshift affairs, lacking even contemporary organisation and administration. The conduct of all the battles, owing to a lack of trained staff officers, was sketchy in the extreme. Every defeat, or victory, by either was usually the result of muddle on the one side, or mistakes on the other. Rarely has the skill and guidance of the professional been so missed by the amateur. Never has the term 'enthusiastic amateur' been so applicable.

King Charles raised his standard at Nottingham and then marched to Worcester. Essex followed him and a minor cavalry skirmish took place, Prince Rupert easily dispersing the Round-heads.

Charles then decided to march to London to reclaim his capital. Bad staff work by Essex allowed Charles to by-pass him, and the Royalists gained a lead of seven miles on their opponents.

King Charles now had a difficult problem before him. Should he turn and shake off his enemy—or continue his march to the east. Spurred on by his youthful, dashing nephew, Prince Rupert, he turned and occupied the ridge of Edgehill, near Banbury.

The Roundheads, among whom was a Captain Oliver Cromwell, attacked and were repulsed, the cavalry 'improved' the victory and the King continued his march to London, while Essex retired west-ward. The King had won his first victory.

On approaching London, however, Charles found at Turnham Green a force of 24,000 Londoners, armed with pitchforks, hatchets, sticks and stones, barring his way. Despite his superior equipment and horses, he recognised that not only were these Londoners un-trained, unled and unorganised civilians but they were also his subjects. He declined to run them down and force his way through to his capital; he retired to Oxford. His army was never to get so near the capital again.

In the second year of the war, Atherton Moor in Yorkshire was a victory for the King. Bristol was captured by Rupert and the

Roundheads defeated at Roundway Down in Wiltshire, and at Chalgrove, near Oxford.

In September 1643, a year after the war had started the tide turned. Another concentrated move on London organised by the King meant that several of his smaller forces, recruited in the areas where they lived, and in which they had marched and fought, would thus leave unguarded their homes. These would be at the mercy not only of the Parliamentary army but also of their neighbours whom they knew to be unsympathetic to the King.

Many men deserted, though several complete forces remained loyal but refused to leave their home areas.

The King advanced to besiege Gloucester but fought an indecisive battle at Newbury and for the next eight months minor engagements took place. Neither side secured any real advantage. None were in any way part of any organised plan. It was largely guerrilla warfare and there were numberless incidents of cruelty, atrocity, sackings, burnings by both sides. Never have Englishmen been so set against each other. Every man, unless recruited into one of the two armies, was suspected by his neighbour of being a traitor to the King or to democracy. Everyday life in England was very similar to that in the Wars of the Roses, when even individuals from the same family might be on opposite sides, each eyeing the other with dislike and distrust.

In July 1644 came the great Royalist defeat at Marston Moor, near York. A large force of Cavaliers had been besieged in York by Scots mercenaries employed by Parliament, and Roundheads under their new general, Fairfax. After Rupert had relieved York he turned on the combined forces surrounding the city and attacked his opponents. The battle was notable for the large number of men engaged. The Royalists had seventeen thousand while the Parliamentarians mustered twenty-six thousand. Again it was a great cavalry battle, and Rupert as a cavalry leader met his match.

Oliver Cromwell had now become the equivalent of a brigadier, and commanded the cavalry in one of Fairfax's three divisions. By his bold yet controlled tactics he defeated Rupert's cavalry, then charged the Royalist infantry, annihilating them. It was Cromwell who won Marston Moor. Indeed three of his brother Roundhead generals, although on the ultimately winning side, had at one period left the field.

Both the general conduct and the military efficiency of the Roundhead forces at Marston Moor, and three months later at the second battle of Newbury, brought to a head the dissatisfaction Cromwell and others felt about their men and their leaders. As a result the whole Parliamentarian army was reorganised, several generals were retired being not up to their work, pay was increased, more capable officers appointed, Fairfax took command, asking for Cromwell to command the cavalry.

In this largely reorganised army, the New Model Army, discipline was tighened up. Morale rose, too, as it always will when regiments are firmly commanded. The officers and men saw that their cause, democracy and self-government, had not been prospering so far. The new regulations, uniforms, pay and discipline did much to wield them into quite a different force from that which had so far been opposing the Royalists.

Sixteen years later, at the Restoration of Charles's son, Charles II, to the throne, the New Model Army, having won the Civil War for Parliament and people, was disbanded, with the exception of one regiment, then and today known as the Coldstream Guards.

A year after Marston Moor the King, irresolute, perhaps a little doubtful of his ultimate success, was stationed with the bulk of his army around Daventry, doing very little. The New Model Army's first task on its reorganisation was besieging Oxford.

On 5th June, Fairfax broke up his camp before Oxford, deciding to search for and engage with all his strength the Royal Army near Daventry. Parliament gave Fairfax a completely free hand, and his skill as a tactician together with the new spirit of enterprise and discipline in his troops made his army a formidable force. It had Cromwell as second-in-command, and commanding the cavalry, whereas the King had no one to show against them. His senior general was sixty-six years old—equivalent today to seventy-three —Rupert, only twenty-five was becoming more and more independent, while Charles, though titular head of the Royal army and worshipped by his men, had little military skill. Lastly, and always an important factor, the Roundheads had a superiority of nearly two to one, 14,000 against 7,500 Cavaliers. The morale on both sides was high. The Royalist's recent capture of Leicester had made them even more contemptuous of their opponents, whom anyway they considered upstarts, common men—their officers included— while the arrival of Cromwell put the New Model Army's confidence high. Both sides felt certain of victory in the obviously impending battle.

On 12th June, Fairfax, from Oxford, and pushing forward vigorously, was eight miles east of Daventry, driving in some Royal picquets. The Royalist army in Daventry, not ready for battle, took fright and withdrew by night to Market Harborough, being followed by Fairfax. In the evening of 13th June the Roundhead main body had reached the village of Guilsborough, while its advance guard had entered a small village, four miles farther north. There they surprised a Cavalier patrol feasting at an inn, capturing it. The village was Naseby.

The news of this incident reached the King in Market Harborough in the middle of the night. He decided at dawn to move out of the town and take up a defensive position on some high ground two miles to the south. By 6.30 a.m. the position from East Farndon to Oxendon was occupied, and facing south had the village of Naseby and the ridge in front of it in full view. About the same time as the Royalists were occupying the East Farndon ridge, Fairfax, who had also heard of the incident in the inn at Naseby, moved his main body forward, and occupied the Naseby ridge. The position was not unlike that on the morning of Waterloo. Two great armies each occupied a pronounced ridge, observing, and in full view of each other.

The great trial of strength wherein the New Model Army was to be tested and where Charles was to have his last chance was about to begin. It was not one of the decisive battles of the world. But it was one of the decisive battles in British history. By its result dictatorship by the monarch in England was finished for ever. Democracy and rule by the people through Parliament was to survive, flourish and remain.

At about 7.30 a.m. Fairfax, accompanied by his cavalry commander, Cromwell, and with a considerable escort, rode forward down his ridge to reconnoitre the ground. He found the valley between the two ridges very boggy with a little stream crossing the road running north from Naseby to Clipston. He considered holding in strength his present position, well down the ridge, covered as it was by the bog and the stream, but Cromwell intervened. He pointed out that the Royalists were strong in cavalry and that Rupert, out on the Royalist right flank would almost certainly try to turn the position from either flank. It would be better to move the army back up the ridge and so tempt Rupert to attack across the valley, encounter the bog and finally have to charge uphill with his horses blown after negotiating the heavy ground. Cromwell won the argument and Fairfax decided to move to the ridge behind him, and there deploy his main mass of infantry.

As Fairfax withdrew to the top of the ridge, Rupert seeing this retrograde movement, also saw the bog and that the valley was unsuitable for mounted action. Farther to his right, however, he saw more promising ground, ground which his cavalry could use to outflank the Roundheads. Sending back an urgent message for the army to follow him, he struck off to his right, and hit the Clipston–Sibbertoft road.

Rupert's flanking movement was seen by Fairfax, who decided yet again to change his mind as to which position he would take up. In order to counter Rupert's westward move he too decided to side-step to the same flank and at about 9 a.m. both armies were moving westward on almost parallel lines. This move brought them respectively on either side of the head of the valley at its shallowest, the slopes at their most gentle and with now no stream between them.

It forms a fine site for a battle, and is virtually in the centre of England. The stream in the valley flows eastward into the Wash, while only a few hundred yards farther to the west, a mere trickle in a ditch runs south-west into the Avon, and thence into the Severn.

Both armies were now astride the Sibbertoft–Naseby road which roughly bisects both positions.

As in most battles in the sixteenth and seventeenth centuries, both armies were drawn up with a solid phalanx of infantry in the centre, forming an apparently immoveable, certainly awe-inspiring, block. In the centre, pikes down and menacing; on either flank the musketeers facing outwards, hoping by their fire to arrest—or at least disorganise—a mounted flank attack.

On the outer flanks was the cavalry, mounted, waiting to act as a reserve to come down on the flank and counter a successful attack—or to harass violently, perhaps decimate, an unsuccessful, hesitating or badly organised advance.

On the Cavaliers' right flank was Rupert, the most dashing cavalry leader alive, with 3,000 men. On the Roundhead right flank was Cromwell with 2,000 mounted men under his hand. Though not so dashing or so young as Rupert, Cromwell was just as skilful as a subordinate general and had the great advantage of a better disciplined force, both men and horses. The two cavalry leaders on the opposite flank of each army respectively, Sir Marmaduke Langdale, a Cavalier, and Ireton, the Parliamentarian, were not of importance.

Rupert's cavalry was drawn up just to the west of the present 'Prince Rupert's Farm', while Langdale's left flank cavalry rested on the southern tip of Long Hold Spinney. Thus the whole line covered nearly a mile, a wide dispersal for only 9,000 men (5,000 horse and 4,000 foot). Charles kept 1,500 in his hand as a reserve. His command post was at Dust Hill Farm, whence a good view of the whole field could be obtained.

The Parliamentarians were drawn up in similar formation, on the same frontage, and about a mile and a half away. Cromwell's cavalry on the right, owing to a sharp declivity in front of him, was slightly behind the general alignment—which was just behind Red Hill Ridge, though in the view of the Cavaliers.

Out on his left flank, quite separate from his main line, slightly in front of it and facing inwards, Fairfax placed 1,000 dragoons behind Sulby Hedge, under Colonel Okey—a curious position. It was admirably sited to enfilade Rupert's cavalry when they charged the Roundhead left flank—as they were almost certain to do—but if Rupert went very wide he would take Okey in flank—or worse still pass behind him. In fact Rupert passed in front of Sulby Hedge in the first charge on Ireton's force so all was well, but had he chosen to go farther out, Okey's dragoons would have been in great tactical trouble.

Fairfax had all his guns up, but remembering the very small effect they had had at Marston Moor he did not rely on them, and used them little. Owing to the rapid and sudden move to his new position on Dust Hill, Rupert too had left most of his guns behind, and the battle of Naseby became the last major battle in British history wherein artillery played no part. The battle became, as most battles in the Civil War became, largely a cavalry battle, the infantry playing their customary sheet-anchor, self-sacrificing role.

By 10 a.m. both sides were ready, facing each other in full array. An easy firm stretch of ground, known as Broadmore Valley, separated them. Each felt confident of victory, the Cavaliers conscious of social and military superiority, the Roundheads determined to show how efficient the New Model Army was to prove. Which would make the first move?

Probably without the concurrence of Lord Astley, commander of the Royalist infantry, Rupert persuaded Charles to order a general attack. Advancing slightly downhill from Dust Hill and into the shallow little depression the Royal infantry started to ascend the opposite rise. The Roundheads seeing the advance moved forward to meet it, and the two great masses of infantry were very near to each other.

Rupert felt that he too should now advance when all eyes were on the imminent infantry clash. Trotting forward in two lines he was abreast of the two infantry forces in a few minutes. He paused before starting to ascend the slight rise, on top of which he could see Ireton's cavalry, as yet unmoved.

Given the order to charge, his horsemen passed outside the two infantry masses but kept inside the Sulby Hedge. From Okey's dragoons there he received a ragged fire which did little damage, neither impeding nor diverting his charge. Gathering speed as he swept up the gentle slope he crashed into the left of Ireton's line about Red Hill Farm. A considerable mêlée ensued. Some Roundheads advanced to meet the charge, others remained stationary. The sword fight went in favour of the Cavaliers whose inbred and superior swordsmanship prevailed. The opposition dwindled, and some Roundheads slipped away. Rupert gathering his men together into some sort of formation resumed his advance and thereby committed one of the great tactical blunders of military history.

Passing to the rear of the Parliamentarian lines, though not behind it, he galloped on for a good mile for no known reason. Suddenly and unexpectedly he came across the enemy's baggage wagons parked in a small depression to the west of Naseby village. The baggage guard put up a stiff resistance and much time was lost by the Cavaliers in attempting to capture the wagon-laager. Rupert had difficulty in withdrawing his troopers from the plunder and reforming them, often a lengthy task, and it was almost an hour before he reappeared on the main battlefield, where much had been happening in his absence.

It is difficult to excuse this waste of time and Rupert's reputation as a tactician is greatly harmed by it. He totally ignored one of the principles of war, maintenance of the objective (in this case the defeat of the Parliamentary army) and he achieved nothing except

1.   Her Majesty the Queen unveiling the statue of Robert the Bruce at Bannockburn. *National Trust for Scotland.*

2. Sulby Hedge at Naseby. Okey's Dragoons were hidden behind the right-hand hedge when Rupert's cavalry passed them.

3. Relics of the battle—a table, a sword and a spur in the church at Naseby.

4. Culloden, looking towards the English positions. The left of Barrell's was across the road by the first telegraph pole, Wolfe's stood where the bungalow is now. The muddy dip which the Highlanders crossed in their charge is clearly shown.

5. Culloden. The restored Old Leanach Cottage, and the ruins of the barn in which several Highlanders were killed when the English burnt it.

6. Quatre Bras. The sun is shining on the house where the Welch Regiment lost its colour. The Gordon Highlanders stood alongside the enclosed farm buildings in the centre.

the capture of a few baggage wagons, the possession of which would assist neither side. By the waste of time on this trivial incident, during which time he was serving no useful purpose whatever, Rupert probably lost Charles the battle and his throne.

Meanwhile on the battlefield the Royalist infantry, although the slope of the hill was against them, had pushed their opponents back to the crest of their ridge in a retreat that was beginning to have the aspect of a rout. Had Rupert been available with his cavalry to 'improve' this temporary victory the battle of Naseby would have become a Royal victory in two hours.

But Fairfax, 'Fiery Tom', threw in his reserve and managed to hold the Royalist advance.

Rupert's early attack on Ireton's cavalry had defeated, disorganised, almost decimated, only half of the Roundhead's left-wing cavalry, before it had galloped off to the capture of the baggage wagons. The other half with Ireton still in command was intact. Seeing his fellow infantry in the centre hard pressed by the Royalist infantry, Ireton advanced and wheeling to the right came straight into the open flank of Lord Astley's veterans, causing them consternation and an immediate halt. Facing right, however, they held their mounted assailants, but were now fighting on two fronts. Okey's dragoons, seeing the success of Ireton's flank attack on the Royalist right also advanced, joining forces with Ireton, and together they firmly fenced in the Royalist infantry right flank.

But more disasters were to fall upon the Royalists. Out on the Roundhead's right flank, Cromwell saw the left wing of the Royal Cavalry threading their way through furze bushes and broken country at the bottom of the hill below him. As they started to climb the rather steep rise he ordered his subordinate cavalry commander, Colonel Whalley, to advance with the front rank. The troopers thundered down the hill in superior numbers, Langdale's Horse being swept from the field.

Whalley's men, intoxicated with momentary victory as Rupert's had been only a short while before on the opposite flank, galloped on and almost reached Dust Hill, not far from King Charles's headquarters. There, however, they halted, their horses blown, the men disorganised, and they took no further important part in the battle.

Cromwell then wheeled his second and third ranks to their left, and remained mounted and ready. Soon after, he advanced in waves against the devoted Royalist infantry who had given such a good account of themselves up to date. They were now beset on three sides. It was too much and they began to give way, retreating in some disorder to the shallow valley behind them.

Charles now had his last chance, a chance that any general has, the timely use of his reserve; in this case 900 horse and 700 foot. He moved south-east from Dust Hill Farm and along the front edge of Long Hold Spinney. At the southern tip of the spinney, owing to some misunderstanding of Charles's intention, the reserve turned about and were soon back near where it had started. From there it was still practicable to re-enter the battle, perhaps decisively, and advance either against Cromwell whom he would catch in flank, busy with the retreating Royalist infantry or to have ignored Cromwell, 'fetched a compass' and come in on the Roundhead infantry's right flank, or even rear.

But Charles did nothing and remained in observation on Dust Hill with his reserve for nearly an hour, watching a tragedy being enacted in the valley below him.

The Royalist infantry were practically surrounded, for some of Cromwell's horsemen had passed round to their rear. It was to be their end, encircled as they were, with no hope of manoeuvre, or help from their cavalry. The regiments of foot laid down their arms one by one, ammunition expended. All had fought on to the end, extracting admiration from their opponents.

During this slow piece-meal surrender Rupert reappeared on the field. He would have liked to have put in a final charge, but his horses were past it, and for some time would be of little value. Occasions are rare when cavalry can charge, cover a lot of ground, fully laden with soldiers and their equipment, twice within a short period and this was not one of them.

Rupert's feelings must have been bitter as he, a hopeless eyewitness, gazed on the tragedy he had helped to bring about by his rash, pointless and ridiculous affair with the Roundhead baggage wagons. It is for speculation whether he realised he had lost his uncle the throne.

As the last regiment laid down its arms Fairfax, regrouping his infantry began to move them forward, over and through the disarmed Royalists. The King saw that he had lost, turned and rode from the field.

The Royalists lost 4,000 infantrymen almost to a man and their

12 guns that were not used. Their cavalry too suffered heavily, though in lighter proportion. The Parliamentary losses were heavy, especially among Ireton's cavalry and the infantry in the centre, but the total figure is not known.

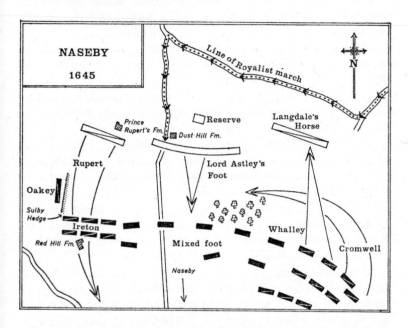

Naseby was very largely a cavalry battle. Five separate groups, Rupert's, Ireton's, Okey's, Whalley's and Cromwell's, all played a part that vastly influenced the final result. As usual the infantry were the pawns, whose flanks were to be protected, or attacked, whose surrender or whose final 'possession of the field' was to be the culminating point, the last episode.

Naseby is ideal cavalry country, with broad, open, gradually rising downs. Visibility is good, the few woods and farmsteads are of little tactical importance. It is one of those areas, not unlike Salisbury Plain, which are so disheartening, perhaps exasperating, to the infantry commander. The position he has taken up is probably no better and no worse than many others he could occupy for a long way round. All can be seen by the enemy. It offers few, sometimes no, physical features to occupy or to defend, yet the farmsteads and woods at Naseby seem to be obvious and of importance.

It is noteworthy that although the names of several farms and woods have been mentioned in this narrative, and appear on the sketch map, largely to designate areas, none of these features influenced the battle once it was joined.

What might have been the result if Rupert, having thrown Ireton's left into confusion, had remained on the field, and after giving his horses a breather, been available for further action?

Firstly it could have prevented the other undefeated half of Ireton's cavalry, and the whole of Okey's, from molesting the right flank of Astley's Royalist infantry as it assaulted the Roundheads. Despite the pressure of Ireton it very nearly succeeded in defeating them anyway, and Rupert as a flank guard could have seen the Royalist infantry home.

But what of Cromwell while this was happening? He could have attacked the left flank of the Royalist infantry as he in fact eventually did—but always having to keep an eye on Rupert, whom he knew to be dashing, volatile, adventurous and liable to appear anywhere his horses could carry men. Langdale was an element always to be considered and although Whalley had put him to flight, his horses were blown and by the time they reached the limit of their charge, Whalley's men were of little further use.

By now the defeat by the Royalist foot of the Roundhead infantry would have been complete, and the latter eliminated. On the western side of the battle would have stood the undefeated half of Ireton's force, which together with that of Okey would be contained by Rupert. This leaves Cromwell, less Whalley, to defeat the victorious Royalist infantry. Could he have done it? Propably not because the King's reserve would have thrown in their weight on Cromwell's outer flank, and so embarrassed him that he would call off his last desperate attacks on the Royalist infantry and left the field, but with his cavalry undefeated.

But Rupert was not available to operate and so King Charles lost the battle of Naseby, the campaign, his throne and, finally his head.

The battle was decisive militarily. It was also important politically. In the baggage captured at the King's headquarters were found documents which showed clearly that Charles had been intriguing with foreign powers, asking for military assistance if he lost the Civil War. These requests could only be construed as invitations to invade, and the nation almost to a man turned against him. At the time of his trial barely half the people wanted him to be beheaded—but ninety per cent wanted him removed from his throne and all power.

The battlefield of Naseby seems much changed since 1645. This is but an illusion, however, which is caused by a large number of simple hedges planted when the small fields were enclosed in 1830. Otherwise there is little change, except for Red Hill Farm, Prince Rupert's Farm, Broadmoor Farm, and Dust Hill Farm, each a group of buildings occupying a very small area only. They have been built since the battle, are of comparative youth, and are of no interest to this story. In the 17th century, isolated farms such as are common today, did not exist in this part of England and all the workers, farmers, labourers, stockmen etc., lived in the near-by village, a very tight little community.

Sulby Hedge still stands as it did in 1645—for the most part two rows of trees some twenty yards apart growing on turf-covered banks. Towards its northern end it becomes only a single row—and the turf track between the hedges peters out.

The ground is open farm land. If the new hedges can be eliminated from one's mind's eye, a very clear picture of the battlefield emerges.

The steep declivity in front of Cromwell's cavalry is not so considerable as anticipated. At its foot the rabbit warrens and gorse have disappeared, and the land is now under the plough. The hollow in which Fairfax's baggage laager was hidden is quite clear but is less of a hollow than a falling-back of the ground down towards the western outskirts of the village.

But by far the most interesting things to see at Naseby are in the church. Here is the table round which the Royalist outpost was sitting, feasting, when surprised and captured by the Parliamentarian scouts. For some years it was at the Inn, and later removed to the Manor House. Here, although treasured for many years, it was eventually discarded and turned out into the yard at the back of the Manor, exposed to the snow and rain of many winters.

However, the predecessor of the present vicar spotted the table and got permission from the owner of the manor to have it restored. It now stands in the north aisle of the church, well worn, but all rot stopped. It is in quite remarkable condition.

Above the table, and firmly secured to the wall is a sword picked up on the field, and one stirrup iron. The sword has a few inches broken off its blade, doubtless caused in the action.

These two relics are naturally very darkly stained with rust—
are indeed almost black—but the corroding has been arrested and
they too are in remarkable condition.

In the vestry and locked up are a pair of spurs, and two cannon
balls. One of them is of beautifully polished and rounded stone—
the other of iron. One musket and one pistol ball complete this
fascinating collection.

The parish of Naseby has been fortunate in its present vicar and
his predecessor. Both keen amateur historians they have done much
to keep the relics carefully, and the atmosphere so true. The present
incumbent in particular, Mr. Mansell, is the most erudite and
knowledgable amateur historian the author has had the privilege of
knowing.

Malplaquet

1709

THE causes of the war of Marlborough's great victories, the War of the Spanish Succession, have always been obscure.

Louis XIV had been ruling France from 1661 until 1702. During these forty-one years, following his minority of eighteen years, he had ruled efficiently and successfully. He was the greatest monarch of his age, and by the end of the 17th century he, and France under him, entirely dominated Europe. He was eventually King of France for seventy-two years, the longest reign in history in any country. He was worshipped by his subjects, as most successful leaders are. His people called him 'Le Roi Soleil', and he is still known by this colloquial title today.

Charles II of Spain, a sickly and dying man in 1699, had no children, and on his death left his throne to his nephew, Philip of Anjou, who was also the grandson of Louis XIV. Charles II died in 1700, and Louis immediately helped his grandson to come into his inheritance. Thus a Bourbon replaced a Hapsburg on the throne of Madrid. Two Frenchmen related by blood and marriage ruled two neighbouring, vast, and friendly countries. 'The Pyrenees no longer exist', as Louis might have said.

By this somewhat ruthless diplomacy, France had secured an enormous accretion to her already great territory and underlined the fact that she was now more than ever the most powerful military and economic power on the continent of Europe.

Diplomatically the succession of Philip to the throne of Spain did not immediately lead to anything more serious than grave disquiet among the British, the Dutch and the Holy Roman Empire. The British as the leader of this coalition and always difficult to rouse unless in acute danger or when insulted, took no action. The sensation subsided, gradually quietening down into an acceptance of a *fait accompli*. A comfortable argument was that after all it was only Louis's second and not his eldest grandson that had succeeded, and perhaps there was no real danger.

Then Louis did a tactless thing. The exiled James II of England lay dying in Paris—and Louis there told him that he would immediately recognise James's son, the 'Old Pretender', as James III of England.

This insult to the reigning William III of England, an officially 'friendly' monarch, was in very poor taste. To the British people who had accepted William as their joint monarch with Queen Mary II, had crowned him, publicly acclaiming him, the insult roused them as no far-off vague danger could.

But there was a much larger and more general question to consider. It was no less than the defence of Austria—more properly the Empire—against the overwhelming and still obviously growing power of France. The British people began to feel concerned, and William, seeing that the tide of public opinion had yet again turned against France, dissolved his Tory Parliament, which favoured peace, perhaps appeasement, and led the newly elected Whig majority to arms. His sudden death from a fall from his horse placed on his sister-in-law, Queen Anne, the burden of declaring, and waging, war against France.

The continent of Europe had not seen a British soldier since Agincourt, almost three hundred years before; both the two other members of the Coalition, and the French, forgot that the British in their long absence might have developed and grown-up as they themselves had done. They imagined the British still used bows and arrows, that knights still fought in armour on horse-back, that all the trappings and customs of mediaeval warfare still held good.

The monarchical struggles of the Wars of the Roses, the religious struggles of the Reformation and the political struggles in the 17th century against the Crown had built up and closely knit the British character in these three hundred years. In this time the British, patriotic to a degree, were now, as a result of their experiences, violently anti-tyranny, ready to fight for freedom or to disperse a growing over-lordship. They made a dangerous enemy, and one which was also very wealthy.

The allies of the Coalition, at the end of 1701, heard with surprise that Great Britain supported whole-heartedly the alliance against Louis XIV—that she voted an army of 40,000 men, all of whom were to be both kept in supplies and paid for by the British—and most surprising of all, that 18,000 of these soldiers would be from Great Britain.

The quality of the British Army in the 18th century was superb—perhaps the best it has ever attained. The officers, all well-born, were accustomed to give orders, to be obeyed, and to take responsibility. They were the descendants of the nobles, the knights and the squires who had led at Poitiers and Agincourt. Mostly from the aristocracy or the county families, they were held in much esteem and not a little awe by the men they led and who so implicitly obeyed them. These men, from the plough and the small county towns, were long-service professionals, bound by an iron discipline. At no period in the history of the British Army had there been such a large social gap between the men and the officers. At no time, except perhaps in August 1914, had the officers been more aware of their responsibilities to their men, often from their father's estate. The Army was the cream of a nation that was emerging into a world beyond the English Channel, a nation that was as one man, all white, all Anglo-Saxon, all speaking the same language, a nation that was well on its way up the hill of world dominance.

The 40,000 men, British, Dutch, Germans and Austrians assembled in the leisurely manner then usual, in the spring of 1702.

England and her allies had yet another great asset—Marlborough. 'The greatest soldier that ever wore a red coat' was appointed to share the post of Commander-in-Chief of the Allies with firstly the Dutch Commissioner, and, later, with Prince Louis of Baden. The former proved a most cautious civilian who listened to Marlborough's professional advice and grudgingly (and often too late) gave his agreement to policy, manoeuvres, and moves, and it says much for Marlborough's negotiating skill and patience that he was to achieve so much in the first two campaigning seasons.

The War of the Spanish Succession, as Marlborough's great campaigns came to be known, was to last for eight years. In the first eighteen months Marlborough established himself as master of the eastern Netherlands, capturing several fortresses in the first campaigning season. In the second (1703) he was less successful, failing to capture Antwerp, but causing the French Army considerable embarrassment by much marching and countermarching, although unable to bring it to battle.

1704 was his great year. It included his march to the Danube and his great victory over the French at Blenheim, one of the fifteen decisive battles in world history, the first in his 'Great Quadrilateral'.

1705 was another unsatisfactory year but was followed, in 1706, by the success at Ramillies, where sixty thousand French soldiers were attacked in a poorish defensive position, outflanked and utterly defeated, eleven thousand being killed or wounded and five thousand captured together with many guns, and much baggage. This great victory was followed by another blank year (1707).

In 1708, a campaign very similar to that of 1706 was fought. The French, their memories of Blenheim and Ramillies fading, made great efforts to concentrate a re-organised army, and they drew troops from all quarters to Flanders. Moving north to threaten Louvain, however, they suddenly lost heart and moved away from Marlborough to the west towards the town of Hal, passing over the battlefield-to-be of Waterloo on the way. Five days later they marched to Oudenarde, where Marlborough, coming up with them, defeated them in the third of his four great victories.

The last corner of the Quadrilateral, Malplaquet, came at the end of the 1709 campaign.

The French, once again reinforced and fearing an invasion and a march on Paris, had built a strong line of entrenchments to protect Arras, the north-eastern gate of France. Facing north-east, it extended from La Bassée to south of Mons, and was intended to be impregnable. The only undefeated French General, Marshal Villars, was in command and there he lay, while to the north Marlborough at his leisure besieged and captured Tournai, invested round the French position. The southward path was to be through the gap between the woods of Lanières and Sars, about a mile to the north of the little village of Malplaquet.

Villars, by excellent reconnaisance and intelligence, discovered the move, and leaving the great entrenchment, moved forward into Mons, and reconnoitred the enemy's line.

Believing them to be too formidable to be forced, the Allied Army side-stepped to the east, intending then to turn south and pass the gap which Marlborough was approaching, and the two armies lay facing each other on the night of the 29th August.

Everything pointed to a general action next day and Marlborough hoped to turn west and attack the French right flank, possibly coming behind the main French entrenchments before the French

could fully erect new defences. The arrival of the Dutch Commissioner, however, upset and delayed matters, and Marlborough
was forced to postpone his attack for twenty-four hours until the
31st. Villars naturally spent the whole day as he had spent the
previous night, in strengthening his position, which by the afternoon of the 30th was already formidable.

Three rows of new trenches joined the two woods at the narrowest
point of the gap, and were thus about a mile and a half in length.
The inner sides of the two woods, facing inwards across the gap
were roughly parallel, and continued for two miles. The woods were
by no means impenetrable and formed excellent cover for any flanking movements. Between them and half a mile short of the trenches
was a small isolated copse, the Wood of Tiry. Lanières Wood was
three-quarters of a mile deep, while that of Sars straggled far out to
the west and at its farthest point was three miles deep.

The French held the now very strong triple line of trenches in
great strength, while the inner sides of the two woods were held
for some distance forward by units facing inwards towards each
other. Detachments in some rear trenches behind the main position
guarded Malplaquet, and finally, in the rear of all, stood the cavalry.
There were ninety-five thousand French soldiers on the defensive.

Two very strong detachments of German and Austrian troops,
started the action for the Allies at about eight o'clock by attacking
the northern and eastern faces of Sars Wood, on the left of the
French position. The main British infantry were drawn up in the
centre, ready to advance down the gap when their right flank had
been guarded by the clearing of Sars Wood. A strong detachment
under General Withers with nineteen battalions and two cavalry
regiments moved far out to their right, to encircle Sars Wood and
turn the extreme French left.

The attack on the eastern face of the wood proceeded well at
first. The Austrians passed through marshes and streams coming
nearer and nearer to the French position but after a slight penetration were eventually held up by fire from deep inside the wood.
Extending their left, and in full deployment, they could make little
further headway.

The Germans fared little better. Pressing into the northern point
of the wood they, too, advanced, driving in French outposts and,
later, some isolated enemy regiments but they also were brought to
a halt by the western end of the main trench line, held by Picardie,

the senior French regiment of the line, which would not yield. Three
British regiments, the Buffs, the Bedfords, and Temple's were sent
by Marlborough in reinforcement around the right but were met by
a strong reserve of twelve enemy battalions in counter attack. This
British brigade would have been cut up had Villars not caught sight
of Marlborough leading the supporting cavalry, and immediately
withdrew the counter attack. The three British regiments were now
able to move forward, Picardie at last fell back and the Germans
and Austrians advanced again. The wood, however, becomes very
dense at its southern end, and all touch with neighbouring units was
lost. French parties left behind in the orderly withdrawal became
mixed up with Germans, Austrians and British, and soon small
parties, all sense of direction gone, were stalking each other in great
confusion. The left flank of the main enemy trenches was uncovered
but scarcely threatened.

Impatient at not being allowed to move while the Sars Wood
battle was progressing, the Prince of Orange, commanding a large
force on the Allied left, advanced without orders against the northern end of the Lanières Wood, across the gap. The trenches on the
edge of this wood were well sited, and bravely held and Orange's
attack was greatly slowed by very accurate French musket fire.
Most of the Prince's staff were shot, and his own horse under him.
Nevertheless he continued to lead them on foot until they came
within range of artillery on their left flank. This caused further
heavy casualties but somehow they continued their advance and
finally reached the first entrenchments inside the wood. A counter-
attack, however, drove them back, with very heavy losses. Six
thousand men were killed in this unauthorised operation and
Orange's precipitation had brought about little less than a disaster,
badly upsetting Marlborough's over-all plan.

By now the English, Germans, and Austrians in Sars Wood were
struggling forward again. Tripping over felled trees, forcing their
way through thick undergrowth and bog, guided only by flashes of
musket fire in front of them, they nearly met with Withers's extreme
right flank movement. Villars, seeing the danger, again rapidly
moved several regiments from the main trench between the two
woods to counter-attack, an attack that was at first successful,
driving the British and Germans back, but Withers arrived just
when he was wanted.

His advance through the wood had been led by the Royal Irish—

the 18th Foot—and they met, and repulsed, the French Royal Regiment of Ireland. The French counter-attack withdrew.

The moment for which Marlborough had waited now came. In the centre a forty-gun battery was moved forward down the gap between the woods until within range of the main line of trenches. After a heavy bombardment, Lord Orkney led the main British infantry division through and round the guns and assaulted the enemy's main position, capturing it at the first advance, though with considerable losses. Orange advanced again and splitting his force into two passed round the great battery, and came up on either flank of the newly captured French front position, now held by the British infantry. Cavalry passed through, attacked the still stubbornly resisting French infantry in their third line, now some hundreds of yards behind their original position, and in front of Malplaquet village.

Villars, who had been badly wounded and was now unconscious, was succeeded by his second-in-command, old Bouflers, a retired French general who had come up to Malplaquet the night before and offered to serve under the much younger and junior Villars. Bouflers recognised defeat when he saw it, and ordered a general withdrawal.

The Great Quadrilateral had been completed. Four times in five years Marlborough had attacked and beaten the great French Army led by experienced generals. His fame, as a general who never lost a battle, had been assured.

The French withdrawal was admirably conducted as the French, though beaten, were not routed, while the Allies were too exhausted to pursue with any vigour. The French lost twelve thousand men, killed and wounded, five hundred prisoners, fifty sets of colours, and sixteen guns.

The Allied losses were far heavier. Twenty thousand men were killed or wounded, largely due to the mad onset of the Prince of Orange. The Dutch lost eight thousand from thirty battalions, or more than half their number. The British lost two thousand from twenty battalions. Until Le Cateau in 1914, there were more casualties at Malplaquet in proportion to numbers engaged than in any previous battle in history.

This heavy casualty list must not be laid at Marlborough's feet. An attack which was obvious, and for which he was ready on 30th August, had he not been delayed by the Dutch Commissioner, would have brought him greater success, while Orange's disobedience lost many lives unnecesarily.

Three days had to pass before the army was fit to return to the siege of Mons. Three weeks later the town capitulated and the campaign came to an end.

The battlefield of Malplaquet is very flat, being more often pasture than plough. In order to keep the cattle and sheep within the bounds of their owners, fences with one or two strands of wire are plentiful everywhere. Most of the posts in the fences are ordinary but now and again a very old twisted knarled part of a tree is seen, and it is likely that these old posts were taken from the revetments of the great French trench. Doubtless the French soldiers in the thirty-six hours allowed them before the battle commenced, cut these posts from the woods of Sars and Lanières and after the battle, when the armies had passed on, the local peasants had salvaged them to re-erect the fences knocked down in the fighting. A very similar situation is seen on the old 1914–18 Front Line in France and Belgium—where returning villagers in 1919 salvaged screw picquets, angle-irons and barbed wire from the trenches all around them for their cottage and farmstead enclosures and corrugated iron from old dug-outs for pigsties, much of which can be seen today.

At Malplaquet no trace of the line of the great trenches can be seen at all, but its approximate position can be closely fixed. It ran along the line of the present Franco-Belgian frontier, midway between the two modern customs posts (about 500 yards apart). Between them is a large obelisk commemorating the Frenchmen killed in the battle. A large plaque on its front facing the road carries two cameo relief portraits of Villars and Bouflers, the former superimposed on the latter, and around the rim with their names the words 'Soldats de la France'.

Across the battlefield and down the road past the two customs posts, the memorial, and over the cross roads marched the regiments of the 3rd Division in August 1914, in the retreat from Mons. Here again, on the battlefield of Malplaquet three days before the Armistice in November 1918, the advancing British Army had a minor engagement with a retreating German rear-guard. Three officers and five men of the Royal Warwicks were killed, and are buried in the village cemetery, half a mile behind the battlefield of 1709.

On Armistice Day a company of the Dorsets of the 11th Division, which had been in the landing at Suvla Bay in Gallipoli in 1915, was marching along the road northward. It was passing the obelisk commemorating Malplaquet when a motor-cycle despatch rider arrived with a message for the Company Commander, Captain Clayton, saying that the Armistice had been signed. He halted the Company, and his men joining hands, danced a 'Ring-a-Ring of Roses' round the memorial. Captain Clayton told the author in 1962 that never had he felt more light-hearted than at this news of the Armistice. His fealing was akin to being slightly intoxicated, although he had tasted no alcohol for several days.

Five hundred yards north-east of the cross roads, behind the line of trenches, and about two hundred to the east of the probable first-line, stood (and still stands) the farm of Blairon. In a barely discernible depression, it completely covers all ground around it for several hundred yards. It seems obvious that the French must have garrisoned it, as its capture by Marlborough's troops would have been a great embarrassment. However, not one account of the battle carries any mention of it as a tactical feature, although the farm appears on the contemporary maps of 1709. In the final advance by the British regiments down the gap between the two woods Blairon must have been liquidated before the main trench could be taken. The French being by no means routed, it is evident that considerable fighting must have occurred here before the British advance could continue to its great objective. The farmhouse today is a modern building and its barns and outhouses, though much older, have obviously been built again since 1709. But that the present farm stands on the exact site of the original is undoubted.

The wood of Sars is less changed in shape and condition than Lanières. A mile long, and about a quarter of a mile wide, today the eastern, inner edge is the original. It is still very boggy, with much water lying about, the undergrowth is very dense, and it is very easy to imagine, almost visualise, the confusion and complete loss of direction by British regiments, and their subordinate sub-units particularly, fighting their way forward or in the orderly withdrawals by the French. Visibility is rarely more than thirty yards, and the smoke from the musket fire, a feature of 18th and 19th century warfare unknown today, must have added greatly to the already existing confusion.

Lanières Wood is much altered. Cottages, gardens, barns and other buildings have been built, and, although the shape of the wood can still be seen, its character has changed. Tiry Wood, however, is totally unchanged and presents a curious appearance. Completely circular and standing on a slight mound its trees are very tall, equally spaced and not close. The prevailing south-west wind has inclined them in one direction and from a distance these tall, well-spaced trees, with parallel trunks, looks as though they are all about to fall over together. The copse makes an unmistakable land-mark.

The cross roads around which the French Guards stood in reserve is a magnificent position. All the ground forward to Tiry and the Sars Wood is under observation, and an attack by cavalry or later by bombardment were the only ones that could possibly succeed. Just behind the trenches or more probably in their third line, the presence of that famous regiment—comparable to the Maison du Roi—must have given great confidence to the troops in the fore-most line.

The scene of the Prince of Orange's unauthorised and disastrous attack is difficult to establish owing to the changed and shrunken shape of Lanières. The temptation to go, however, must have been very great, as the wood, its inner edge closer than today, must have presented an inviting target.

In the village school at Malplaquet, about a mile behind the battlefield are several relics picked up from the field itself. Nothing nowadays is turned up by the plough, while on the pasture fields nature and the feet of cattle and sheep have long since trodden into the ground anything remaining.

In Sars Wood, owing to the boggy nature of the soil, nothing is to be seen. However there must have been a number of men killed therein, from the Royal Irish, the Austrian and German battalions in their two advances. Doubtless most were buried there. However, owing to the extremely close nature of the undergrowth it is prob-able that many bodies were not seen by any burial parties and that they lay there for many years. The uniforms and bodies decompos-ing, the muskets and metal accoutrements would be left—gradually they would be engulfed in the mud of the bog. Little digging would be needed there today to disinter them, and from the author's observation it is quite certain that there is much there—in the water-logged ground—not far below the surface.

In the Malplaquet village church is a large marble plaque, placed there in 1909, two hundred years after the battle. On it are carved the names of about a dozen titled senior French officers killed in the battle. On it every year on the anniversary day, a wreath is placed by the Curé.

At Sars-la-Bruyère, four miles to the north is a large almost ruined tower. It was the keep of a mediaeval château and today from its roof a magnificent panorama-view is obtainable. Marlborough surveyed the ground from its roof and made his plan for the battle, giving his orders in the one great room below. Sir Winston Churchill mounted the narrow and steep stair-way also to view the battlefield before writing his chapter on Malplaquet for his 'Life of Marlborough'. The French Government is to restore the tower next year.

In Bavai—four miles to the south—and where Sir John French had his G.H.Q. for the battle of Mons—lives a very old man, eighty years of age, a lawyer, a retired judge, and a highly cultured man. His grandfather picked up three circular lead bullets about half an inch in diameter on the battlefield about, the old judge thinks, 1825. When proudly shewn them by the old gentleman, the author was unable to decide whether they were English or French, but there is no question that they are 'right' and would adorn any military museum.

Culloden

1746

TO understand fully the ''45' and Culloden, it is necessary to go back to 1714, the year before Queen Anne's death.

The lawful heir of James II had been his only son James, the baby alleged to have been brought into the palace in a warming-pan—the 'Old Pretender'. But he was brought up as a Roman Catholic and under the Bill of Rights of 1689 no person being a Roman Catholic or married to one could succeed to the throne of England. In any case, when James II escaped to France this child had little chance of being recognised as King. His father's behaviour, and eventual desertion of his country and indeed the evil reputation all the Stuarts had earned for themselves generally in the past eighty-five years had ruined for a long while all interest in or loyalty to them.

James II's successor in 1688 when he deserted, was his eldest daughter Mary, who with William III ruled England until 1702. On William's death, his sister-in-law Queen Anne succeeded to the throne.

While Anne lived, married and with several children there was no problem as to the successor. It was all clearly laid down and provided for. But all her children died young, only the Duke of Gloucester reaching the age of ten when he, too, died. (Many authorities believe that Mary's childlessness—and the succession of the tragic infant deaths of Anne's children was due to syphilis passed to them by their grandmother, Anne Hyde, who contracted it from her husband—James II). The death of the Duke of Gloucester immediately created a great problem of the succession.

In the last years of Anne's life the mass of the English people was Tory. Thirty-five per cent were Roman Catholics, most had forgotten the evils and near-dictatorship of James II before his desertion. All they remembered of the previous twenty years was the quiet, prosperous stodgy reigns of William, Mary and Anne, and in the case of the latter, the great victories of Marlborough. They were quite ready to accept a Stuart monarch again.

Under the Bill of Rights any failure of the succession after the death of Anne was to result in a Protestant granddaughter of James I—Sophia—married to the Elector of Hanover, as then being the rightful monarch of England. But Sophia and her son, George, were completely unknown in England, the English people regarded them as 'foreigners' upon whom the English have always looked down, and the fact that neither Sophia nor George could speak English made them doubly unpopular.

Just prior to Anne's death there was much scheming to avoid these Hanoverians coming over, and to boost the Stuart claims of the Old Pretender. Scottish noblemen were given positions of influence and trust, Harley, the leader of the ministry (there was no Prime Minister in those days) a brilliant but irresolute man, and a mild supporter of Sophia and her son, was elbowed out of the leadership by Bolingbroke who stepped up the plans for a Stuart succession.

But two things prevented this succession. Firstly young James in France again refused to change his religion. Consequently the Tories, the ruling party in Parliament, were torn between their adherence to the Protestant cause and their allegiance to the Stuart dynasty.

Secondly, Anne died suddenly and too soon. Had she survived another three months, it is believed that Bolingbroke would have persuaded young James to come over and claim the throne. But Bolingbroke's plans had not quite matured—and the Whigs proclaimed George King of England (Sophia, his mother, had died two months before Anne). Legally the Whigs were right and although they had not the authority to do so, being the Opposition at the time, were only observing the Bill of Rights, and the Tories had to concede that George was, in fact, the lawful King. The peaceful succession of the House of Hanover has been called the greatest miracle in our history.

But George I was in no hurry to claim his unexpected inheritance. He did not cross over from Hanover for six weeks, and on his arrival found—through interpreters—that not only was there a strong government with a good majority which had been against his succession, but also that a rival claimant, popular, able, and only just across the Channel, was very much alive. No monarch of England has ever come into or faced such a dangerous position. The stage was set both for the ''15' and the ''45'.

George quickly added to his initial unpopularity by his personal character, appearance and habits. He was over fifty, and separated from his wife, finally having her imprisoned. He had little idea of being a monarch with dignity, he quarrelled with his son—the future George II—and never attempted to learn any English. The English thought him a thoroughly unpleasant character but, they felt, what else could one expect from a foreigner.

The Tory desire for a Stuart king, whom they knew would be a cultured, English-speaking patriot, was very much alive—and riots in London between the Tory and Whig mobs were frequent. An insurrection broke out in Scotland, some 1,400 Highlanders advanced into Lancashire with the intention of reaching London and presumably there proclaim James as king—despite his religion. At Preston, however, this invading force was defeated and surrounded by the royal troops. As a last desperate effort to save his cause James landed in Scotland, attended by six friends. But he was unable to rouse the Scots to take any definite, certainly no military, action on his behalf, and he left hurriedly for France, never to set foot in the British Isles again.

In the next thirty years little was heard of the Stuarts, or the succession. England was very busy with the bitter animosity between the Whigs and the Tories, scandals such as the South Sea Bubble where thousands of families were reduced to beggary, wars on the Continent against France, including England's defeat at Fontenoy, and, in 1727, the death of the King.

In 1745—when George II, succeeding George I, had been on the throne for 18 years, the exiled Stuarts decided that the embarrassments of England on the Continent and at home might be a suitable occasion to try and recover their lost inheritance. The son of the Old Pretender, Charles Edward, 'Bonnie Prince Charlie' sailed from France with two ships and a staff of seven to conquer his rightful homeland. One of his ships was intercepted off Brest by a British man-of-war, and there forced to return to harbour, while the other containing the Prince sailed round Ireland. He landed on the west coast of Scotland in July and from there, gaining the support of the great clans Cameron and MacDonald, he marched south.

He reached Perth, where he proclaimed his father as James VII of Scotland, and then went on to Edinburgh, where without opposition he installed himself in the residence of Holyrood House.

Some 3,000 royalist soldiers were at Inverness, and hearing that Charles Edward had not only landed but reached Edinburgh, they were embarked at Aberdeen and landed at Dunbar. From there they marched towards Edinburgh, to meet Charles, who by now also had 3,000 men, but of poorer training.

Prince Charles must have been fearful as to the outcome of his great adventure. To land on a coast, admittedly friendly, there to gather only 3,000 adherents, and advance southwards towards a country that might well be hostile was indeed a gamble. His soldiers were but clansmen, primitively armed, almost unorganised, un-trained, with no discipline other than patriotism. They were to meet the trained regulars of the English Army, men who had fought at Dettingen and Fontenoy, men who knew their trade.

At Prestonpans—ten miles east of Edinburgh—the two armies came in contact. Charles had marched his force eastward, through the night, and then veering south-east, passed right round the English Army and wormed up for battle now facing west, astride the road from Cockenzie to Tranent. The English, surprised at dawn to find the Highlanders east of them hurriedly took up a line to face them and occupied ground along which the modern railway now runs. Their right rested on the Prestonpans–Longniddry road at Meadow Mill.

By a sudden onslaught of the Highlanders at dawn driven on-wards by the idea that they were expelling a 'foreign' army from their homeland they scattered the English forces within an hour. All the artillery, colours, baggage and treasure-chest were captured. Charles had not only won the first round but by an overwhelming margin. As a result nearly all the wavering partisans now recog-nised Charles as their leader. He was in possession of Scotland.

The psychological result of the victory of Prestonpans was great. It was comparable to Marathon and Valmy, and showed what enthusiastic, dedicated, though untrained patriots could do in the defence of their country, though facing organised trained regulars.

Charles now held most of the cards. A victory, high morale, a greatly enlarged force, the initiative were all his. A swift return to Edinburgh and then south to the Border might well have brought

him to London, where the greatest consternation had been caused
by the news of his landing and victory at Prestonpans.

He did not show urgency, though, and loitered in Edinburgh for
six weeks. Then with 5,000 men behind him he advanced into
England, via Carlisle, Lancaster, Manchester and reached Derby,
more than half-way to London.

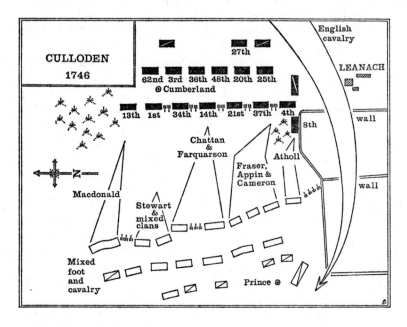

Although received with cheers and welcomes he did not attract
many recruits to his cause, Manchester only finding 299 men to
join him.

Charles' subordinate chiefs, disappointed at the indifference of
the English Jacobites, and very aware of the dangers of their
position, strongly advocated retreat. They knew that the Duke of
Cumberland, George II's son, and commander of the English army
was somewhere in front with 10,000 men, and they suspected that
a similar force was possibly between them and Scotland. Charles
remonstrated in vain, begging them to press on with him southward,
but they refused and a dejected Prince had to turn his army back.

A fighting withdrawal was skilfully carried out, and at Penrith,
between Kendal and Carlisle, Cumberland's advance was checked

and thrown back. Retreat via Glasgow and Stirling was achieved with safety but many Highlanders lost heart and withdrew to their homes. The Stuart cause was virtually lost.

Three months of bitter winter saw the Scotsmen wandering around in the Grampians, and in April a force of six thousand assembled at Inverness.

The English Army under Cumberland marched north via Stirling and Aberdeen, and then west through Elgin and Nairn. On the 14th April Prince Charles heard that the English had reached Nairn and were probably about to move on to Inverness and attack him. He marched out six miles eastward along the Nairn road to meet them and on Culloden Moor halted, bivouacking there for the night.

At dawn on the 15th the Highlanders were drawn up in order of battle. When the men were allowed to fall out for a while they mostly went off in search of food to supplement their day's ration of one biscuit each.

During the day a plan was made to advance across country to Nairn through the night and there surprise the English asleep in their tents. But at dusk, when the Assembly was sounded, at least a third of the men had not returned from their search for food. However, Charles decided not to wait for them and started off with 4,500 men to attack an enemy assessed to be 18,000 strong, twelve miles away.

All might have gone well had some sort of formation been possible. But the men went forward in single file, through forests and marshes and in the dark complete chaos developed. Many of the men were weak from the lack of food and could not go on, many lost their way, and towards daybreak only 2,000 men were afoot.

As the exhausted force approached the English camp, a drum was heard to beat therein, indicating that Cumberland's men were awake. The Scots advance guard halted and its leader, Lord George Murray, realising that any chance that might have existed of surprising the English had virtually vanished, ordered a withdrawal.

Prince Charles' aide-de-camp galloped up to expostulate at a withdrawal not ordered by his master, but Murray took no notice. The turn-about continued and meeting Charles, showed him that he had no alternative but to go back to Culloden. Most of the officers agreed with the necessity of retreating, but their morale and that of the Highlanders, already low from lack of food and an abortive night march, sank even lower. By 6 a.m. the whole force was back on Culloden Moor, in its old positions, no one, including the senior leaders, thinking of anything but sleep, and if possible, food.

Little was done by Charles' army, staff, or troops for some hours. Everyone slept; even the quest for food took second place.

Many woke at about 9 a.m. Among the leaders (it is impossible to call them generals or even subordinates) there was much discussion and free advice given to Charles as to whether he should fall back behind the little stream running across the Moor—or fall back on Inverness—or stay where he was. Advocates of the third course again disagreed among themselves and argued with Charles not only as to which physical features on the Moor should be held or ignored, but also as to which clan-regiment should be posted where. There was much ill-feeling because the Camerons were not allowed to have the post of honour on the right, being replaced by the Atholl Brigade. Lord George Murray complained that it was his turn to be on the right, but Charles' Staff Officer replied that the Camerons had had the honour on the previous day. The fact that there had been no fighting on that day was not considered a valid reason—nor was there time to make a change.

One of the most striking features of the battle of Culloden was the lack of a firm dominating commander who could make a plan, make decisions, issue orders. It was made worse by the absence of any lower-formation organisation. There were no brigades—or groups—only a number of 'clan-regiments' and these had no interior organisation within themselves. No one co-ordinated moves between the clans, no one allocated areas, or saw to supports or reserves. Each clan fought almost as it pleased and largely according to the patriotism, ability and health of its Laird. Most were sensible enough to form a line and so prevent an English penetration, but there were no tactics, and it says a great deal for the patriotism of the Highlanders that in fact they lasted so long and did so comparatively well, the more so in view of their near-starvation and extreme fatigue.

Culloden Moor is about a mile and a half from north to south and a mile from east to west. It is a moor in every respect. It is still, today, such a coarse piece of ground as to be quite unsuitable for the roughest agriculture. The turf is springy and clearly peat is not far below the surface. It is heavy going and in the lower levels of the Moor—it is slightly undulating—bogs still exist. Between the final positions taken up by the opposing armies ran a slight hollow fifty yards wide containing heavy muddy ground. (A mass of pine trees is now growing, the plantations being subsequent to the battle).

There were two large 'enclosures' whose drystone walling has now mostly disappeared, on either side of the road running across the Moor from Nairn to Inverness. The walls formed suitable cover for defending infantry, and being loosely built of large stones could easily be breached to let the defenders through should an advance be possible. Surprisingly the Highlanders made little use of these walls thereby showing the absence of professional military knowledge or 'eye for ground'. The right-hand enclosure, 'Culloden Park', had two cottages 200 yards out beyond its northern wall, Leanach Barn. The gap across the road, between the two 'enclosures' was about 700 yards wide. There was a bog just out beyond the western end of the gap. By about 11.00 a.m. the vast majority of the clans were in position in the gap, their flanks protected to a certain extent by the walls on the two outer flanks.

Reveille had been sounded in the Duke of Cumberland's camp at Nairn at 4 o'clock in the morning, and at 5.30 a.m. the royal army advanced towards Inverness in three columns of five regiments, each preceded by a light advance guard of cavalry.

At about 11 o'clock the opposing armies were in full view of each other, $2\frac{1}{2}$ miles apart. After another advance of half a mile Cumberland halted, drew up his line of battle, and issued an astonishing order. In effect he told his army that if any officer or man through timidity, conscience or inclination felt unsure of himself, he was to fall out and retire from the field of battle and that none should be penalised for so doing. He added that he would rather command one thousand brave and resolute men than ten thousand who through cowardice or misbehaviour might injure the chance of victory. This brave, perhaps risky, statement is not unlike that which Shakespeare put in the mouth of Henry V the night before Agincourt. It is probable that Cumberland remembered the words and the gesture. However, no man took advantage of the offer, although doubtless some would have liked to do so, and would have done so but for public opinion.

The royal advance then continued, with colours flying and drums beating. When it was 600 yards from the Highlander's line all could see its greatly superior numbers, its perfect discipline and organisation. Its appearance did nothing to raise the spirits of the already tired Scotsmen.

The Macdonald clan had just arrived on the battlefield, and with no instructions to do so, marched off to the left of the line, having found the right which they too claimed already occupied. Here they elbowed the then incumbent regiment off to its right and forced their way into the gap they had created alongside the wall. The congestion in the 700 yards between the two enclosures now became so acute that regiments could not have all their men in the front line, some having to form third and fourth lines. Defence in depth was not known in those days and depth merely meant a reduction of muskets in front. An example of the confusion caused by the lack of a strong hand at the top, allowing bickering and ill-feeling between the clans, was the fact that later in the day the Macdonald's refused to join in the general advance because they were not allowed to be on the right of the line. They remained sulking in their lines on the extreme left.

When 500 yards away, Cumberland ordered up his ten 3-pounder guns, and opened fire soon after 1 o'clock. The Prince returned the fire at once, one shot narrowly missing Cumberland, but the royal cannonade became a decisive factor in the battle. Prince Charles' guns were ill-served, most being manned by scratch crews who when counter-battery fire was directed on them turned and fled.

Meanwhile a party of Cumberland's cavalry moved out to its left, and fetching a wide circle came up against the north-east wall of 'Culloden Park'. They dismounted, pulled the wall down and remounting, advanced again to the opposite wall on the other side of the 'Park'. This too they negotiated, hoping to take the High-landers in flank, but were forestalled by some Campbells who were sent to repair the breaches, and so entrap the small party of royal cavalry.

A Highland leader, probably the Duke of Perth, ordered Lord Ogilvy's Regiment of two 'groups' to form flank to the east, and thus engage this cavalry flank attack. Had this cavalry party been of considerable strength it might well have charged into the right flank of the Highlanders, and thrown them into such confusion that, with their lack of training and discipline, they would have disintegrated.

The royal artillery fire was increased and irreparable damage was inflicted on the Highlanders, while Cumberland's men suffered practically no casualties. Clearly he had no need to advance, and only had to wait for his enemy to retire—or better still to advance against his regular infantry regiments and their musketry.

His regiments in the front line were, from the left:—

Barrell's (4th, today The King's Own)
Monro's (37th, today The Hampshire Regiment)
Royal Scots Fusiliers (21st)
Price's (14th, now the West Yorks)
Cholmondeley's (34th, now the Border Regiment)
The Royal Scots (1st)
Pulteney's (13th, now the Somerset Light Infantry)—with
Wolfe's (8th, now the King's Liverpool) forming a defensive left
    flank, facing inwards.

About 2.30 p.m. the royal artillery fire changed from solid cannon balls to grape-shot and the Highlanders suffered severely, not having previously experienced this type of fire. The regiments in the front became impatient at being kept stationary as 'cannon fodder' and were with difficulty restrained from charging forward haphazardly.

Several requests were sent to Prince Charles to allow an advance, which eventually he sanctioned. Several messengers were sent to the clan-leaders in the front, but there was no co-ordinated advance and most clans moved forward as soon as they received permission, irrespective of whether those on their right or left were moving or not. The centre of the line surged forward first, closely followed by several regiments on the right wing, but the still disgruntled Macdonalds on the left refused to obey.

Leading the charge in the centre was Clan Chattan, led by MacGillivray. The men were by now so exasperated at lack of food and the punishment they had received from the royal artillery fire that they raced towards the English lines, many of them throwing away their muskets as hindering their speed. Half-way across the 'no-man's land' the Clan suddenly swung to the right masking many of the Prince's best men in the right-wing regiments and thus preventing them from coming to grips with the enemy. By this swerve to the right, the fire from the West Yorks and the Royal Scots Fusiliers caught the Highlanders in semi-enfilade and caused many casualties.

Because of this confusion caused by the swerve the right-hand

regiments became packed against the park wall, and became so
inextricably mixed as they advanced that some fifteen hundred men
surged forward in nothing more than mob-formation.

By sheer force of numbers they got forward and found facing
them Barrell's Regiment—and Monro's. These two regiments, with
fixed bayonets and in three ranks, waited until the enemy was
within 30 yards, when they opened fire. It was impossible to miss.
Yet many Highlanders survived, and passing through, virtually
split the regiments into two halves. The very weight of their charge
carried them on, past the cannon in the area between the front and
second line of infantry battalions, until they were brought to a halt
by the fire from Bligh's (20th, now the Lancashire Fusiliers) in the
second line, which virtually exterminated them. The loss of men in
both Barrell's and Monro's Regiment was very heavy not only from
the almost maddened Scotsmen, but from the fire of the regiments
in the second line who brought the charge to its halt. Barrell's loss
from killed and wounded was a hundred and twenty officers and
men out of a total of four hundred and fifty; this figure is one-third
of the total English casualties that day. Of the fifteen hundred
Highlanders who started the charge five hundred penetrated
Barrell's and Monro's. Very few of these five hundred eventually
survived, as many who fought their way back were caught by the
fire of Wolfe's flank guard.

On the Highlanders' left wing little happened. One company only
of Farquarsons joined in the great charge of the right and the
centre, and there was general disinclination to advance. The
Macdonald's, to a man, refused to move through pique. To their
right four Scottish regiments now fled the field, leaving a gap of
several hundred yards between the Macdonalds and the next troops
in the centre. Soon the remnants of the great charge on the right
came back and also left the field—and the Macdonalds followed
them. Cumberland 'improved' his victory by letting his cavalry
go into pursuit. It encountered no resistance, though two small
parties were held up by ultra-brave Jacobites who, sheltering behind
one of the walls surrounding 'Culloden Park' were able to ambush
the little parties of cavalry.

Other parties of horsemen tried to round up the fleeing Highlanders and it is to the disgrace of these royalist horsemen that they
cruelly hacked with their swords, or rode down, the fugitives. Few
prisoners were taken.

Cumberland having despatched his cavalry on their task was in no hurry to follow his defeated enemy, and ordered his regiments to 'dress their lines'. When all was ready he slowly advanced, leaving Barrell's and Monro's regiments behind to lick their wounds.

As the royal army passed over the battlefield, and disappeared towards Inverness, hordes of camp followers, soliers' wives, civilians from near-by crofts, deserters, swarmed over the ground searching for husbands or plunder. Several wounded Highlanders had taken refuge in Leanach Barn, but a particularly savage royal captain with fifty men whose task it was to succour the English wounded found them in the barn and, locking the doors, set the building on fire. 32 charred bodies were removed later.

Culloden was an easy victory for Cumberland. Of his fifteen regular battalions five did not fire a shot and a total casualty list of three hundred and sixty officers and men out of his probable total engaged on the Moor, 8,000, is but a little over four per cent.

It must have been a victory. Cumberland had double the number of men that Charles had. They were trained, equipped, disciplined regulars of experience—were well fed and although tired after their early reveille and a ten-mile march across country were not nearly so tired—or hungry—as their opponents.

Had the Highlanders been under the command of a professional middle-aged experienced general, who had dominance, the ability to make up his mind and to make a plan and see it carried out—and, most importantly, one who allowed no argument with himself, no bickering or quarrelling between his subordinates, no 'belly-aching'—then the royal army would have had a very different experience. They must have won in the end with their vast superiority in numbers and training, but they lacked the burning enthusiasm of the Scots whose dash and *élan* carried them so far into the English lines, and they would have been hard put to it to hold these lines.

Today, regrettably from the military historian's point of view, by far the greater part of the battlefield is covered by a fairly modern, closely planted wood of pines and firs. There is, however, a strip about a hundred and fifty yards by three hundred yards left largely untouched along the eastern side of the battlefield and where most of the action took place. There is much to be seen in it.

The little cluster of three or four farm buildings at Leanach Barn is now reduced to one and the ruined foundations of another. The one remaining is virtually as it was in 1746 with little restoration. It stood just behind Wolfe's 8th Foot, and slightly to the rear of Barrell's left flank. It was thus in the middle of the fight. It was occupied as a crofter's residence until 1912 and is now an attractive and romantic little museum. A few yards away are the foundations of the barn where the wounded Highlanders were found by the English and whose door they locked. The burning of this barn and thus the murder of the thirty-two helpless soldiers inside was typical of the totally unnecessary harshness and cruelty practised by the royal army for some days after their victory. It has not been forgotten by the Scots.

In the 'no-man's land' between the two opposing armies, at its eastern end lie the mass graves of many of the clans. Each has a rough-hewn weather-worn stone at the outer end of each mound, about three feet high, with the name of the clan crudely carved upon it. Just in front of Wolfe's Regiment's left flank is the mass grave of the English dead with a simple and brief statement of the losses.

Alongside the left flank of the second line of English regiments is a large car park, with a building containing an excellent exhibition of photos, plans, aerial photos, books and pamphlets not only of the '45 and Culloden, but of Scottish history in general. This exhibition is well-housed in a modern building, does a roaring trade in selling the books and photos, and once an hour in a darkened room shows an audio-visual account of the whole of Prince Charles's campaign of 1745 and 1746. The exhibition is very similar to that at Bannockburn.

A striking feature of this small area—another shrine of Scottish history—is the number of visitors. On a week-day in the summer an average of one hundred visitors an hour arrive, and the weekly average is 8,000. Most are Scots, of course, but many non-Scots accents are heard, including those of foreigners.

The exact sites of most regiments, both English and Scots are almost impossible to fix, owing to the thickly planted wood and considerable undergrowth. An exception is the two left-hand English regiments, Barrell's and Wolfe's—whose positions were clear of the modern wood. They can be pin-pointed very accurately to within twenty yards, but the position of the regiments on the right of Barrell's cannot be even conjectured after a few yards walk into the wood. Indeed it is quite easy to lose direction and one's whereabouts, so reduced is the visibility.

All the military historians who have described the Battle of Culloden, together with official brochures issued by the National Trust for Scotland and the local authorities in Inverness state that the stone walls on the battlefield which played a considerable tactical part have long since disappeared.

The author, after four visits and many careful searches, is unable to accept this unanimous and sweeping assertion. The wall against which the swerving Chattan Clan forced the Atholl Highlanders against the Camerons, and there joining them, inextricably mixed up as a football mob—is still standing and can be found if carefully looked for. A small copse on the main Highland right flank before the charge ends abruptly where lie the graves of some Campbells who had been sent out to repair the wall. This wall is now the boundary of the big field out beyond the copse. It is four feet high, is made of large boulders at the bottom, smaller ones as is rises, and is largely covered with turf. Perhaps the most incontrovertible evidence of its being the original wall is the fact that for about a hundred yards it follows the precise line of the original wall shewn on the sketch maps of all the authorities, and alleged to have long since disappeared in its entirety.

The little muddy dip between the lines of the two opposing armies and across which some of the Highlanders charged, throwing away their arms, is still there. It is still muddy, and enables the almost exact positions of Barrell's and Wolfe's regiments to be closely identified. For the military historian it is a pity that the new and dense wood precludes similar siting of the other front-line regiments, no matter how approximate.

Direction-posts on the roads for some distance out, indicating Culloden, are numerous and well sited. Two hours on the battlefield are sufficient to see everything in this small area. They will be absorbingly interesting.

Quatre Bras

1815

E ARLY in April 1815, Napoleon, after a disastrous three
years of defeats, abdicated his throne. He was banished to
the little island of Elba where he set up a miniature court,
with 1,200 French soldiers and played at being an Emperor and
'His Majesty' for ten months. About the same time Wellington,
with the prestige of four years of successful campaigning in the
Peninsula behind him, was appointed British Ambassador to the
Court of the restored Louis XVIII in Paris.

In October the congress of Vienna assembled to settle new
national boundaries disrupted by Napoleon's nineteen years of war,
to distribute the spoils made available by the defeat of France, and
for the Heads of Governments, and in some cases their monarchs, to
meet together to discuss those matters which Summit Conferences
generally discuss. Castlereagh for Great Britain, Metternich for
Austria and Talleyrand for France were present, while the Czar of
Russia, the Emperor of Austria, and the King of Prussia attended
for some time.

Castlereagh, being required in London on party political matters,
was recalled and Wellington was switched from his ambassadorial
post in Paris to be Great Britain's representative in Vienna. He
arrived early in February and quickly dominated the Congress. On
7th March, when the Conference was about to adjourn for four
months, word reached him that Napoleon had left Elba, presumably
for France. Wellington was at once appointed Commander-in-Chief
of all the British, Dutch, Belgian and Hanoverian troops in the Low
Countries. The Prussians were to form up behind him around Namur
and the Austrian Army to cross the Southern Rhine and move
westward.

But what if Napoleon had left Elba a week later; the Congress of
Vienna would have adjourned, its members dispersed. Lacking any
means of communication faster than a horseman, the leaders of the

several Allied countries must have taken a very long time indeed to re-assemble, to reform the Coalition, to devise a plan and appoint a Commander-in-Chief to implement it.

But the Congress had not dispersed and Napoleon knew that he must work fast before the concentration against him, doubtless arranged in Vienna, could become effective. By superhuman efforts he re-organised in Paris what was left of his great army after the Abdication, enlisted four hundred thousand recruits, fed, clothed, equipped and armed them all, and marched them up to the north-east corner of France. This staggering and classic performance of administration took eighty-five days.

One of the great mistakes in history was made by Napoleon in not finding out when the Conference was to end, or even adjourn. Had he delayed his departure from Elba until after the leaders of the great powers had dispersed and when agreements made when they could still sit round a table were no longer even remotely possible, he must have had many more weeks for his 'reconquest' of France and her mobilisation.

The majority of the new French Army were recruits. Most of the old soldiers from the Peninsula and those that had survived Moscow were transferred to the Guard and the Army was very uneven in its quality, training, experience and discipline. It was bound together, however, by the bonds of enthusiasm for their brilliant leader, their disillusionment with the recently restored and inefficient monarchy, by the spirit of revenge, and lastly by the legend of the glory and the invincibility of 'La Grande Armée'—which was not entirely justified.

The great names of England's victories, Agincourt, Minden, Blenheim, Balaclava, Ypres and El Alamein, names outstanding in British history, are all overshadowed by that of Waterloo. Head and shoulders over all the others, its notoriety and glamour still attract thousands of visitors every year.

The importance of Waterloo is great. It brought to an end for almost a hundred years the presence of British troops on the Continent. It brought to an end the last campaign in Europe before the introduction of the railway, which was to effect the strategy and tactics of war so vastly. It was the last important European battle when solid cannon balls were used. It brought to an end a hundred years of military dominance by France.

Active operations in the Waterloo campaign began in the early hours of 15th June, 1815—when the French crossed the Sambre and attacked the Prussians—and ended in the early hours of the 19th. In these ninety-six hours, the shortest campaign in British military history, or at least the shortest period covering active operations, three great battles were fought, some 11,000 soldiers both Allied and French lost their lives, Napoleon, the colossus of Europe, perhaps the greatest captain in history, was irrecoverably overthrown. The British infantry in their squares became a legend, and a symbol of British steadfastness, stability, and reliability. In ninety-six hours Great Britain and Europe passed from mortal danger to the beginning of ninety-nine years of safety.

The Allies under Wellington were in billets around Brussels, and neighbouring towns, covering a frontage from Oudenarde on the north-west to Quatre Bras on the east, a distance of forty-five miles. Of the 100,000 men, infantry, cavalry and artillery under Wellington's command, approximately one-third were British, the others being Germans, Dutch and Belgians.

Napoleon crossed the Sambre on the evening of 15th June, and next day the greater part of his army under his personal command attacked the Prussians at Ligny. Forced back with heavy casualties the Prussians withdrew in the darkness, not north-east to their lines of communication as anticipated by Napoleon but north and then north-west to maintain touch with Wellington.

Prudently, Napoleon before attacking the Prussians detached two corps under his favourite general, Ney, to contain the British Army and its allies, under Wellington, and so protect the left flank of the attack on Ligny. Ney's orders were not to commit himself to a headlong clash with the British if encountered (as seemed probable), not to get even deeply involved but by his presence and that of his 38,000 men present such a menace to Wellington that he must remain on the defensive and be unable to move to the help of old Blücher at Ligny. Wellington was to be gripped by Napoleon's left hand Ney, meanwhile with his right hand he smashed the Prussians.

Wellington on the evening of June 15th, while he and many of his officers were attending the Duchess of Richmond's famous ball in Brussels, heard that Napoleon had advanced over the Sambre against the Prussians that evening. Immediately he ordered Picton's Division of British infantry to march out to Quatre Bras, an important cross roads, twenty miles south of Brussels, ten miles beyond the ridge at Waterloo and seven miles north-west of Ligny.

Picton's division left at 4 a.m. and Wellington rode out of Brussels at 7 a.m., Wellington overtaking it on the road. Despite the early hour he was cheered by several regiments as he cantered past.

On arrival at Quatre Bras where the great main road from Brussels to Charleroi is crossed almost at right angles by one scarcely less important from Nivelles to Namur, he found that there were no enemy in immediate view. A brigade of his Dutch troops had fought and repulsed a probing attack by French cavalry the previous evening at the village of Frasnes, some miles farther down the main road. They were now retreating, although they had been unmolested for more than twelve hours.

Wellington reached Quatre Bras about 9 a.m. and at once ordered the Dutch troops withdrawing from Frasnes to stand fast around the cross roads. Then realising that Picton's division could not arrive before 11 a.m. he cantered off to the south-east to meet Blücher at Ligny, about to be attacked in strength. They arranged to keep touch and if either were driven back that each would converge on the probable line of withdrawal of the other. To prevent Napoleon, after defeating one of them, coming between them must be avoided at all costs and was only to observe the principles of war of concentration, and co-operation.

Wellington then rode back to Quatre Bras and realised the immense importance of the Nivelles–Namur road. After running south-east over the cross roads at Quatre Bras it passed within two miles of Ligny, Blücher's battlefield. The road must be kept open as the great link between the two Allied armies.

The position of Quatre Bras is not unlike Waterloo in that it is at the top of a gradual, easy rise, the crest of which gives a good position for infantry. A mile in front of it lies another lesser ridge. Down the centre runs the great main road, Brussels to Charleroi, exactly bisecting the battlefield. From the cross roads and veering away to the south-west was a large wood, the wood of Bossu, one and a half miles long, and five hundred yards wide. On the other side of the main road and in front of the forward ridge stood the large farmhouse of Gemioncourt.

A forced march brought Picton's division to the cross roads by 11 a.m.—where Pack's leading brigade of the Royal Scots, Black Watch, Essex Regiment and the Gordon Highlanders took over from an outpost position of Dutch-Belgian cavalry, and lined the Namur road running south-east from Quatre Bras. Kempt's brigade of the Gloucesters, Dukes and Camerons arriving soon after, was sent to extend further the left and to deny that flank to the enemy. The Rifle Brigade went out to the extreme far left of the line and moving to their right attacked and captured the village of Piraumont.

About 1 p.m. Ney, one of whose Corps had been resting at Gossellies, twelve miles to the south, advanced until held up by a Dutch battalion holding the farm of Gemioncourt. A most gallant and protracted defence by the battalion delayed Ney's corps for a long time.

Eventually it was entirely overrun by cavalry and thus isolated. But it gained invaluable time for the steady and continuous arrival of other British and Allied units at the cross roads, and later in the day was relieved. A brigade of Hanoverians on arrival was sent down to the forward ridge, behind Gemioncourt while the Dutch-Belgian Division of Perponcher, moving round to the right, entered the wood of Bossu extending the Hanoverian line on the forward ridge.

This wood of Bossu was the most important tactical feature on the battlefield, running parallel to the main road, and is the obvious French line of advance. It could shield any manoeuvre by them far out on their left, and at least cover any advance of French infantry through it, which if successful could have brought them behind the Hanoverians, and on the exposed right flank of the British. Its importance to the defence was as great as that of the woods of Sars and Lanières at Malplaquet, a hundred and six years before. Villars there had seen the two covered lines of approach available to the British and filled both with considerable forces. Wellington, too, saw the danger, and feeling not fully confident that Perponcher's Dutch-Belgians were sufficient to hold the dangerous wood, sent two brigades of Guards on their arrival down to its forward edge.

At 3 p.m. Ney sent Jerome Bonaparte's division of 8,000 men and eight guns against the Bossu Wood. The Dutch-Belgians were forced back into the wood where, the Guards just arriving, the French attack was much slowed down, and finally held, on an extension of the line across the main road by the Hanoverians. About the same time a separate attack by the French up the centre had some success, the Hanoverians being forced back. Another unco-ordinated French attack on Picton's division lining the road to Namur from Quatre Bras was driven back, though its left contingent got almost up to the cross roads, where the Gordons repulsed it.

During all these operations new and fresh regiments, both British and Allied were arriving, and by 5 p.m. Wellington had a numerical superiority over the French, with 26,000 men against Ney's 22,000 —an unusual situation for any British army to find itself in when on the defensive.

On the repulse of the attack on Picton's division, Ney ordered Kellerman's cavalry brigade of 800 Cuirassiers to charge up the Brussels road, a hopeless task for so small a force against a well-disciplined and deployed line. British regiments formed square and caused great casualties but the impetus of the charging cavalry carried them up to the Namur road, on the way bursting through the ranks of the Welch Regiment newly arrived, seizing the King's Colour. In 1909 Captain Jeffcock of the Inniskilling Dragoons, when on holiday in the Château country, saw this Colour for sale in an antique shop at Azay-le-Rideau and bought it. It was the only Colour ever lost in an army commanded by Wellington.

The regiment has a story that the C.O. tried to conceal the loss of the Colour and that night set the regimental tailors to work to make a substitute that might pass as the original. However, this seems hardly possible. The tailors could scarcely have got at their gear in the first line transport that night and it is extremely unlikely that any materials even remotely suitable would be available. In addition these tailors, like all other 'employed men', were, in those days, ordinary soldiers in the ranks. Together with the cooks, shoe-makers, batmen, farriers, armourers etc., they were in the ranks by the squares and only carried out these additional specialist duties when the action was over—or the regiment off parade. Consequently at the end of the day they were as tired as the ordinary men in the ranks. They too had been on the march, in battle, and on their feet since 6 a.m. They were not in much condition to use needle and thread in the open air by candlelight that night. The next day a ten-mile march in pouring rain back to the ridge at Mont St. Jean would not leave much time, opportunity, or inclination to get down again to such fine sewing when greater affairs were afoot. It seems probable that this story of the tailors is only a fable.

After the Colour was found by Captain Jeffcock in 1909 it remained with his family until 1953—when his grandson gave it back to the regiment.

This Colour, now very fragile, heavily netted and framed between glass, is once again in the possession of the Welch Regiment at Cardiff.

Attacking the East Lancs, and Duke of Wellington's Regiment, next in the line, the Cuirassiers lapped round both squares.

Wellington, anxious to show himself to these battalions whose ordeal was considerable remained outside any of the squares. At one moment he found himself almost surrounded by individual French cavalrymen, practically out of control of their officers.

Galloping up to the Gordon Highlanders, who were lining both sides of the main road at the cross roads, he shouted to them to lower their bayonets and to crouch low. This they did, and he then jumped the line, clearing the Highlanders easily and taking shelter in the square then forming.

It was claimed by a few uncharitable and ill-informed people in London that Wellington's personal courage when under fire in the Peninsula had not been conspicuous. It seems possible that this libellous rumour had reached him and that his almost foolhardy bravery in the face of this French cavalry onslaught was deliberately staged by him to prove the opposite.

By now the French cavalry charge had lost all impetus and the timely arrival of two light guns of the King's German Legion dispersed them with a few well-aimed rounds.

At 7 o'clock the two Guards Brigades were able to advance again in Bossu Wood which they cleared and soon afterwards two British brigades on the main position along the Namur Road advanced astride the Brussels road, reaching the forward ridge from which the Hanoverians had been evicted. Past 8 o'clock the Grenadiers moved out of Bossu Wood, reaching Pierrepont Farm, several hundred yards in front, but were driven back to their wood by a last desperate charge of French Lancers. Wellington ordered Pack's brigade, now on the forward ridge to assault Gemioncourt village, which fell after a feeble resistance. Ney's forces withdrew in the failing light from their forward positions, while the 'victors' slept on the battlefield, some of the regiments having been on their feet for twenty hours.

Quatre Bras is usually considered inconclusive since darkness had stopped the fight before the French had been driven from their morning positions. For this reason the Battle of Quatre Bras is not considered a victory and its name appears on no regiment's Colours.

Nevertheless it is difficult to argue that Quatre Bras was not a victory. The Allied forces occupied a defensive position dictated by the position of the Prussians at Ligny, the cross roads, and the vital communicating road to Namur, a position accepted by Wellington and turned by him to the best advantage.

In this position they were eventually attacked. They repulsed the enemy and then moved forward, the enemy withdrawing into the night. The Allies were left in possession of the field. Surely the Allies should have advanced? Surely the withdrawal of the French after the failure of their attacks indicated their defeat? The with-holding of the battle-honour 'Quatre Bras' was unjustified and its bestowal today would not be out of place.

Quatre Bras could so easily have been a victory for Ney. The British and their allies could have been pushed back, Napoleon could have got between them and the Prussians, finally defeating each in turn, Brussels captured, Louis XVIII forced to leave the Continent, and Napoleon firmly fixed in the saddle again. But Ney, a brave soldier but a mediocre general, and Napoleon between them made an appalling muddle over the employment of D'Erlon's Corps.

At about 4 p.m., under Ney's command, this corps of four divi-sions was moving north from Gossellies through Frasnes towards Quatre Bras, as part of the main body. Without Ney being informed it received orders direct from Napoleon to leave Ney and march at once back to Ligny, there to encircle Blücher's right flank. It was some time before Ney discovered that D'Erlon's corps had left him and not knowing that it had been ordered back to Ligny by Napoleon personally, was understandably furious. Seeing that the chance of capturing the Quatre Bras cross roads was fading Ney sent abrupt orders to D'Erlon to return at once. D'Erlon turned yet again, although he had now reached the edge of the Ligny battle-field, and marched back to Ney. Moving across country the corps could not concentrate at Frasnes until 9 p.m., by which time the action of Quatre Bras was over and darkness falling.

The corps fired not a shot all day which was spent solely in waiting, marching and counter-marching. Had Napoleon not re-called it from the Quatre Bras action, Ney would have thrown it into the balance, and Wellington would have been overpowered. Had Ney not recalled it from Ligny the Prussian right flank would have been encircled and Blücher destroyed. A classic example of 'order, counter-order, disorder'.

Today two of the three buildings at the great cross roads of Quatre Bras are very old. They must have been there in 1815, and

still show slight scars of battle. Unfortunately most Belgian farmers
have a habit of lavishly plastering the upper walls of their farm
houses and barns with whitewash, and this naturally tends to
obliterate battle scars. However, there is no doubt that under the
half-inch layer of whitewash the bullet holes are still there. These
farm buildings at the cross roads, unusually high, must have received many hits, owing to their size and position. The positions of
the squares, especially that of the Welch Regiment around which
Kellerman's absurd cavalry charged roamed, are very clear and
obvious. A modern café, and, opposite, a filling-station do little to
lessen the atmosphere of this very important cross roads.

When the French cavalry withdrew, Picton's two British brigades
fell back slightly to avoid enemy artillery fire and they resumed
line formation. They were now only just in front of the vital Namur
road seen running off to the left of the cross roads in illustration
number 6. The retreat of the French cavalry allowed the enemy
guns to open up again and the regiments, now once again very vulnerable, had no ground to cover. However, the tall rye crop gave
cover from view to a certain extent, while the narrow ditch on the
north side of the road sheltered the Gloucesters and the Dukes
for some time. This ditch can still be seen along the side of the road.

In front of the forward, lesser, ridge the farm of Gemioncourt
still stands—a very considerable farmstead, mostly enclosed in
walls. Marks of bullet holes abound below the level of the whitewash on its south, east and west sides from the French attacks, and
on its north side from the British counter-attack. The whitewash
here is old and peeling, and allows much to be seen.

The position of Gemincourt is curiously like that of Blairon at
Malplaquet. Although contemporary maps show it to be very close
to the road it is, in fact, about two hundred yards to the east of the
main road bisecting the battlefield. It lies in the slightest possible
depression, yet dominates all the ground around it for several hundred yards, and threatens the use of the main road to any troops.
It again speaks badly for Ney's tactics that when his early moves
were held up by this isolated obstacle, he did not see the obvious
path round to the west through the Bossu Wood (the wood would
have hidden any move from Gemioncourt) or equally to by-pass the
wood to the east where there is much ground available, suitable
both for cavalry and infantry. He may have felt that Gemioncourt
was only part of an important forward position and that its capture

before a general advance could follow was essential. The absence of fire, however, from anywhere in the vicinity or, early in the action, anywhere at all, should have made it obvious that it was only an isolated outpost. One brigade to contain it would have allowed the rest of his force easily to by-pass it on either flank.

The wood of Bossu has entirely disappeared. The ground it covered is now under the plough and from the road to Nivelles just to the west of the cross roads an excellent totally unobstructed view of all the ground on which it stood is obtained. Assuming that the shape and size of the wood as shown on the contemporary maps are accurate, the wood formed a nasty obstacle on Wellington's right front and tactically he was compelled not only to occupy it, but to go right forward and out beyond its southern face. If Ney had pushed hard and captured this southern edge the defending Guards would have been badly embroiled in wood fighting, and probably forced gradually to withdraw. If Ney had exploited this in strength he could have cleared the wood and found himself on the Nivelles road, and thus behind the right flank of Picton's division holding the Namur road.

The Namur road on its 1815 foundations has been widened from its original ten feet and is now eighteen feet wide. The shallow ditch is now about five feet to the north of its position in 1815. The positions of the battalion squares of Kempt's and Pack's brigades cannot be pinpointed, but the area in which they stood is obvious. It extended for 1,200 yards along and to the south of the Namur road. The foremost battalion (which it was cannot be ascertained) was probably about six or seven hundred yards south of the road before all were forced back northward by French artillery fire.

Marlborough was unhorsed at Ramillies and very nearly captured in a cavalry mêlée. Wellington too was caught up in the French cavalry charge on the Gordons at the cross roads, and he too might have been killed or captured. What might have been the results of such a disaster?

Surprisingly such a calamity would have had little effect immediately. The fresh regiments—there were not many more to come up by about 5 p.m. when Wellington's casualty might have occurred —were mainly filling gaps, or reinforcing weak spots. The battle of Quatre Bras was in fact fighting itself by the evening and Wellington's personal presence and influence were barely necessary. It is true that those regiments in the immediate vicinity and seeing such a disastrous event would have been greatly shocked, but Pack's brigade would never have wavered. Bad news travels fast but it must inevitably have taken a long time before such news reached the majority of the Army. Meanwhile the British were getting stronger every hour and the French less active. The domination of Wellington's presence and personality was not an essential ingredient in the last few hours before darkness fell and the French withdrew southward.

The next senior general at Quatre Bras was the Prince of Orange. He was not a great soldier and was only present because a large number of his Dutch-Belgian units were part of Wellington's army. It is easy to imagine the resentment and distrust felt by some of the British divisional commanders at such a succession of command. Men like Picton, Alten, Cooke, Clinton, all with long and successful experience in the Peninsular War, only three years ended, must have resented Orange's assumption of chief command. But to whom could they protest? Their own innate discipline would ensure respect for seniority, but their patriotism and sense of urgency must have compelled them, jointly and severally, to insist that one of them took over by mutual agreement. If Orange had been adamant, the friction that must have arisen is evident.

But perhaps Orange would have seen the force of their arguments, the weakness of his own position, and gracefully withdrawn. Probably he might have agreed loyally to serve under the command of the next Peninsular man.

But the day after Quatre Bras would have shewn the vast gap left by Wellington's disappearance. No general was ever more needed than he was in the ensuing forty-eight hours. The decision to withdraw about midday on the 17th, the area to be occupied, the implementation of the agreement wtih Blücher, the personal control during the withdrawal; most important of all, the conduct of the great Battle of Waterloo, all could only be fulfilled by him, and his presence during these critical hours was indispensable.

He is credited with many sayings, all blunt and to the point. None was more apt than the one he spoke on the night after Waterloo— 'By God, I don't think it would have done if I had not been there.' It is claimed that no man is indispensible. Wellington at Waterloo is the exception that proves the rule.

The Siege of Ladysmith

1900

I N ALL the three hundred and thirty years of South Africa's
turbulent history there have been three outstanding dates.

In 1652 the Dutch landed at what is now Cape Town, looking
for water and finding an uninhabited near-desert. They founded a
colony and then a country.

In 1814, as a result of the Treaty of Vienna after the Napoleonic
Wars, the Dutch sovereignty in the Cape, now extending to sixty
thousand square miles and with a white population of thirty
thousand, was transferred to Great Britain by Holland on a payment of six million pounds.

In 1961 this British sovereignty was repudiated—U.D.I. was
declared and South Africa became a republic owing allegiance and
loyalty to no one but herself.

1814 is the most important of these three dates. The imposition of
British rule on the then one hundred and sixty-two-year-old Dutch
colony has never been forgotten, forgiven or morally accepted.

The Dutch had not, by British standards, been good colonisers.
For over a hundred years they had been the only inhabitants of
the first three hundred miles of territory to the north and east from
the Cape. On first meeting the negroes on the Great Fish River in
1760 they made primitive treaties with them regarding raiding and
cattle-rustling, and then encouraged them individually to come
down into Cape Colony as labourers. Here the Bantu was not
treated as the British settlers living among the Dutch felt he should
be, and on the transference of power from the Dutch to the British
in 1814 a new deal for the negro was made. Slavery was forbidden,
proper wages had to be paid, farmers were punished for ill-treat-
ment of their staff. Flogging was forbidden.

This Christian, humane, and correct treatment of the negroes
infuriated the Boer farmers. There was nothing in the Bible—the
only book many of the Boers had ever possessed or read—to forbid

slavery, they said. Clearly the black man was an inferior being, very much a third-class citizen, barely human, and was never intended to be anything else than a hewer of wood, a drawer of water, the servant of the white man.

The payment of wages greatly upset the economy. Profits and the few luxuries available became more difficult to come by. This transference of power to the hated British had ruined the Dutch paradise which their ancestors from Holland had found, developed and improved. No wonder the simple burghers resented the new regime, the new conditions forced upon them, when the old ones had been so adequate, so prosperous and so happy.

Understandably they also felt resentment that the transference of power was not because they had been beaten in battle, were bankrupt, or had suffered an interior revolution. They had just not been consulted, the wishes of the majority had not been ascertained. Lastly they felt, not unreasonably, that the price of six million pounds was paltry.

This widespread and deep-seated resentment smouldered hotly for twenty years after the transference of sovereignty. Then a large and exasperated number of Dutch farmers, the Boers, started one of the greatest migrations of history, an attempt to get away from it all—the Great Trek.

Many families, selling what they could, packed their belongings onto their wagons and drove off across the veldt, driving their cattle before them. There was no central controlling brain, no headquarters, no plan, no objective beyond the all-powerful urge to get away from the hated English, with their ridiculous ideas and restrictions. After nearly two hundred years of complete family independence they refused any longer to be told what to do by strangers. Their ancestors had found a new country and so successfully colonised it. They, too, would find one and again be independent and successful.

After incredible hardships—some families were on the move for six months—they reached what became known as the Orange River Colony, and the Transvaal. Here they set up two republics and existed, no more, for fifty years. Townships grew up and two very loose forms of central government, from Bloemfontein in the Orange River Colony and Pretoria in the Transvaal tried to rule, or at least control, the highly individualistic and independent Boer 'groups'.

Life was chaotic. There were frequent clashes with British regiments and the Zulus on the 'frontiers' and life became dangerous with the lack of a firm central government. White men other than Boers received scant courtesy, while the treatment of the negroes reverted to the habits, methods and principles of the Cape prior to 1814.

Then in 1885 an epoch-making event occurred. Gold was discovered in the Transvaal, on the Rand, a few miles south of Pretoria, an area entirely pastoral and covered with large and prosperous farms.

The news spread round the world, and adventurers from Great Britain, Germany, Italy, America, poured in. Jews, craftsmen, traders, financiers, speculators, Australians with their 'know-how' from Ballarat arrived, and in two years a large shanty-town had sprung up, along a broad, unmade High Street inches deep in dust. It was flanked by diggers' huts, drinking and gambling saloons, a so-called hotel, a post office, a few simple shops—Johannesburg-to-be, the golden city of Africa.

In twelve years it had a population of 100,000—no city in the world has grown so quickly. Only 5,000 were Boers, mostly Transvaal Government officials, who regarded the other 95,000 as foreigners, newcomers and outsiders—*Uitlanders*.

These miners worked, and played, very hard. The few Boers in the city, and those in Pretoria, only twenty miles away, looked with great disfavour on the wild irreligious life led by these 'outsiders' and determined to offer little co-operation to these Godless people or to their Godless trade.

As the years passed most of the early cosmopolitan settlers moved into middle age and began to look more soberly at their future and the future of Johannesburg. Suddenly they realised that many taxes were punitive, that restrictions were aimed against them and that they had no say whatever in taxation or its application. They provided seven-eighths of the total revenue of the Transvaal but had no vote. They banded themselves into some sort of organisation and not only demanded the vote but also the right to elect their own representatives to the Transvaal parliament. Neither request was granted.

Appeal after appeal was made and eventually Queen Victoria was petitioned to exert her influence to redress their grievances. Beyond a mild letter from the British Colonial Secretary to Pretoria, which was ignored, no action was taken.

The ridiculous and rather pathetic Jameson Raid, from near Mafeking, to 'relieve' Johannesburg was easily repulsed by the Boers who regarded it as an infringement of their territory by a neighbouring 'friendly' state. It further hardened their intransigent attitude. They refused even to consider giving the vote to the *Uitlanders*, many of whom had now been living in Johannesburg for twelve years.

The Boers knew that if they did give even a modified franchise to the *Uitlanders* on no matter how restricted a scale, it must quite soon produce a parliamentary majority largely non-Boer. Thus they would be swamped and then governed by the despised gold-diggers, a people whose whole outlook and way of life was so alien to their own narrow, bigoted, religious attitude. To be governed in one's own country, a country of one's own making, by a lot of evil-living foreigners was no better than going back to 1814 when at the Cape they had been forced to cede their sovereignty to the English. There was a worse aspect. A 'foreign' majority would almost certainly insist on a liberal attitude towards the Negroes. They would be given rights, equality before the Law, an admission to consideration, those liberalities their grandfathers and grandmothers had trekked north to avoid sixty-five years ago. This fear of emancipation of the negroes was by far the greatest cause of the South African war.

Tension in Johannesburg and Pretoria slowly increased, the Boers as determined as ever not to increase the franchise, Downing Street equally insistent that justice must be done to the *Uitlanders*. During August and September large numbers of Boer 'soldiers' together with their professional artillery, moved down to the Natal frontier and it became increasingly evident that the Transvaal was fully prepared for war. In October the British Government agreed to reinforcements being sent out, and on the 7th October 'the Army Corps' was mobilised. The announcement of this step in London caused grave resentment and alarm in Pretoria and two days later the famous Transvaal ultimatum was issued. It demanded that all troops on its southern border be instantly withdrawn, that all recently arrived reinforcements be sent back to the coast and that troops on their way to South Africa by sea should not be landed. This humiliating ultimatum was of course rejected. Within 48 hours the Transvaal armed forces crossed the frontier, invaded Natal and attacked Dundee.

The frontier between Natal and the Transvaal is very irregular. At the north-west corner of the British Colony it makes an ugly north-pointing salient with the little town of Dundee well forward, only five miles from the Transvaal to the east. Fifty-five miles to the south lies Ladysmith, then Dundee's nearest white settlement and garrison.

Lieutenant-General Sir George White, very recently appointed to be Commander-in-Chief in Natal, with headquarters at Ladysmith, had seen service in the Indian Mutiny, had won the V.C. on the famous march to Kandahar in 1878, had much experience in native wars and was 64 years of age. On arrival at Ladysmith in mid-October he was dismayed to find that Major-General Penn Symons had sometime previously established himself at Dundee in the salient, with four battalions from the Ladysmith garrison.

This outpost position was indeed precarious. However, Sir George White's suggestion that Dundee, exposed to attack or raid from three sides should be evacuated was opposed by Penn Symons, a zealous but over-confident officer, and the four battalions in huts and tents around the town remained, living their almost peace-time existence.

In the early morning of the 20th of October 1899 life in Dundee and in the garrison was normal. Early parade had been dismissed, horses had been led off to the stream to water and the men were waiting at the cookhouses for their breakfast. About 8 a.m. a shell, fired apparently from Talana Hill two thousand yards away, fell in the camp a few yards from General Penn Symons's tent. The Second Boer War had started.

Talana Hill is a long, regular, whale-back hill a thousand yards long and three hundred feet high. At its foot on the Dundee side flows a small stream, the Sand Spruit, with five-foot banks, from where the ground rises very slowly for a thousand yards back to the huts occupied by the soldiers.

The noise of the shell quickly followed by a second one fired at the town itself created some confusion and several of the horses being led back after watering bolted, adding to the confusion. The alarm sounded, all ranks hurriedly equipped themselves and companies doubled forward down the long slope to the cover of the river banks, where chaos reigned. The Irish Fusiliers, 60th Rifles and Dublin Fusiliers were in no sort of order or formation. Commanding officers did not know whether missing companies were up or down stream, adjutants had difficulty in getting through the crowd, company commanders could not find battalion headquarters and a long time was spent in collecting the three battalions in some sort of order. Colonel Yule, second-in-command of the force, succeeded partially, though not completely, and at about 10 a.m. the three battalions advanced in line out of the river bed towards the hill.

A considerable plantation of blue gum-trees extending along most of the lower slopes of Talana Hill afforded some cover, which was quickly reached. In the middle of this plantation lay Smith's Farm, a considerable homestead with numerous outbuildings where General Penn Symons and at least one battalion set up some form of headquarters. Beyond the plantation the hill itself at once becomes a series of gigantic steps, each terminating in a low cliff on the top of which rough stone walls are built. Between the wall and the next small cliff the ground is pasture.

Six hundred Boers were now on the hilltop and on the two upper steps, having a perfect view of the troops leaving the river bed, then disappearing into the cover of the plantation and then reappearing as they climbed forward and upward over the low walls. The enemy, firing downhill at an angle of 30 degrees, always a difficult task, frequently lost sight of the troops as they gained the shelter of the successive walls and considerable progress was made, although the original disorganisation at the start was never overcome completely. General Penn Symons, believing the advance through the plantation and up the hill was not as speedy as he thought possible, rode forward through the trees from the farm and dismounted. Climbing on to the first wall, from where he exhorted the Dublin Fusiliers to greater urgency, he was an easy target for some Boer behind the nearest wall and he was shot down, mortally wounded.

The enemy, rather shaken by the tenacity, discipline and bravery of the British soldiers, qualities which they had not encountered at Majuba eighteen years previously, wavered as the summit was approached and they could see the British bayonets getting closer. Not wanting or waiting to fight it out they turned and ran down the reverse slope of the hill, jumped on their ponies and fled. Two squadrons of 18th Hussars under their C.O. Colonel Moller had been posted out on the left flank of the British advance and now were gallantly but foolishly led at the gallop round the hill and into the retreating Boers streaming across the plain. At first the shock of this totally unexpected attack on the vulnerable flank of the enemy's retreat was successful but soon the eight hundred Boers realised that the three hundred British cavalrymen were no match for them. Reining in, they surrounded the Hussars, drove them off their line of retreat and, cornering them in some broken country, captured most of them.

At the other end of Talana Hill and after a small depression rises another lower *kopje*, Lennox Hill. Here the Boers had originally posted two hundred men under Commandant Lukas Meyer, later one of their successful leaders, presumably with the object of enfilading the British infantry as it emerged from the plantation. This force on Lennox Hill could have so held up the main advance as it climbed the walls as to turn the action into a British defeat, especially as Penn Symons had no reserve to deal with it, having left the Leicesters in Dundee to guard the town. But this party of Boers fired not a shot throughout the battle and its presence was quite unknown until after the action. It was the first engagement of the war, the targets were easily seen and the range was right. The inertia and supineness of this considerable party remains to this day inexplicable.

Up and over the Nek between Talana and Lennox Hills— 'Smith's Nek'—runs a road from Dundee to Vryheid. As Talana Hill was carried a battery of field artillery advanced up the road to the top of the rise and there saw the Boers in their initial panic fleeing across the plain. The Battery Commander was about to open up with shrapnel on this ideal target when he noticed a white flag —which had been flying all day, out of sight—on a small building which is still standing, on the enemy's side of the hill. Thinking naturally that the Boers had surrendered he held his hand for some minutes, the opportunity passed never to return and the vast majority of the enemy escaped, including the Lennox Hill detachment which had slipped quietly away. In the battle the British lost fifty men killed with a hundred and eighty wounded while the Boer losses were not less than three hundred.

The battlefield of Talana Hill is exactly similar to what maps, sketches, and descriptions have led the visitor to expect. The steps, with their pasture bounded by low cliffs topped by the walls are still there and are very obviously difficult and arduous to climb. The complete cover from view provided by the last few yards of each terrace under the lee of the wall above it is very clear.

Lennox Hill, a hard, bare, rocky feature, shows what a nasty enfilading fire position out on the right flank it could have been. Good riflemen as the Boers were they could so easily have held up the attack.

The absence of explosive shell-fire in this battle has of course left no sign of bombardment but on many of the rocks in the walls can still be seen the 'splashes' of the rifle bullets. The top of the hill, almost flat, and about forty yards wide, is very heavy going. Rocks three or four feet high, stones and boulders underfoot, long grass and cactus plants provide wonderful cover for the rifleman but make movement difficult. There is little doubt that on that hopelessly tangled ground empty Mauser cartridge cases are still to be found today.

The Sand Spruit River where the three battalions congregated seems little changed. The plantation of blue gums through which the regiments advanced seems to have neither shrunk nor spread and in the middle of it lies Smith's Farm. Rebuilt some twenty years ago on precisely the same site as the original it is surrounded by several outhouses, barns, and sheds, some of which have not been rebuilt. These were standing on the 20th of October 1899. The Smith who owned and worked the farm then died in 1941 at the age of 101, and today his great-granddaughter owns Smith's Farm, her husband farming the land. It was a great privilege for the author to have tea with this lady in her farmhouse in the middle of the battlefield. Near by in the plantation is the small family cemetery where nearly all the names on the tombstones are Smith. An extension encloses the mass grave of the men of the three regiments who were killed.

The troops remained on the hill for several hours after their victory and that night, evacuating Talana Hill, returned to their camp at Dundee. Constant pressure by small mounted parties of the enemy from the direction of both frontiers and disquieting reports of converging commandos decided Colonel Yule, now in command, to withdraw to Ladysmith.

The march of fifty-five miles was arduous. Carried out in almost incessant rain, constantly pressed by sniping patrols on both flanks, bivouacking every night with no hot food, the march took four days. Sir George White, already partly surrounded in Ladysmith, kept the way open for the Dundee force by fighting the battle of Elandslaagte, and on the 26th of October the nearly exhausted brigade marched back into the town which it should never have left and where it was to be besieged for four months.

Fourteen miles to the north-east of Ladysmith, and well outside the perimeter being taken up by the enemy, the village of Elandslaagte, with its railway station, was occupied by the enemy, cutting the Dundee force's line of retreat.

Sir George White was determined to keep open this road to allow the Dundee brigade to reach the shelter of Ladysmith. Hearing that the Boer line at Elandslaagte could be forced he ordered Major-General John French—who had a Chief-of-Staff named Major Douglas Haig—to lead out a mounted force to recapture the little town of Elandslaagte. The Boers, though not in strength, were too much for French's two cavalry regiments, which had to withdraw.

White then sent out from Ladysmith a brigade of three regiments, Devons, Manchesters, and Gordons under a Colonel Ian Hamilton, the third soldier taking a part in this very minor and local tactical exercise who was to reach eminence in the Great War, sixteen years later.

Colonel Sir Henry Rawlinson, senior General Staff Officer to Sir George White, was the fourth senior officer in the siege of Ladysmith to rise to great heights in the Great War. Three of them, French, Haig, and Hamilton, became Commanders-in-Chief, while Rawlinson commanded the Fourth Army. Sir Hubert Gough, who was to command the famous Fifth Army in France in March 1918, commanded the cavalry regiment first to enter Ladysmith on its relief. It would seem that these five officers learnt so greatly from their active service experiences in South Africa that they found success against the new enemy fourteen years later in Europe. Yet this new enemy of 1914 was highly trained, professional and rigidly disciplined, so different from the Boers. Conditions at Ladysmith and Le Cateau, at Elandslaagte and Gallipoli could hardly have been more different. It says much for the elasticity of their minds that they could so drastically re-adapt themselves.

Hamilton sent the Devons across open, undulating country to attack the enemy's right and in their full view, while his other two battalions worked round the Boer left flank. The advance of the Devons was in a formation never before seen in European warfare. Until now all infantry in the attack in any army had moved almost shoulder to shoulder. But the growing power of modern small-arms fire and of artillery turned these almost solid blocks of men from being a menace to become a superb target for the defender and at heavy cost to the attacker.

But Hamilton ordered the Devons to deploy the men at intervals of two yards, which enabled them to advance almost unscathed across the open country and to be in a position to manoeuvre across rough ground. The outstanding success of this new formation was obvious. The lesson was well learnt and the British Army thence onward always attacked in this open formation, the original 'extended order'. German rigidity of thought, however, prevented them from adopting it in 1914 until the 1st Battle of Ypres in October, after fearful casualties had been suffered at Mons, Le Cateau and Landrècies. Many British soldiers from Elandslaagte onward were to owe their lives to Hamilton's innovation and originality of thought.

The holding attack of the Devons took much of the attention of the Boers, and the Manchesters got well forward on the enemy's left, where they were held. The Gordons came through them, rolling up the defences, capturing the little town, and reopening the road from Dundee. Twenty-four hours later the four battalions from Dundee marched—staggered—through the cordon and, covered by General French's cavalry, both forces entered Ladysmith, the garrison turning out to cheer them in. The Boers re-occupied Elandslaagte and the ring was again closed. 14,000 soldiers, a mass of stores and a swollen civilian population, many of whom were white farmer-families seeking the shelter of the garrison, were to be besieged for over four months.

The town of Ladysmith was ideal both for defence and investment, being largely encircled by low hills. The enemy was provided with excellent observation posts and heavy gun positions, while the besieged had ample defensive areas. The town itself was, and still is, a typical colonial 'small-town'. On the High Street, running through the town, stand the bigger shops, the church, the Town Hall and the Royal Hotel. The population was very largely white, with a high percentage of British people, which included people from every grade of society. Around the town the country is flat, pastoral but not very fertile. There are some prominent hills about five miles out from the town, but these were not occupied by the British troops.

To the immediate south of the town one large ridge, only two

miles out and running east and west, had an almost flat top—
'Caesar's Camp'. After a slight dip towards its western end, it rose
again into the pronounced rise of Wagon Hill. It dominated both the
town and the undulating plain running south to the Tugela Heights
fifteen miles away. Because of its proximity to the town, it was
occupied. It was in fact the only tactical area to be so used for
some time after war broke out, and before the investment was
complete.

Very shortly after the investment was complete, Sir George White
decided to make two sorties to push the enemy off the hills to the
east and north. He hoped to prevent the embarrassment of having
Boers in good positions so near him, to deny them observation, to
start them looking back over their shoulders towards their own
frontier, and to secure these good positions for his own troops,
which he ought to have occupied immediately news of the withdrawal from Dundee reached him.

One sortie—to the north—was to hold Nicholson's Nek, a narrow
defile through the hills, six miles away. It consisted of six companies
of the Irish Fusiliers, five of the Gloucesters and a mountain battery,
with a hundred pack mules carrying entrenching tools for building
a defensive post.

A long delay in starting caused the force to be caught climbing
the defile at daybreak. One mule then bolted. The remaining ninety-
nine took fright, shook themselves loose from their soldier-leaders
(who had little experience of that most intractable animal), and
stampeded through the mountain battery whose animals enthusi-
astically joined them. The Gloucesters, coming up the defile in
column, were in the way, and the rout of the regiment was painful
and undignified.

Some attempts were made to rectify the chaos but the Boers,
fully alerted by all the noise, opened fire and the infantry who had
lost their guns and reserve ammunition were surrounded, and killed
or captured.

To the east, and at the same time that the Nicholson's Nek
adventure started from Ladysmith, another sortie left the town to
capture the high ground around Farquahar's Farm, Lombards Kop,
Long Hill and Pepworth Hill. Sir George White's additional intention here was to drive the Boers north and north-west on to the
Gloucesters and Irish Fusiliers now holding Nicholson's Nek—
as he hoped.

The leading brigade of this second sorties consisting of the King's Liverpools, the Leicesters, and two battalions of the 60th Rifles, was commanded by a Colonel Grimwood, C.O. of one of the battalions. His appointment to the command had been a matter of hours only, he had never commanded a brigade even on peace-time manoeuvres, he did not welcome the task and, as he admitted afterwards, he was not up to it.

After an early start and during the remaining hours of darkness both cohesion and direction were lost—and two battalions going off on their own captured a hill unknown, and unoccupied. The remainder of the brigade then attacked and captured Lombard's Kop, the defeated enemy withdrawing eastward instead of westward towards Nicholson's Nek—as had been hoped.

The troops were now extended on a line some three miles long, in two unequal halves, out of touch and out of sight of each other and with a brigade-commander who was quite incapable of gripping the situation. Little had been achieved except chaos.

Sir George White then sent a second brigade out from Ladysmith consisting of Devons, Manchesters, Gordons and Rifle Brigade under Ian Hamilton, to reinforce Grimwood's firing line, to pass through it and attacking the enemy's left (eastern) flank, restore the 'intention' of driving them on to the Nicholson's Nek force. The Manchesters and the Gordons were drawn up for the advance.

Unluckily the two battalions with Grimwood, the Leicesters and the 60th, now began to fall back from Lombard's Kop, which was immediately reoccupied by the Boers. The retreating battalions, under a devastating fire from their rear, now almost panicked and ran through the Manchesters and Gordons awaiting the word to advance, causing great confusion. Sir George White up at Ian Hamilton's headquarters, seeing the chaos and disorganisation, and hearing of the set-back at Nicholson's Nek ordered a general withdrawal back to Ladysmith. The men of Grimwood's brigade obeyed this, the first sensible order they had received, with alacrity. General French's cavalry, on Grimwood's right flank protected the withdrawal and the eight battalions got safely back into the town. It must be accepted that in largely superior numbers, all long service regulars, these units were repulsed, disorganised and defeated by a smaller force of semi-amateur, unorganised 'farmer-soldiers'.

This disastrous sortie, designed to capture four considerable, clearly visible hills not only failed to hold any of them but completed the day of defeat for the defenders of Ladysmith—'Mournful Monday'. Never has it been truer to say that by nightfall 'they were back where they started'. Had the enemy shewn real initiative, on their horses they could well have driven the British right through Ladysmith where near-panic was rising, and out on the other side.

The ring was closed. To the north, north-east, east, south-east, and south wherein all roads and the two railway lines ran, the Boers were settling themselves in to conduct a long siege. All communications were cut, including telegraph lines, and the only contact with the outside world was by heliograph, not a very satisfactory method. To the west lay open country, almost desert. No sortie that way could lead anywhere—while no relieving force coming that way could depend on any lines of supply behind it.

In this humiliating position lay 14,000 British troops, almost throttled by only half that number of Boers, sitting on the hills round them. Stores and rations in Ladysmith were plentiful but clearly they would not last for ever, and there was not the slightest chance of replenishing except by a strong relieving army from the south able to brush aside the 7,000 Boers.

The British troops occupied most of the lesser and nearer hills by posts, manned by night, and used as O.P.s by day, and quickly the regiments settled into a weekly routine of guard duties on the hills alternating with peace-time life in barracks or tents. There was little or no activity, no patrolling by either defenders or besiegers and life became monotonous and dull.

The weather, mid-summer, was hot and dry and, as rations were gradually reduced, dysentery and enteric fever appeared. By the end of the year, 1,600 men were in hospital with one of these diseases. Water was severely rationed.

Yet the siege had its lighter moments. Concerts, at which officers' wives sang, whist drives, and dances were organised to entertain the garrison. Cricket and football matches abounded as they always will where the British soldier can find the opportunity and the ground. Polo for the officers was possible, small dinner parties were even arranged.

But the enemy was strengthening his grip. Mounting heavy guns on his hills, he was able to cause dismay and casualties by indiscriminate shelling of the town. One such gun position was raided early in December and the gun destroyed at the cost of twenty-one men wounded. A few days later a similar raid was also successful, but fifty-four casualties were suffered and such raids were therefore discontinued.

When the ring had closed round the town the Boers had brought forward one of their five 'Long Toms', a 6-inch Creusot siege-gun, and mounted it on a special platform on Pepworth Hill overlooking the town, within two miles of its centre. It fired a ninety-four pound shell and was to prove, with the dwindling rations, perhaps the greatest hardship of the siege.

Throughout December the bombardment continued, though with surprisingly little effect. By Christmas five thousand shells from 'Long Tom' and the other besieging guns had fallen on the town but only thirty people had been killed. The tower of the Town Hall was hit and suffered several large holes, but it survived. The Royal Hotel, an imposing and prominent building in the middle of the High Street, two hundred yards from the Town Hall, was a favourite target. The enemy knew that officers often lunched therein, including Doctor Jameson (of Jameson Raid fame), Colonel Frank Rhodes, brother of Cecil, now besieged in Kimberley, and General French with his senior staff officers. One shell landed on the front *stoep*[1] of the hotel, just outside the main entrance, on what is now the public pavement. It did not explode. It was left intact where it buried itself, and is there today, now worn smooth and highly polished by seventy years of passing pedestrians.

One shell hit Sir George White's residence, but luckily he and all his staff were out. Sand-bag repairs were made but eventually the Headquarters had to move to a less obvious house.

Many private householders built themselves shelters, especially those whose houses were on a slightly rising slope of ground. Primitive caves excavated into a hillside, no matter how insignificant, were an expression of 'Ladysmith can take it'. These caves may have saved a few lives but more importantly they satisfied a subconscious urge to resist, a determination to stick it. They were the forerunners of the deep dug-outs on the Somme of 1916 and the air raid shelters in Hyde Park in 1941.

Morale remained high for some time. The operations at Talana Hill, the withdrawal into Ladysmith, and the keeping open of the road at Elandslaagte were regarded as victories, being only very slightly offset by the twin defeats of Nicholson's Nek and Lom-

[1] A stone platform attached to the walls of some South African houses.

bard's Kop. The strict but not yet meagre rations were regarded as inevitable. The British are always philosophical in danger or under pressure and there was little doubt that the people of Ladysmith would have given as warm a reception to any Boer incursion as the Home Guard and the people of Kent and Sussex would have shown to a German invasion after Dunkirk.

The first sign of lowering morale was the news of the defeat of Colenso in December, when four British brigades of 15 battalions, the biggest force to attack an enemy since the Alma in 1854, were utterly repulsed by the Boers, losing 1,100 men and 10 guns. Every person in Ladysmith, soldier and civilian, knew that their relief was the object of the battle of Colenso and the rebuff made everyone feel, perhaps not quite apprehensive, but certainly not quite so sure. Immediately after the battle the news of Buller's advice to Sir George White to burn his documents, fire off his ammunition, and surrender, leaked out and was unfortunately accompanied by a further substantial, but necessary, reduction of rations. At this height of mid-summer and in a heat-wave dysentery and enteric were raging, and by the New Year, the first in the new century, both morale and health had sunk.

However, it quickly, but only temporarily rose again. The repulse of the Boer attack on 'Caesar's Camp' and Wagon Hill on 7th January, acted as a great tonic.

During the siege the normal garrison of this long flat ridge was five battalions. Early in the New Year they were the King's, the Manchesters, the 60th Rifles, the Gordons and the Rifle Brigade. Its local commander was Colonel Ian Hamilton.

At about 4 a.m. on 7th January 1900, the Boers attacked the great east- and west-running ridge in strength, trying to encircle Wagon Hill, with four minor assaults on other parts of the ridge. Considerable success was achieved, largely by surprise in the dark.

In addition to the boring wait by the British soldiers for several weeks with little happening, coupled with the lowered vitality due to the new rationing, a low standard of sentry-vigilance had resulted and indeed the Boers thought for a while that the ridge had been evacuated. Wagon Hill was quickly surrounded on three sides while considerable penetration was made further along the ridge, Manchester Fort in the centre and on the highest point being captured and Ian Hamilton's headquarters, close by, surrounded.

Hamilton himself was out on a dawn inspection. Caught in the battle he rallied the troops at Wagon Hill, personally led a minor counter attack and shot several Boers with his own revolver.

But by 8 a.m. the Boers had a firm footing on a number of points on their crest of the ridge and on Wagon Hill they had met great success. Crossing the entirely flat summit, they had penetrated three hundred yards to reach the inner crest of the ridge overlooking the town and had completely cut the whole British position in half, but their salient was only two hundred yards wide. Although they had created a very serious and unpleasant tactical situation for the defenders, the Boer position in this long, narrow salient in broad daylight, was untenable.

Elsewhere, however, the British regiments in small, frequently isolated parties were holding firm, and by close-range rifle fire easily prevented any further enemy movement. At midday, five companies of the Devons were ordered out from the town to recapture the north face of Wagon Hill and liquidate the enemy salient. Climbing the steep slope quickly and skilfully and then using the bayonet ruthlessly, they drove the enemy off the hill, a classic example of the use of the British steel which the Boers so feared. The remaining pockets of Boer penetration, seeing the success of the Devon's charge, started to withdraw gradually and by nightfall Caesar's Camp and Wagon Hill were again in British occupation. The close-range rifle fire and excellent fire positions of the British infantry had caused many Boer casualties, and their wounded barely out-numbered the dead.

Today there are many signs of earth-works along the ridge. Manchester Fort, about the size of a tennis court, is very clear, its sangar-like walls being still four feet high and the various divisions within the fort are visible. Owing to the hard rocky soil, little digging was possible and there is a wealth of small isolated breastworks on the ridge a few feet high, all showing skilful siting with excellent fields of fire. The whole position being so narrow, there was little room for defence in depth, but the principle of mutually supporting posts on the outer (southern) crest was clearly recognised, cross-lines of fire being frequently used. Had great surprise not been achieved the enemy must have suffered heavily from small-arms fire from these defended localities, and possibly been repulsed at the outset.

The scene of the Devons' bayonet charge, about one hundred and fifty yards of the level top of the hill, is easily found. It completely over-ran the sharp point of the salient, capturing many Boers and forcing a pocket deep into the enemy's newly-won positions.

Further to the left the great plateau of Caesar's Camp itself still shows many earthworks around its edges, all with the same good fields of fire. In the middle, a row of six rectangular enclosures, twenty feet square and with low turf walls on three sides, indicates a battery position. Owing to the extreme flatness of the ground all round them and their distance of three hundred yards from the steeply descending sides of the plateau, this battery position must have been invisible except from the enemy's position at Umbulwana, three miles away. Vague tracks and paths are still discernible in the grass, which in spite of the rocky soil, is for once quite rich and luxurious.

Ian Hamilton's Headquarters, a small sangar of enormous stones, is in almost as good condition as Manchester Fort, while fifty yards in front of it, in a little cluster of rocks and cacti, was a company headquarters. On one of the smooth rocks can still be seen, in faint white paint: 'D Company, Manchesters'.

A notable feature of Caesar's Camp and Wagon Hill is the excellence of the siting of the battalion, company, and section positions. All show many of the defensive principles of 1918—and it is evident that Ian Hamilton by his new tactical use of the Devons in the attack at Elandslaagte, and then in the defence of Caesar's Camp, was not only a great tactician but in 1900 far in advance of his contemporaries in his thinking and methods, and their application. He had learned much from his experiences in the first South African war (especially at Majuba), on the North-West Frontier of India, where he had taken part in two campaigns, and Burma. It was sad that with his long service and great experience he should fail so lamentably when his great chance came as Commander-in-Chief at Gallipoli in 1915. He was removed from his command and never employed again.

The repulse of the Boers from Caesar's Camp raised morale again but life was no easier for the garrison or the town. Dysentery and enteric increased. Sentry and guard duties had to be extended on account of the surprise attack on Caesar's Camp. No news came in from Buller, still south of the Tugela fifteen miles away, and there seemed to be no future in anything.

Then suddenly Buller became active again after the three weeks stagnation following his defeat at Colenso. Announcing that he had found the key to Ladysmith he marched two-thirds of his army, now amounting to thirty thousand men, to the west and crossed the Tugela, obviously to attack or even outflank the enemy extreme right. The news again raised hopes in Ladysmith and on the 24th the sound of firing could be heard all day. Through glasses could be seen numberless figures on the summit of Spion Kop, the highest feature for some miles to the south-west. Doubtless Spion Kop had been captured, the Boers defeated. Relief was only a matter of two or three days now.

But the sound of the field-guns died away, instead of getting nearer, and there was no sign of British cavalry on the plain where they should be now if Spion Kop had been captured and the enemy's flank turned. Gradually it dawned on Ladysmith that things had gone wrong again.

Morale was pushed yet further downhill two weeks later when a lesser attack by Buller on Vaalkrantz petered out. (It was not, largely, defeated by the enemy.)

Rations had again to be reduced, water got scarce and smelly, shelling went on and disease increased. The energies of the troops sank more and more and their clothing which could not be replaced got tattered and torn. Their general condition was desperate and deplorable. However, as usual they did not know when they were beaten.

The enemy successes at Spion Kop and Vaalkrantz were not significant except as a surprise for the British and as local tactical victories for the Boers. Indeed, the latter had suffered considerable casualties and would have preferred to forego the two successes, retaining their men, munitions and morale. A general withdrawal took place, and Buller, returning to Colenso, was able to cross the Tugela at last, and without much opposition. Advancing through the Tugela Heights he found enemy resistance to be less and less, until on 28th February, on the capture of the last of the hills, the enemy broke and fled, dispersing to the north and north-east.

Next day White heliographed to Buller that his rations were half a pound of inferior bread per person a day and that he could hold out only until the 1st April. In Ladysmith these last days of the siege were miserable. Few men had the strength and none the heart for cricket or football, while concerts and entertainments fell flatter and flatter. There was no defeatism in Ladysmith but there was hunger and the depression that hunger, accompanied by in-action, brings.

During the afternoon of the 28th the Boer dispersal and retreat could be seen from Ladysmith and the sight of their wagons moving across the veldt away from Buller's army seemed to be too good to be true. The shelling of the town stopped and the removal of the big gun on Bulwana Ridge could be seen.

At 6 o'clock a squadron from a mounted infantry regiment rode up the High Street. They were strangers, their horses were in excel-lent condition and the riders had the air of conquerors. They were the advance guard of the relief column.

Major Hubert Gough commanded the regiment and entered Ladysmith at 6.15. He was taken to Sir George White, whom he found a grey-faced stooping figure weakened by illness and depri-vation, walking with the help of a stick.

As the cavalry rode up into the town the relieved soldiers of the garrison, tattered, thin and pale, lined the streets feebly cheering their relievers. The cavalry soldiers threw them chocolates, cigar-ettes and tobacco, but it was some days before adequate supplies could be brought in.

Buller, with his usual caution, this time justified, tried to find the Boers. He planned attacks on Bulwana Ridge and Van Renan's Pass, twenty miles to the north-west. The hills around the town were searched by the cavalry but no Boers were found and he judged correctly that he had defeated the enemy, relieved Ladysmith and that his three-months task was accomplished.

On 3rd March he made his formal entry into Ladysmith, riding with his staff down the High Street, followed by several infantry battalions, well dressed, well fed—at great contrast to the ragged, thin Ladysmith garrison which lined the street. At the town hall he met Sir George White with his staff, their meeting and shaking hands being the subject of a well-known picture, reminiscent of the meeting of Wellington and Blücher at La Belle Alliance after Waterloo.

By the time the official entry was made some of the food brought up by the relieving army had been distributed and the troops and civilians in Ladysmith were already looking better and feeling more cheerful. But the three-months siege had taken a great toll of the health of the garrison and there was little energy or life in the town. Buller's relieving army, too, was tired, needing a week's rest, and 'care and maintenance' and no action was taken to find or chase the Boers.

The siege, however, was over—Ladysmith had been relieved.

In Northern Natal there are many war memorials, individual graves, commemoration stones and mass graves. The Zulu War, the Majuba campaign, the siege of Ladysmith and its relief have each provided several. They are easily found. although often in almost inaccessible spots. All are well kept-up, due to the untiring and enthusiastic work of the Natal Historical and Archaeological Society. Occasionally a memorial or grave has to be repaired after the skylarking of the Zulu herd-boys, who, naturally enough, have little reverence or respect for the memorials. Their depredations are quite unpolitical and non-racial and might well be expected in more civilised countries.

The author, on his first visit to the South African battlefields, was in Ladysmith in 1961 when the memorial to the King's Regiment near Pepworth Hill, having been repaired, was rededicated. The vicar of Ladysmith conducted the simple little open-air service on the hill-top. The Mayor of the town and the town clerk attended in state. The chairman of the Natal Historical and Archaeological Society, Major Stevenson, was the outstanding figure and as the driving force of his organisation unveiled the repaired memorial. Several old soldiers from 1900 from either side now living in the town or its vicinity were present in the modest little gathering, one of whom had been a lance-corporal in the King's battalion, sixty-one years previously.

It so happened that the King's Regiment at the time of the rededication ceremony in 1961 was stationed at Nairobi in Kenya. The father of its C.O. had in 1900 been adjutant in Ladysmith during the siege. The 1961 C.O. sent down his son, a second-lieutenant in the battalion, to represent the Regiment—and the family—at the rededication.

Four years later the author was again fortunate enough to be in Ladysmith when a not-unsimilar ceremony was held. This time it was not the rededication of a sixty-year-old, repaired war memorial, but the unveiling by the Administrator of Natal—a Government and political official—of a new memorial to a Dutch priest who had, with great bravery, administered to the wounded of both sides, Boer and British, during the battle of Caesar's Camp and Wagon Hill in 1900.

It is possible to get jeeps up Wagon Hill and an assembly of perhaps fifty people were present at the service around the monument. There were Boers, descendants of the attackers at Caesar's Camp in 1900, civilians from the town of Ladysmith, whose grandparents in many cases had been in the siege, and visitors. It was noticeable that the non-partisan attitude of the brave and unselfish priest of 1900 was reflected in the demeanour of the assembly in 1961.

Most sensible people in South Africa today realise that the differences between the Dutch and the British, born at the transference of power in 1814, and accentuated by Majuba, the Boer War, the concentration camps and the declaration of the republic in 1961 had better be forgotten. Most realise that they are now South Africans, and no longer British or Dutch. The occasional ceremonies at these memorials around Ladysmith and in Natal assist this patriotic, common-sense, forward-looking attitude.

The siege of Ladysmith in 1900 and its memorials today were and are important steps in making a new nation a united nation.

The Relief of Ladysmith

1900

THE South African War—the Boer War—was in fact two separate campaigns which eventually merged into one. In each case the objective was to relieve a town which had been surrounded and cut off by the Boers immediately after their invasion of Natal and the Cape Colony without a declaration of war.

On the western side of the Continent the siege of Kimberley, 'the Diamond City', besieged as an obviously important centre and a railway junction did not include military events of such moment. It lasted only a hundred days and was chiefly noteworthy for the presence in the beleaguered city of the most powerful Englishman in South Africa, Cecil Rhodes, who was caught in the siege. The senior military officer was Colonel Kekewich, who, when the Boer ring was closed, became automatically the supreme authority in the town. He was a stolid, efficient, dedicated, perhaps unimaginative soldier, whose qualities and exercise of his duties infuriated Cecil Rhodes, who disliked soldiers anyway. Friction between these so contrasting characters became so acute that Kekewich had to prevent by force Rhodes using his own and the de Beers private telegraph out of the town, and himself to ask for confirmation by telegraph from the Commander-in-Chief that he was, in fact, the supreme authority.

Attempts to relieve Kimberley were made by General Lord Methuen up the railway from De Aar. After some not very convincing victories at Belmont, Graspan, Enslin and Modder River, he was finally brought to a halt by the disastrous defeat of the Highland Brigade at Magersfontein, one of the three defeats in the 'Black Week'.

Lord Roberts, sent out as a new Commander-in-Chief, took over on this front and by brilliant re-organisation, and then tactics, defeated the enemy at Paardeburg, and relieved Kimberley.

7. Aftermath of Spion Kop. Boers collect arms and equipment while a medical orderly attends the wounded. *National Army Museum.*

8. The summit of Spion Kop today.

9. The Town Hall at Ladysmith during the siege.

10. Ladysmith. Manchester Fort, Caesar's Camp, today.

11. The relief of Ladysmith. Buller's army enters the town.

12. Le Cateau. The sunken lane in which the Norfolk Regiment were positioned and the successor to the Great Tree.

13. Gallipoli. The Landing from the *River Clyde*. From a painting by Charles Davies.

On the eastern side of the Continent, the town of Ladysmith with its siege and relief was the focal point of the other sub-campaign. The engagements of Talana Hill, Elandslaagte, the closing of the Boer ring, Lombard's Kop, Nicholson's Nek, Caesar's Camp and Wagon Hill, have been reviewed in the previous chapter, together with some notes of conditions inside the town during the siege.

The importance of relieving Kimberley had lain in the diamond mines, the railway junction—and Cecil Rhodes. The urgency of relieving Ladysmith was for a very different reason. In the town were nine battalions, and a total force of 8,000 men with a large number of civilians. Stocks of food were limited and the reasons for relief were humanitarian rather than material.

After the failure of the Bloemfontein Conference between the British High Commissioner, Sir Alfred Milner, and the Boer President, Paul Kruger in May 1899, tension in Johannesburg had steadily mounted. This conference had been convened by Sir Alfred and agreed to by Kruger. Its object was to settle the political and financial position of the *Uitlanders*.

The *Uitlanders* were the inhabitants of Johannesburg; they came from many countries in the world, were all white men, and were mostly gold diggers.

Because of their wild, immoral life they were loathed in Pretoria, the capital of the Transvaal, and were denied the vote. Yet they provided nine-tenths of the Transvaal's income and formed seven-eighth's of its white population. That they had no say in the Government nor in the application of taxation from which they suffered severely seemed a monstrous injustice. By October 1899 the British Government felt the situation was deteriorating to such an extent that massive reinforcements were needed. Accordingly the two divisions comprising the Army Corps were ordered out from home and General Sir Redvers Buller, Adjutant General in the War Office, was appointed as Supreme Commander.

He had just completed the biggest achievement of his career— the birth, formation and organisation of the Army Service Corps from the old, hopelessly out-of-date Commissariat and Transport Department, mostly manned by civilians. He was a great organiser and administrator and utilised his long experience as a regimental officer on active service, and then on the staff of the War Office to good purpose. His new 'child', which he conceived and nurtured so well was and still is one of the most efficient units in the Army.

During two and a half years in France and Italy in the First World
War the author cannot recall any occasion when the rations, ammunition, water, even letters, failed to arrive in the front trenches,
no matter how arduous the conditions were. The Army Service
Corps was Buller's masterpiece. But he was not a great commander—still less a tactician.

On arrival at Cape Town, and after the latest assessment of the
situation, he decided to take personal command of the eastern campaign, to relieve Ladysmith and to leave Methuen alone to relieve
Kimberley. He accordingly re-embarked and sailed for Durban,
which he reached at the end of November 1899.

General Buller was a typical late-nineteenth-century British
General. An old Etonian, he was pompous, upright, limited, unable
to suffer fools gladly or otherwise, and irascible, but he looked after
his men's welfare most assiduously. He was vastly experienced,
having been present at the engagements of Fort Garry in Winnipeg,
in the Zulu War (where he won his V.C. as a lieutenant-colonel),
at Tel-el-Kebir, Suakin, Abu Klea and in the Ashanti War.

He had served in the 60th Rifles as a regimental officer for fifteen
years and had passed through the Staff College. He had commanded
units at all levels and by 1899 he had forty-one years service.
Obviously he was able, intelligent, and experienced. Like all his contemporaries he was very concious of his own seniority and extremely loyal to his superior officers and his subordinates. He was
very wealthy; fond of the good things of life and in his more
senior years, campaigned with a case of champagne.

During his three weeks stay in Cape Town he exercised to the
full his powers of organisation. Realising the extreme paucity of
transport and lack of military rail organisation — on his arrival the
latter consisted of one officer, a lieutenant-colonel, one batman,
one horse and one groom—he and his staff performed prodigies
of improvisation. The Army Corps was split into two unequal
halves, the smaller part going up to reinforce Methuen in relieving
Kimberley, the major portion being re-embarked and sent round to
Durban by sea, to help relieve Ladysmith. Mules and horses were
commandeered, trained and ridden by civilian volunteers, the South
African Colonial Corps, whose enthusiasm later became efficiency.
Stores, rations and forage were collected and despatched to the front.
Buller was in his element, and full of confidence.

On his arrival at Durban he again threw himself into the organisation of his now considerable army of 20,000 men, and their advance further up country.

He made his forward base at Frere, ten miles south of the Tugela River at Colenso, where the Boers had established themselves, blowing up the road and railway bridges over the river at the little town and entrenching themselves on the north bank. A small force of 2,000 men from Frere consisting of regular soldiers, volunteers and police was stationed at Colenso as an outpost.

Frere became an enormous military base. Besides the men's tents there were the rapidly accumulating stocks of food, forage, horses, ammunition, vehicles, guns and medical stores for the field hospitals. In addition there were the officer's kits.

In those spacious and leisurely days, officers liked to carry many comforts and amenities on active service. There seems to have been no restrictions on the number of horses, both riding and pack, that each officer was allowed as well as private carts. Most officers would carry cases of wine, plain clothes, long-horned gramophones, baths and polo sticks. Often a small chest of drawers would be included. The camp at Frere grew and grew.

Buller's army naturally took some time to assemble at Frere and except for cavalry, including the newly recruited volunteer Colonial units, there was little for it to do. The mounted units were kept very busy on reconnaissances and patrol duties and the recently recruited units in their inexperience had many horses off-duty with sore backs. But the chief diversion for the infantry was to see the daily departure of the armoured train up the line to Colenso. It was intended both for reconnaissance and to show the flag and there was considerable competition to be selected as its daily complement. On its narrow one-track line frequently passing through cuttings and round, for a railway, acute blind corners, it was bound to be ambushed sooner or later.

On the 15th November the train went out on its almost daily sortie, its crew being one company of the Dublin Fusiliers, one of the newly raised Durban Light Infantry, with a few sailors to man the 7-pounder naval gun that had been installed on one of the trucks. Some plate-layers to repair the line if at all damaged were included and one War Correspondent, the young Winston Churchill, aged 25.

It got as far as the little town of Chieveley, ten miles up the line, and then turned back. Some mounted Boers, who had seen it going on its way in the morning, ambushed it on its return journey by placing rocks on the line. Into these the train ran, derailing the leading truck. The train was immediately surrounded, but the engine and tender were uncoupled and got away. Seventy prisoners were taken, including Churchill, and Captain Aylmer Haldane, the O.C. train. (He commanded a brigade at Le Cateau and finished his career in 1918 as a Corps Commander). All were taken up to Pretoria and there interned, being correctly treated as prisoners of war. Churchill managed to escape and found his way through Portuguese East Africa to Lourenço Marques—from where he rejoined Buller's army.

By mid-December Buller was ready to relieve Ladysmith. His first plan was to send a brigade up to Colenso, ten miles to the north, to 'demonstrate' his intention of forcing the Tugela there while he marched the whole of the rest of his army off to the west, intending to cross the river at Potgeiters Drift, eleven miles from Frere and so come round the Boers' right flank in the Tugela Heights — a goodish plan, but it overlooked the Boer mobility and the positions of observation they could have used along the line of the hills.

However, on the 13th December, he heard of the defeats at Magersfontein and Stormburg, the beginning of the 'Black Week', and then realised that he was Commander-in-Chief in the whole of South Africa, and not only in Natal. Clearly he was indirectly responsible for these defeats and he felt that something must be done quickly to counteract them. A quick success was imperative and its news must arrive in London very soon.

Accordingly he abandoned the Potgeiters Drift plan entirely and decided to attack Colenso with his whole strength. He rode up from Frere to Chieveley on the 14th and that afternoon he told his brigadiers that he would attack Colenso in the morning and, having crossed the Tugela, bivouac on the far bank. It was to be his first great attempt, and he lead out next morning the finest and largest force which any British general had handled since the Alma. Four brigades of four battalions each, two regular cavalry regiments with six regular and five other batteries of field artillery with sixteen naval guns under command made up a force of twenty-one thousand.

The plan was simple. A line of three brigades was to advance to the river and cross it where possible. Objectives allotted to each brigade were very vague and almost unspecified.

The left brigade consisting of three Irish regiments and the Border Regiment moved out to their left-front, trying to find a ford which a local civilian thought he knew well. He was wrong, and disappeared and the brigade blundered on into the 'Loop', an area surrounded on three sides by a great curve of the unfordable Tugela, a mile long and half a mile wide. The Boers around two sides of the 'Loop' waited until the brigade had halted well inside the trap, and had sent one of the scouts out to find a ford. Then fire opened, heavy casualties were caused and in spite of gallant attempts by companies and individual men to rush forward down to the water's edge, not one man reached it, and not one man of the enemy was seen. The brigade withdrew, badly shaken.

The centre brigade, of four typical English country regiments, Queen's, Devons, West Yorks and East Surreys, fared scarcely better. Under the cover of the village of Colenso itself they advanced well for a while, making for the two bridges, rail and road, that crossed the river five hundred yards beyond the last houses. The fact that no battalion in this brigade had been given a specific bridge as an objective was of little matter, as all were held up soon after leaving the cover of the houses and gardens, by rifle fire from across the river. The two leading battalions, Queen's and Devons, infiltrated up the water's edge and the two bridges but could not cross, while the reinforcing West Yorks only added to the targets along the river bank. Not a man crossed the river.

On the right the Fusilier Brigade, of Royal, Scots, Welsh and Irish Fusiliers, advancing sometime after the other two brigades were in action had orders to probe for the river and act as a right flank guard. Its latter task was unnecessary and like the other brigades it too was held up by accurate rifle fire from across the river and pinned to its ground. A flanking movement by one battalion out to the right petered out.

Three brigades were now halted short of, or only just up to, the river bank, not a man was over the water and the enemy was still concealed in the superb cover in the foot-hills over the river.

But the biggest disaster of all occurred in the centre, between the English and the Fusilier Brigades. Here Colonel Long, commanding the artillery, had been ordered to support with two batteries the advance of the centre and right brigades. He was a zealous and dashing officer with very distinct ideas of his own on the tactical employment of guns. His previous battle experience, always against natives whose rifles were usually obsolete and their marksmanship rudimentary, had taught him to fear little from defensive small-arms fire.

His principle, always successful previously, of getting his guns up into action quickly, close to the enemy, was put into practice yet again. Getting his two batteries forward at the trot he quickly got in front of the brigades he was supposed to support and advanced across the open plain in line, eventually outdistancing the Fusilier and the English Brigades by nearly a mile.

Seven hundred yards from the line of the tree-covered river bank and well short of the cover provided by the houses, gardens and railway station, in full view, with no infantry near him and the nearest cavalry far out on his right flank he halted, and his twelve guns, neatly drawn up as though on Queen's Parade at Aldershot, meticulously carried out all points of drill. The teams were led away to a donga three hundred yards in the rear and Colonel Long was about to open fire at the clear low scrub-covered hills only a few hundred yards away, and where he thought the enemy might be.

The Boers anticipated his order to fire by a few seconds, and several hundred of the finest marksmen in the world, firing from behind cover, opened up. Heavy casualties occurred at once, among the first being Colonel Long, who was mortally wounded. He and those that could be moved were carried back to the donga where the horses were sheltering, and where he died that evening.

The gun detachments, as might be expected, fought their guns to the end despite devastating casualties. Their target was the low hills beyond the river, eight hundred yards away—wherein the enemy casualties were negligible—and they fired until their ammunition was exausted. Then withdrawing to the shelter of the donga, they waited, the guns silent. Captain Reed, one of the battery captains, galloped up some scratch teams to pull out the guns, but was driven back losing seven men out of thirteen, and thirteen horses out of twenty-two. Buller then called for volunteers from his staff to bring the guns in, and miraculously two were saved. Their casualties, though, were heavy, among them Lieutenant Roberts, son of the field-marshal, who died in hospital two days later. The V.C. was awarded to him after his death, as it also was to three other officers and a driver. Among the Indian bearers who carried back the wounded was a young man called Gandhi, who learned here the hatred of violence that made him so successful in his campaign of non-violence in India, twenty-six years later. The remaining ten guns were left out on the plain, and after dark were removed by the Boers who used them against the British at Ladysmith a month later. At dusk the centre and right brigades withdrew as best they could, and next morning the force marched back to Chieveley.

Nine hundred men were killed or wounded with two hundred and fifty missing. The latter were mostly wounded who could not be moved from the donga or the 'Loop' and who were taken prisoner.

The disaster at Colenso, when none of the sixteen battalions reached their objective and ten of the twelve field-guns were lost was General Buller's greatest defeat. As a result of the 'Black Week' Lord Roberts was ordered out to South Africa as Commander-in-Chief. On his arrival it was thought that he did not remove Buller from his command because Lieutenant Roberts had been killed whilst on Buller's staff, and he feared that a removal might be taken personally.

Today Colenso is a thriving and rapidly expanding town of 2,500 inhabitants. The site of the furthest advance to the river by the Queen's and Devons of the centre brigade has been completely built over and it is impossible to define any tactical features. The donga where the gun teams sheltered and where Colonel Long died, is easily found, three hundred yards behind the gun line. It is merely a sluggish stream in a shallow bed, but gives good cover. The cairns marking the site of Lieutenant Roberts' death and the memorial to Colonel Long's two batteries have both been removed further back to make room for a new railway siding. They are out of position, and consequently rather misleading. In 1902, after the war, twelve small cairns of white-washed stones were erected on the exact site of the twelve guns. Later they were removed at the request of Lady Roberts, who did not wish the site of her only son's death to be perpetuated. Recently, however, after careful search in the grass in this area the author discovered the original foundations of three of these twelve cairns, twenty yards apart in a straight line and facing the enemy position. The exposed position of the two batteries with their long and methodical advance over open ground ahead of the infantry and in face of almost certain enemy resistance is very obvious.

Most of the graves of men killed in this battle, buried where they fell, are now in most unsuitable places. The expanding town, extensions to the railway yard, a sewage farm and housing estates now surround many graves. The worst situations are having the bodies exhumed and re-buried on a special site two miles from the town. Here all memorials and graves are eventually to be concentrated, and a Garden of Remembrance laid out.

Buller was much depressed by this defeat. It was the third in a week—the 'Black Week'—and he was deeply disappointed that a resounding success had not been achieved, to show alongside the two defeats elsewhere. His never-optimistic nature now became defeatist and he informed London and his goal, Ladysmith, that he could not succeed, advised the latter to destroy all documents, fire away all ammunition and to surrender. He sat back, not knowing what to do next. Severely reprimanded by Downing Street for his defeatist attitude he awaited supercession, but none came. Instead yet another division was ordered out in reinforcement.

Its Commander was Major-General Sir Charles Warren. He was a difficult man to get on with, with a distinct tinge of acerbity in his temper and tongue. Buller was brusque, with an overbearing manner and the frequent clashes between them must have been most unedifying to those of their staff who overheard them.

Roberts had telegraphed Buller to remain on the defensive and attempt no further advance until he, Roberts, and the new division had arrived. But Buller, however, being somewhat affronted by his coming supercession in the Chief Command by Roberts, whom he knew and disliked, suddenly changed drastically his recent defeatist policy for the relief of Ladysmith. He determined to have another try while still his own master. Telling his army that he had found the key to Ladysmith, he left Chieveley on 10th January for the west, marching along the line of the river barrier. Reinforced by Warren's division he had now 30,000 men, 20,000 of whom he took with him.

It was a slow and tedious march. Usually the leading unit had reached its night's destination before the last wagons had marched out of the previous camp, and it took five days to cover the sixteen miles to Springfield, where Buller set up his advanced H.Q.

Not only was the vast column frequently in sight from the Tugela Heights on its right, but the incessant dust cloud indicated its whereabouts. The Boers marching through the hills on the far side of the river kept up with the British, having no difficulty whatever in assessing their enemy's moves and intentions. When the British halted, they halted too, and the two marches were parallel—the only difference being that every British move was seen in full view whereas the movements of the Boers were not only invisible but their presence largely unsuspected.

Pushing on from Springfield the army reached the village and ridge of Spearman's, opposite two drifts over the river and beyond which were a high and imposing series of hills. Several days were spent here while preparations were made to cross the Tugela. The two drifts available had to have their approaches widened and metalled, water points set up on the far bank, roads improved, bakeries built, the Boers having as perfect a view from the hills of the preparations and obvious intentions of their enemy as they could possibly wish. During these five days of waiting (when the infantry and artillery were much employed in finding work parties for the sappers building or expanding the crossing and other works) the cavalry crossed to the north bank and probed for the enemy.

Buller now took an extraordinary step. He handed over the command of the whole force at Spearman's to Warren, leaving him only with his normal divisional staff to command a large force, and convoy it across a difficult river into rugged unreconnoitred country in which a dangerous enemy might or might not be lurking. He withdrew from the growing camp to his new headquarters at Springfield, some four miles away.

Meanwhile the cavalry found no sign of the enemy on one of the great mountains, Tabanyama, the most westerly of the group. The cavalry Brigade Commander, Lord Dundonald, reported this to Warren, asked for reinforcements and permission to push on and round the north side of the range of hills. It was a sensible and feasible tactical move. But this was too enterprising for Warren and he not only refused both reinforcements and permission but severely reprimanded Dundonald for presumption. However he did send one brigade on a rather half-hearted attack on Tabanyama, which was recalled for no apparent reason when within sight of success.

During these days while the crossings were being enlarged, and the Tabanyama operations were carried out, General Buller frequently rode over from Springfield to see Warren, bombarding him with advice, suggestions, and criticisms—but no orders. Warren seemed quite unable to make up his mind as to the best tactical course to take, and Buller became more and more impatient. Finally Warren selected the next hill to Tabanyama, Spion Kop, for attack, although he admitted he did not like the look of it. Buller acquiesced, thankful to have some plan made at last.

On the late evening of 23rd January, the Lancashire Brigade of
Royal Lancasters, Lancashire Fusiliers, South Lancashires and
Thorneycroft's Mounted Infantry left camp, and started to climb
the hill, the most formidable, and the highest in the whole range,
1,500 feet above the river. The night was dark, a fine drizzle was
falling and the going very difficult. Moreover, the Brigade Commander, Major-General Woodgate, an ex-Royal Lancasters C.O.,
was fifty-five years of age and in poor health. The operation bore
many similarities to the disaster of Majuba, nineteen years earlier.

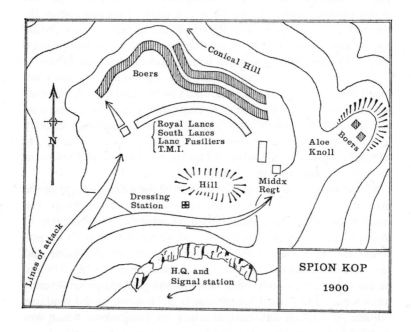

Spion Kop has three very steep sides, with one convenient and
less acute shoulder up which the brigade climbed. Towards the end
of the climb the hill flattens out considerably, the top being a shallow inverted saucer. At the farther (northern) end the high ground
runs away into a long narrow saddle, terminating in a pronounced
knoll. To the east and two hundred feet below the main hill, and
quite separate from it, rises another small feature, Aloe Knoll.

Advancing on a two-battalion front, the Royal Lancasters on the
left and the Lancashire Fusiliers on the right followed by Thorney-

croft's Mounted Infantry and led by the Brigade Commander in person, the brigade reached the first 'flattening out' without incident after climbing for most of the night. Owing to their weight and the noise inseparable from carrying them, many of the picks and shovels were dumped, but the men were still encumbered with greatcoats and ammunition, though not with rations or water. At about 6 a.m. the thick dawn mist gave the impression that the summit had been reached, the only Boer encountered had been bayoneted and the men ordered to give three cheers to indicate success to Warren below.

An hour or so later the mist suddenly lifted to disclose the summit two hundred yards further on up the hill. The ensuing movement on to the hilltop in the now broad sunlight warned the main enemy force on the far side of the hill and on the plain below of the occupation, and they immediately started to climb the Aloe Knoll and the north-western end of the main feature at the end of the saddle. From the former they were soon able to accurately enfilade the shallow trench being built on the summit by the Lancashire Fusiliers on the right, while the Royal Lancasters, prolonging the line to the left, came under accurate though frontal fire from the knoll at the far end of the saddle. From Tabanyama Hill, three thousand yards to their left front across the intervening valley, an enemy battery enfiladed both battalions.

The extreme rockiness of the hill precluded any serious trench digging although both battalions scraped together some skeleton form of breastwork two feet high. The picks left behind would now have come in useful, although the Lancashire Fusiliers could only have protected themselves from the accurate enfilade fire from Aloe Knoll by changing direction through 90 degrees. Even then it is doubtful whether much entrenching could have been done under this fire.

Thorneycroft's Mounted Infantry passed through the two battalions and tried to reach the far end of the inverted saucer, but were prevented from doing so by the fire from the north-west knoll. A few men from the two left-hand companies of the Royal Lancasters managed to crawl forward individually, around the left (outer) flank of the M.I., meeting some success but also meeting enemy scouts who had crept up along the saddle on to the far segment of the saucer. Attempting to relieve this complete hold-up, the South Lancashires were ordered forward to support. They too were quickly pinned down before reaching the three forward battalions. About an hour after the two forward battalions had commenced their trench digging, General Woodgate was mortally wounded, standing at the right of the Lancashire Fusiliers trench—the nearest man to Aloe Knoll. He was carried down the hill and died in hospital some days later.

Woodgate left chaos behind him in the command on the hill and Colonel Crofton, C.O. of the Royal Lancasters, as the senior officer present, assumed command. Losing his head he sent a panic signal to Warren below: 'Reinforce at once or all is lost. General dead'. Buller intercepted this message before it reached Warren and he rode over with his usual advice, suggesting that an officer more vigorous than Crofton should be appointed. Warren chose Thorneycroft, and as he was junior to Crofton heliographed to him his promotion to Brigadier-General. The news of his promotion reached Thorneycroft later but he neglected to tell Crofton.

Later in the day Warren sent up the Middlesex to the summit, and the Scottish Rifles to work round the right flank, in order to relieve the pressure on the Lancashire Fusiliers. They were unsuccessful, however, and not only added to the general confusion on the hill, but also to the problem of command. Colonel Hill of the Middlesex was senior to both Crofton and Thorneycroft.

When Hill arrived he assumed command at the eastern end of the summit, while Thorneycroft was commanding with vigour at the other end. They did not meet for several hours. The commander of the brigade to which the Middlesex and Scottish Rifles belonged, Major-General Talbot-Coke, felt that he too should ascend the hill to see his two battalions and was then, of course, the senior officer present. However, he did not attempt to take command and the delicate point as to who was in fact the commander on the hilltop was never settled.

During the afternoon the C.O. of the 60th Rifles (from yet another brigade), acting on his own initiative and without orders from any superior officer, moved his regiment far out to its right and, climbing a long low ridge, came up behind the Boers on Aloe Knoll, causing them considerable casualties from long range fire. The Boers, seeing the British were in front of and now apparently behind them, were about to leave the Knoll, when General Buller rode up to Warren and demanded to know who had ordered the 60th on its lone though effective mission. On hearing that the C.O. had done so without orders Buller immediately and peremptorily ordered the battalion to withdraw, on the grounds that he would not tolerate such independence, almost amounting to impertinence.

At dusk the problem of who in fact was in command on the hill-top became acute. General Talbot-Coke advised Colonel Hill, whom both believed to be in charge, to retire to the plain during the night. Thorneycroft at the other end of the hill had now run into Crofton. Both felt that they should stay for some time yet and therefore sent a heliograph message to Warren for orders. Warren had by now heard from Hill, advising retirement, yet Thorneycroft was, as far as Warren knew, in command. However, Warren took Hill's advice and ordered withdrawal. As the left-hand units were on their way down they met Hill, who, having my now changed his mind, ordered them back. Thorneycroft came along and met Hill and, after a considerable wrangle, the latter had to admit that Thorneycroft as a Brigadier-General was the senior. The withdrawal continued.

And so the British left their objective leaving three hundred dead behind them. Probably at about the same time, the Boers, quite certain that the British troops were immovable, withdrew too, and for several hours Spion Kop remained unoccupied. At dawn next day a Boer scout, finding the hill empty, signalled to his commander below and the hill was re-occupied.

It must be remembered that Woodgate's brigade did not capture Spion Kop. It took possession of it on finding it untenanted after the climb—and there remained unmolested for some hours. Had the Lancashire Fusiliers only advanced another 300 yards over the top to the far rim, they would have reached the edge of the plateau and so seen the Boers leave their laager on the plain below when commencing their climb. To assault such a slope against the fire of the defending British infantry was an impossible task for the enemy, no matter how mediocre the British shooting. But Woodgate did not see the obvious advantage he held.

Amongst the might-have-beens that are found in every account of every defeat must appear Warren's failure during the day to visit the hill-top where seven of his battalions, parts of his three brigades, were closely in action. A firm grip of the situation taken there must have shown a general with dominance how the battle could be controlled. The *junta* of five or six colonels on the site was quite incapable of doing so.

By 4 a.m. the next morning the last battalion had left Spion Kop, and rejoined the camp at Spearman's. When it was all over Buller moved Warren's command away to the east again, and out of range of Boer guns.

Apart from six memorials to the dead, and two mass graves, Spion Kop is, in 1970, unchanged from 1900. The Lancashire Fusiliers' trench was largely filled, after the battle, with their dead, large stones being piled over the bodies. Four feet wide and 40 yards long, enclosed in a neat wire fence, the cairn shows all too clearly the tragic and entirely fortuitous coincidence of its alignment with Aloe Knoll only 400 yards away. Every man hit by a Boer bullet must have received it in his right forehead or side. Close beside this cairn the author, in 1966, picked up a fired Boer cartridge case, and a 'soft-nosed' bullet.

Further to the left, the dead of the Royal Lancasters and Thorney-croft's M.I. were laid out in a straight row, head to foot, and there covered with big stones. This cairn, too, is white-washed yearly and enclosed in a wire fence. The ground here is quite impossible to dig and nearby are the remains of the trench the Royal Lancasters tried to build. They succeeded only in rolling together some boulders, often no more than a football size, and many are still in position. Slight depressions behind the stones show some scraping out of soil but the cover was woefully inadequate against the Boer shellfire from Tabanyama.

Spion Kop is very difficult to reach and then climb. The author was taken nearly to the top in a private car by a friend but the road was so bad that regrettably a broken back-axle was the result, and the only way to drive up is in a very sturdy Land-Rover, and even then the passenger will have to hold on with both hands. The other alternative is of course to walk up but it is not a suitable occupation for men over fifty. A good deal of the easiest route which the Royal Lancasters took involves the use of hands as well as feet, and the following of this route demonstrates how fit and hardy these young men must have been to make the climb in the dark.

The atmosphere at the top of the hill is the driest anywhere encountered. On the author's last visit the few hundred yards' walk from the stranded car followed by an hour of walking round the position on a very hot day carrying maps and field glasses resulted in no suggestion whatever of perspiration. It was in the middle of the South African summer.

After Spion Kop a curious psychological change came over the

Boers along the Tugela. They knew they had successfully invaded Natal, had surrounded and were now successfully besieging behind them a garrison of eight thousand British soldiers, had won resounding victories at Colenso and Spion Kop, all in less than three months. Their morale should indeed have been high. But it wasn't.

Many of them felt they had done enough and that their farms and families were now again top-priority. Many applied for, and got, leave for 'private affairs' and went back to Transvaal. Others, more fearful, wondered whether they had not taken on too much. They felt that their invasion of friendly territory and then the defeats of their enemy would sooner or later bring retribution on them from the ever-growing and professional British Army. These Boers did not apply for leave. They quietly left their comrades in the hours of darkness and also rode back to Transvaal. By the time the next British advance took place there were only 4,000 Boers to face Buller's 20,000 British soldiers.

Unlike his behaviour after Colenso, Buller did not have a fit of deep depression following his defeat at Spion Kop. Instead he decided to have another go at a small hill, Vaal Krantz, six miles farther to the east.

Vaal Krantz was much lower than Spion Kop and had it been captured the cavalry could comfortably have passed round both its east and west extremities. They would then have found themselves in a plain with little or no obstacles in front of them and from where they could have taken the Boers in the rear and from both flanks.

After a week's rest and excellent rations of vegetables and fresh meat, the British soldiers were full of high spirits and very ready to go again. But the attack on Vaal Krantz was miserably slow.

It began at 6 a.m. when Wynne's Brigade (which had been Woodgate's and had led the assault on Spion Kop) advanced up to the Tugela, making a feint attack. It advanced well towards a smaller hill to the right of the Vaal Krantz but failed to draw the Boer fire.

A pontoon bridge was then built in front of the main hill and Buller led the remainder of his forces across it. It took time for the several thousands of men, in double file only, to cross the swaying bridge and the horse-drawn guns had to go very slowly. The Boers were left in no doubt as to where the attack would come.

The day passed into afternoon, the sun got hotter and hotter, the crossing of the bridge took longer and longer and Buller's natural pessimism returned. He decided to give up any idea of an attack

in force that day, and told General Lyttelton, the commander of the
leading brigade: 'You'll never carry the hill before dark, we had
better put it off'. Lyttelton replied: 'Let me go now, and I'll guaran-
tee I'll be on the top of Vaal Krantz by 4 o'clock'. Buller let him
go.

The Durham Light Infantry led the attack and, after stiff resistance from the naturally very thinly-spread Boers, reached the top of
the ridge—soon followed by the Rifle Brigade—at precisely
4 o'clock.

But the position now became like Spion Kop. The top of the hill
was taken but no reinforcements arrived and the Boers on the next
hill were able to enfilade the Rifle Brigade. Buller, with his
customary pessimism, ordered Lyttelton to withdraw—but Lyttelton
ignored the order, and advised an additional attack on Green Hill
whence the fire enfilading the Rifle Brigade was coming. But Buller
would have nothing to do with such a common-sense suggestion,
and decided to leave Lyttelton, exposed and unsupported, with no
attempt to help him, on the hill all night. Buller then went to bed.

It was a very similar situation to that at Sulva Bay in the Gallipoli
campaign in 1915, when 900 Turks on a low but clearly defined
ridge several hundred yards inland from the beach held up two
British divisions for three days before Turkish reinforcements arrived.

During the night the enemy concentrated his force, and all his
guns, to defend Vaal Krantz. But for Lyttelton's tactical skill, another Spion Kop would have developed. Next day Buller vacillated
all the morning between telling Lyttelton to withdraw and 'asking'
him to hang on, and then reached the nadir of his professional incapacity. He telegraphed Roberts, who had just arrived in Cape
Town seven hundred miles away, asking him what he should do
and could he have tactical advice on a situation Roberts did not
know, on ground he had never seen. Roberts replied that Buller
must do what he could to relieve Ladysmith, his prime task, and
that he was the best judge of the situation.

Buller's next step was at least positive. He relieved Lyttelton's
brigade on Vaal Krantz with Hildyard's, which spent that night improving their positions on the ridge. On relief Lyttelton and Major
Wilson (later to be C.I.G.S. in 1918) went to see Buller, who was
dining. He asked them to share his champagne and enquired how
they had got on. Lyttelton was very angry that Buller had failed to

support him and so avoided victory, but the champagne worked wonders and Lyttelton and Wilson returned to their lines.

The next day Warren was sent out personally on reconnaissance, and returned with some sketches he had made of enemy-held territory. Buller saw them, and making only a sarcastic comment called a Council of War of his brigadiers and Warren. Some advised going on, though most advised withdrawal. Buller, glad to have his mind made up for him by a democratic vote, ordered withdrawal. The troops got back accross the Tugela without disturbance, the pontoon bridges were dismantled, and Buller's army marched back to Chieveley again.

Vaal Krantz, the third major defeat for Buller in trying to re-lieve Ladysmith, was much less costly than either Colenso or Spion Kop. Thirty men only were killed with some 300 wounded. The loss of prestige was negligible, it was already very low. Ladysmith was getting used to disappointments and Roberts had his hands full.

The new Boer position holding the Tugela around Colenso was extended two miles further to the east than they had done when Colenso was attacked in December. Buller, now in an optimistic period of thought decided to out-flank this long extension to the east.

A cavalry reconnaissance secured a hill five miles from Chieveley, and Buller arrived with his telescope. The result of his observations was that he ordered everyone back to Chieveley, intending to advance again with his whole army, eastward, along the south bank of the river, as he had done to Spearman's before Spion Kop, hoping to find a crossing.

But the next day when he intended to start was very hot, and the start was postponed for 24 hours. Then for three days the army crawled eastwards parallel to the river, but well to the south. The Boers had, unwisely, left their excellent positions on the north bank and, crossing over, occupied lines not nearly so good in the open country to the south of the river.

On the 18th the British Army turned left and attacked the new Boer lines with two brigades. The Boers nervously concious that they had their backs to the river turned and fled. For two days they were not followed and were allowed to get clear away over the river.

By the 20th Buller was not only in possession of the south bank of the river for several miles, but there was no sign of the enemy on the north bank. He could have crossed anywhere he liked by building pontoon bridges at, presumably, the most suitable sites, suitable both from an engineering point of view and for tactical reasons. But he moved back almost to Colenso where he built one bridge only, leading directly into a hollow surround, enclosed by hills. Despite the expressed opinions of his staff on the unsuitability of this site, he took no notice and fifteen battalions and forty guns got across without opposition. But if anything more than a rear-guard were to oppose them they would indeed be in trouble. But Buller was over the Tugela, his army now very experienced, the weather was gradually cooling, the Boers were obviously failing, and Ladysmith was only seven miles away. The end was in sight.

For three months since the Boers invaded Natal and its withdrawal from Talana Hill at Dundee the British Army had, with the single exception, at Caesar's Camp and Wagon Hill, suffered nothing but setbacks. The retreat to Ladysmith, Elandslaagte, Lombard's Kop, Nicholson's Nek, Pepworth, the armoured train, Colenso Spion Kop and Vaal Krantz had all seen the superiority of the Boer fighting.

But now, over the Tugela at last, everything was to change. The advance through the hills and the actual relief of Ladysmith was pursued with energy, speed, concentration and success. In contrast to the previous eighty days of marching, bivouacking, marching, attacking, marching, withdrawing, covering a tragic thirty miles, littered with defeats, repulses, casualties, depression, the new phase was to be indeed different. The seven miles to Ladysmith was to take seven days only, four successful brigade attacks were to be carried out, the Boers were constantly kept on the run, less than 1,800 total casualties were suffered, of which the vast majority were wounds, frequently not serious. Press correspondents, painfully accustomed to witness assaults that failed, could hardly believe their eyes.

The brigades attacked in succession four sizeable hills, Wynne's Hill, named after the brigade commander, with Green Hill, were the first to be assaulted and it gave the most trouble. It is in fact two abutments of the same feature. Between them is a small re-entrant which peters out before it reaches the summit. The Royal Lancasters led the attack on the twin hills, the left two companies reaching the crest without great difficulty. The right companies were held up by Boer trenches—still to be seen quite clearly along the crest—

and the rather steeper slope, with much more difficult going. The C.O., who had only taken over the command that morning (Colonel Crofton having gone to Brigade in place of General Wynne, wounded earlier in the day), went up to the left companies to assess the situation and make a plan for a flank movement to release the right companies. While there and holding a brief 'O-Group' conference he was shot and mortally wounded. The bullet came almost from the rear, and undoubtedly one of the Boers holding up the right companies whose position was not so far forward, saw the O-Group with all its paraphernalia of officers with swords and maps and took the wonderful opportunity. Shortly after the C.O.'s death the right companies were able to move again and the hill was captured.

The plateau above these two abutments has half a dozen graves which show the line of advance the Royal Lancasters took after reaching the summit.

Next day the Irish Brigade came through and the Royal Inniskilling Fusiliers took Inniskilling Hill a mile further on. This regiment too had considerable resistance to overcome and suffered many casualties. The hill is much more bare than Wynne Hill, with no trees, bushes or grass, and the Boers must have had great difficulty in finding positions. There is no top-soil whatever on the rock, no digging was possible, and the graves are like those on Spion Kop, the bodies being covered with stones and rocks. However, Inniskilling Hill and Wynne being held and forming a strong flank protection, the next hill, Railway Hill, another mile on, was the objective for three days later.

But the plan was changed and the fourth hill, Pieters Hill, of which Railway Hill was an off-shoot, was the next objective. Its capture must 'pinch out' Railway Hill and clearly Buller was beginning to show some tactical knowledge and to use his experience. Indeed his staff could hardly recognise the man they had served for the past two months. His previous pessimism, vacillation and indecision seemed to have disappeared and he had a firm grasp of the operations. He dictated his orders at speed and omitted nothing.

The Fusilier Brigade advanced up to, and captured Pieters, the Irish Fusiliers losing many men. The Scots Fusiliers and the Dublin Fusiliers supported them, and the Dublin Fusiliers were able to open fire on the Boers still on Railway Hill from their rear. The

West Yorks had assaulted this hill as a feint attack, and while containing the Boers thereon, had allowed Buller's 'pinch out' tactics to be successful. Buller then followed up his success with the kind of pressure that no one in his army had ever seen or suspected before. Gunfire continued through the night and next morning, the 28th, the Boers disintegrated, fleeing across the plain past Ladysmith.

That afternoon Lord Dundonald's cavalry brigade entered Ladysmith. The ninety-two days operations were over, and success had at last reached Buller. He had relieved Ladysmith.

The sudden change in Buller's attitude was quite extraordinary. His normal pessimistic, introvert, rude nature could not stand a rebuff or failure or opposition. Hence his colossal defeat at Colenso, his first engagement in the South African War, affected him deeply, greatly shaking his self-confidence and inducing indecision. He remained the same man for two months, set-back following set-back, his doubts always remaining.

Then the first success, when after returning to Chieveley from Vaal Krantz he got his army across the Tugela without opposition. His sudden elation, optimism, vitality, showed him to be a man whom success encouraged, a man who did not like, perhaps couldn't take, hard knocks, but who thrived on good news. Never was there a clearer case of nothing succeeding like success.

There were three main reasons for this sudden wave of victories. Firstly, as had been seen, Buller's character changed because he got over the Tugela without opposition, without losing a man, and thereby regained his self-confidence over-night. He became, at last, a leader.

Secondly, the British soldiers and their regimental officers, accustomed to meeting ill-armed, untutored wild savages for so many years, were at last realising the calibre of their opponents and were learning the skills, the battle 'know-how', of their trade. Their professionalism was gradually proving superior to the untrained and amateur, though natural, tactics of the Boers.

Lastly, there can be no doubt that the very considerable 'thinning-out' of the Boer forces through leave of absence to their farms and what really amounted to desertion by so many others, was of enormous advantage to the British. Always in superior numbers in the Natal campaign since the beginning of the war they now held an overwhelming numerical advantage.

For the visitor the main road, an excellent motor road, south from

Ladysmith to Colenso is of no use beyond the town. It goes nowhere near the four hills of the Tugela Heights, and the only way to visit them is a good three mile walk to where the pontoon bridge was built—or to take a taxi along an execrable 'road'. From there Wynne's Hill is close by.

After a very simple climb which is well worth while—to see the site and the whole area—the road, which closely follows the railway, passes the foot of Inniskilling Hill, Railway Hill, and Pieters Hill. A mile beyond the last, it debouches on to the plain and the surface becomes quite fair.

Apart from the Boer trenches on Wynne and Green Hills, and the scattered graves on both of them and on Inniskilling Hill—there is little for the traveller-historian—for whom this book is primarily written—to see. But for a young officer studying tactics and use of ground, perhaps a Staff College candidate, such an expedition will be of great value, instruction, and professional interest.

Le Cateau
1914

AFTER the battle of Mons on 23rd August, the British Expeditionary Force had disappeared into the night. The Commander-in-Chief, Sir John French, had decided to retire for two days despite close pressure by the enemy and several rear-guard actions, and then to hold a defensive line in the neighbourhood of Le Cateau. Here he intended to give battle again and with replenishments of ammunition, food and some reinforcements, to repeat the defeat he had inflicted on the Germans at Mons.

Forty-eight hours after Mons, I Corps were moving southward to the east of the almost impassable Forêt de Mormal, and II Corps to its west. On the evening of 25th August, II Corps was approaching Le Cateau, the newly arrived 4th Division being rear-guard to the very, very tired 3rd and 5th Divisions.

Late in the afternoon Sir John French heard that General Lanrezac's 5th French Army, on his right, was yet again retiring—again without consultation or even information—and in addition, that large enemy forces were in front of him. He had no alternative, he thought, but to abandon his plan to stand and face the enemy around Le Cateau and to continue the retreat at dawn on the 26th. To risk encirclement, with the French 5th Army already twenty-four hours' march ahead of him, seemed suicidal.

During the forty-eight hours following the withdrawal from the canal bank, the four British divisions covered by the five cavalry brigades had been retreating without rest. However, the enemy were generally kept from seriously interfering, although the unlucky 3rd Division, the division that had borne the brunt of the fighting along the canal bank at Mons on the 23rd, had several times to turn back reserve units and brigades to keep the enemy off. Eventually this division became so exhausted that its march was crossed with that of the 5th Division, who thus took over the role of rear-guard, while the 3rd Division only had to march. This crossing of two divisions in retreat, barely out of contact with the enemy, tired, hungry, slightly disorganised, was a triumph of staff work. There were no dislocations, missing units, or even major delays. This apparently very complex operation lasted a few hours, and in the hands of the experienced, professional staff officers, was a master-piece.

On the 25th the 4th Division, newly arrived from England, came up and took over the rearguard, covering the 5th and 3rd Divisions into Le Cateau and along the main road running north-west to Cambrai. This line was reached by the two very tired divisions during the night of the 25th. All through the night units arrived, and the town, particularly the *place*, became completely jammed with transport, guns, ambulances, battalion, brigade and divisional headquarters, men looking for their units and units trying to find billets for a few hours' rest.

At about midnight Sir Horace Smith-Dorrien issued orders for a further retirement at dawn the next day, in accordance with the C.-in-C.'s decision not to fight around Le Cateau but to continue the retreat. 2 a.m., however, saw the cavalry Divisional Comman-der, General Allenby, telling him that his five cavalry brigades, indeed the regiments themselves, were much scattered and in many cases out of touch. In addition both the men and horses were almost exhausted. He also said that the enemy being so close, the infantry divisions must move back at once, or be forced to fight at daybreak. The G.O.C. 3rd Division who was present said that his infantrymen were so tired that they could not possibly move before 9 a.m.

The 5th Division still coming in was obviously very tired, and its G.O.C., when visited by Smith-Dorrien shortly after 2 a.m., strongly advocated standing and fighting, largely because his men would get a few hours' sleep. The Corps Commander then asked the 4th Division out on his left to act under his orders, to which its G.O.C. agreed, having really no alternative.

Thus, the decision to stand and fight was taken.

For almost three hours nothing happened, and the two armies, both almost exhausted, slept where they could, the majority in the streets or fields.

At dawn on the 26th, one brigade of the 5th Division had its right to the east of Le Cateau and the two other brigades to its west, just south of the Le Cateau–Cambrai main road. Continuing the line along the main road was the very tired 3rd Division. The 4th, which had marched continuously since detraining on the 25th, and then acting as rear-guard all day and night of the 25th/26th, had moved out at dawn to the left of the line around the villages of Fontaine-au-Pire, Haucourt and Esnes. The three divisions, two of which had had no rest for four nights and marched forty miles, held a frontage of thirteen miles.

On the extreme right of the whole line, the Duke of Cornwall's Light Infantry of 5th Division, having not yet received the orders to stand and fight, were forming up in fours on the Le Cateau road preparatory to continuing the retreat as ordered. Suddenly they were fired on from the windows of the houses lining the north side of the road, and men began to drop. Hurriedly they were moved up to the higher ground farther east, where, with two companies of the East Surreys, they held for some hours the rather weak attack by the German advanced elements around the British right flank.

Looking at the position today it seems unlikely that the D.C.L.I. were in fact fired at from the houses, as the official history states. About seventy yards behind these houses, on the enemy side of the road, is a steep bank, almost a cliff, several feet high, and the enemy reaching its top could have fired down at the D.C.L.I. from the cliff top into the gaps between the houses. By wasting time in forcing entry into houses, and climbing stairs, they might well have missed the perfect target of a battalion in fours, stationary.

To the immediate west of Le Cateau the King's Own Yorkshire Light Infantry and the King's Own Scottish Borderers were extended about three hundred yards south of the main road.

On this entirely open and gently sloping forward piece of ground some trenches had been dug by inhabitants of Le Cateau. It is not known what authority decided on this step, who organised the labour and tools, or who directed the work. It seems an impossible task with the chaos in the town, where most civilians were packing to get away, refugees were pouring in, every man looking after his own affairs. Yet these trenches were dug. Only three feet deep, they were not deep enough and the two battalions had to use their own entrenching tools to improve them. They afforded some cover but being on such open ground were very obvious and drew much enemy shellfire.

'B' Company of the K.O.Y.L.I. on the right formed a refused right flank along a lesser road running back from the main road. Today it can be seen to have been a magnificent flank protection, with the men lying down behind the road bank and with an excellent line of fire in front of them.

The enemy artillery had, however, the magnificent target of the civilian-sited trenches and by their fire they greatly helped their infantry regiments forward in their attack across the main road. The K.O.Y.L.I. suffered severely, but refusing to surrender or withdraw caused heavy casualties by their musketry and the one remaining machine-gun. The enemy naturally hesitated to rush in. Several times their bugles sounded the British 'Cease Fire' and an attempt was made to take forward a flag of truce. Each overture was met by renewed defensive fire, but gradually the enemy got round the flanks. Many now came forward from the front and the remaining men of the K.O.Y.L.I. could not fire fast enough to hold them. Finally some Germans came up behind them, and a close-quarter bayonet and fist-fight ensued. Overcome by vastly superior numbers, they were mostly captured, and the battalion, within a few short hours, lost 600 officers and men, the majority being taken prisoner.

The position of both battalions is easily seen today. The wonderful field of fire, and the site of the trenches so exposed to artillery fire are very obvious.

About twelve hundred yards behind the K.O.Y.L.I. position is the village of Reumont. In 1914 the most easterly house in the village, and the biggest, had a ladder in the garden for some roof repairs being carried out. Up it the Divisional Commander, Sir Charles Ferguson, climbed and from there he watched the whole battle taking place. On the house in 1919 a plaque commemorating the fact was placed. This plaque was removed by the Germans in 1940 and in 1950 the house was demolished. A new house has been built on the site with a new plaque bearing the words:

'5th Division, Battle Hd. Qrs. Le Cateau,
26th August 1914.'

Off to the left-front of this house and in a shallow depression behind a wood, the 19th Independent Brigade waited. This brigade belonged to none of the original five divisions, having been made up on the outbreak of war by battalions stationed in Scotland and the Mediterranean. It was used as a reserve at the battle of Mons. During the morning of the battle for Le Cateau on the 26th it was sent to extricate the D.C.L.I., the East Surreys and the Suffolks, all of whom were hard pressed out on the right flank.

The left brigade of the division alongside the left of the K.O.S.B. consisted of the Norfolks, Bedfords, Cheshires, and Dorsets. It was an entirely ordinary brigade, all regiments being English county regiments. There were no Fusiliers, no Light Infantry, no Highlanders and no Irish regiments. The men were very largely from the country, and were very hard to shift. It was one of the best brigades in the B.E.F. At Mons it had been in reserve and had not fired a shot. On the following day, the first day of the Great Retreat, it had been rear-guard to the 5th Division, and the Cheshires had been all but surrounded, losing almost six hundred men.

It was put into the centre of the front line at Le Cateau, with, naturally, the Cheshires as its brigade reserve. Its task was to cover the village of Troisvilles, situated about a quarter of a mile back from the main road. But there was no serious German pressure before mid-day and then very little in the centre, and so in two major actions in five days, the brigade saw little serious fighting. On its front the ground is slightly more broken than that occupied by the K.O.S.B. and K.O.Y.L.I. and there are low banks, ditches and minor features of tactical value which the forward companies occupied, and from which excellent fields of fire are obtainable.

Eastward, and across the main road here, the ground is very level and German infantry advancing over it must have suffered severely, in spite of any artillery support brought down on the Bedfords and Dorsets holding the front line. However, the Germans did not attack here, and these two regiments saw very little action that day.

Headquarters of this brigade were in a sunken lane, with eight-foot banks, to the south of Troisvilles. Alongside headquarters were the Norfolks in reserve digging themselves well into the eastern bank. On the reverse side of the very slight slope that runs back from the main road and the position of the Bedfords, they were unable to understand why so many shells were falling so close to them and brigade headquarters in the sunken lane. Clearly both were out of sight of the enemy. However, on top of one of the banks an entirely isolated tree was standing, large enough to be marked on the map, and very conspicuous. It made a fine aiming-mark for the German gunners. The Norfolks spent a long time trying to cut it down. But as soon as it was cut half through so as to fall to the south, the wind blowing strongly from the south-west threatened to blow it down to the north and thus into and over the sunken lane. This would have been a disaster indeed, blocking the road wherein much transport was already parked—and along which more vehicles must pass if a further retirement became necessary. Having been half cut through it then became necessary to guy it up with ropes, but the wind was very strong and it was only held up with difficulty. Eventually it was brought down on the right side of the sunken road, and the shelling died down considerably.

Today the roots of this great tree are clearly visible. Twenty years ago a sapling was planted among them, which is now half-grown—twenty feet high—and is clearly visible on the bank from a great distance. Its giant predecessor, twice its height, must have been conspicuous indeed, and explains the Germans' interest and attention.

The banks of the sunken lane are higher than they seem, and clearly indicate why the Norfolks, well protected and hidden from enemy view, could not understand the extensive shellfire directed against them. Doubtless it did not take long for some intelligent officer to appreciate the use of the great tree as an aiming-mark, and what a shell-trap the otherwise excellent sunken lane had become.

Farther along the line, and now in the 3rd Division's area, the exact positions of the Royal Scots, Gordons and, over the road in front of the town of Caudry, the South Lancs and the Wiltshires, are easily identified. This part of the line was heavily attacked throughout the day by cavalry, three infantry regiments (six battalions) and consistent heavy artillery fire. Casualties were considerable though not severe. Minor indentations in the line were made but surprisingly were not exploited until nightfall.

At dusk the Corps Commander authorised individual withdrawal by units, but in the 3rd Division this order failed to reach the Gordons. In the fading light they did not see that the South Lancs and the Wiltshires, and on their right the Royal Scots, were moving back. At about 10 p.m., the C.O. having become a casualty, the second-in-command noticed the silence all around him and realised that some sort of a withdrawal must have taken place. Accordingly he concentrated what was left of the battalion and led them back, hopeful that he was moving in the right direction. After about four miles in the dark, complete silence and isolation, he passed through two villages, and then came to a T-junction in the road. Having by now largely lost all sense of direction, he decided to turn left, which led him into the village of Bertry, instead of right which would have led probably to escape. In the village he saw lights in a cottage and heard voices. Forcing his way into the house he found it occupied by many German soldiers. Bertry, small and compact, had been captured by the enemy some hours before, and in no time the Gordons were in the midst of an exultant enemy, who surrounded them, capturing all except a handful of men in the rear company who turned and ran. The chaos in the dark village is easy to imagine.

On reaching the road junction today, and after following the route the Gordons took after passing along the winding lane, it is still necessary, even in broad daylight, to consult the map to establish one's bearings, and decide which road to take. Standing there it is easy to realise how Major Gordon made this mistake in the dark, even if he had a map, and the uncertainty in his mind as he stood at the road junction.

Out on the extreme left flank the still comparatively fresh 4th Division had, at dawn on the 26th, taken up a position on the vulnerable left flank. The 11th Brigade had the Somerset Light Infantry in touch with the left of the 3rd Division and, well out in front, the Rifle Brigade and Hampshires. These three regiments had very similar experiences all day to those of the Wiltshires and South Lancs; they were attacked and shelled all day, without suffering heavily, and at dusk withdrew.

The next brigade, the 12th, faced north-east, to form a refused flank to any German attempt to come in there. This brigade, although fresh by comparison with those troops who had been in action or marching since the Canal engagement, was nevertheless tired. It had detrained at Le Cateau in the early morning of the 25th after twenty-four hours in the train—there was not much sleep to be had in the cattle trucks provided. It had then marched forward all day, and taking over the rear-guard from 5th Division had marched back again, deployed and fought its way all through the night, reaching its position out on the extreme left flank at dawn on the 26th.

The left forward battalion, the Lancashire Fusiliers, started to dig in on high ground north-west of Haucourt, while the right battalion, the King's Own Royal Lancasters, formed mass on the forward slope, piled arms and removed equipment. The men were lying down. It was said that the French cavalry were out in front protecting the brigade.

At about 6 a.m., while most of the King's Own were still asleep, a junior officer reported that he had just seen two or three horsemen ride out from a wood a thousand yards in front, observe the battalion and then withdraw. He added that their uniforms were foreign and he thought not French.

Little notice was taken until, a little later, a wheeled vehicle left the wood, advanced a hundred yards or so and paused, with much activity. In a few moments machine-gun fire, at a range of eight hundred yards, opened on the battalion sleeping in mass. In the first burst eighty-three men were killed including the C.O., and over two hundred wounded. Men rushed to unpile arms, equipment and ammunition was searched for, and general chaos prevailed. Although the machine-gun fire was quickly and accurately followed by shrapnel fire, the second-in-command was able to rally the battalion and withdraw it a hundred yards behind the crest.

Here some reorganisation was possible and a party was sent forward to engage the enemy, who had by now also withdrawn. The Royal Warwicks from the 10th Brigade (in reserve) came forward to support, and later relieved the King's Own, who were withdrawn into reserve at Haucourt.

The exact position of the battalion when surprised can be precisely fixed. The forward open slope continuing evenly down-hill for a thousand yards is very clear, while only fifty yards behind the battalion's position is the crest of the slope and then a sharp drop to the valley of a little stream—an ideal defensive position. To its right there is a slight rise in the ground over which the Hampshires could not be seen. A post on this ridge would have made a link with this unit and also provided further observation over a large area forward. The example of the Lancashire Fusiliers digging in, clearly seen by the King's Own, should have been followed.

On the large situation-map of the battle of Le Cateau at about 8 a.m. on the 26th, the exact position of every infantry battalion and artillery brigade in the three divisions is shown. All those units in the front line, numbering twenty battalions, and many in support are shewn as in 'extended order'—digging-in, presumably. The exception is the King's Own and it is surprising that a regular infantry battalion should be so placed in such circumstances.

The author has visited the site of this disaster three times in the past few years. Each time he is struck with the enormity of the tactical blunder.

There were two courses open to the C.O. He could and should have started to dig a defensive position on the very site where the battalion was in mass—from it a perfect, long field of fire was obtainable for a thousand yards down the slight slope to the trees and houses in front of which and from where, in fact, the Germans emerged into the open. His military knowledge and experience must have suggested this to him and in any case he could see the Lancashire Fusiliers doing this very thing only a few hundred yards away to his left, in full view, and in a similar position.

The other course was to hide the battalion in the perfect, ready-made cover of the pronounced crest only a hundred yards behind him. One company might have lined this crest as a precaution. This course would have at least observed the principles of concealment, and, if attacked, surprise. The mass formation out in front on the forward slope, however, ignored concealment, surprise and security, while the piled arms did nothing to increase the safety of the position.

The C.O. of the King's Own, Lt.-Colonel Dykes, had been adjutant of his regiment at Spion Kop in 1900, had in 1902 received a brevet-majority for his work in the South African War, had passed through the Staff College in 1909, and had been in command of the battalion for a year before August 1914. It is surprising that this obviously able, intelligent and experienced officer, should so completely ignore his 'Field Service Regulations'. It was a blunder which cost him his life and those of 83 of his men.

As the day progressed the Royal Warwicks and the Lancashire Fusiliers were pressed back towards Haucourt and by dusk the Royal Warwicks withdrew through the village, the King's Own thus again becoming the right forward battalion of the 12th Brigade. At about 8 p.m. the permission to withdraw by units was received, and at about the same time the Germans entered the eastern outskirts of Haucourt. Several minor, isolated incidents took place in the darkness while the King's Own were preparing to leave, and one officer and several men were killed. They were later buried in the village cemetery where the Imperial War Graves Commission later preserved the graves and erected grave-stones. Several villages in and just behind the line of battle of Le Cateau have similar little

British corners in their cemeteries, all well tended by the local communities. The bodies of the men killed in the main disaster to the King's Own in the morning were buried where they fell by the enemy some days later.

In the village of Haucourt in 1955 there was living an old man who remembered the battle, the disaster to the King's Own, their withdrawal after dark and the German occupation for the next four years. He also remembered as a child seeing the German troops march through in 1870, and a similar invasion in 1940.

Pressure of enemy attacks had been felt all day along the front, gradually increasing in intensity. The two outer-flank brigades of the Corps were the first to feel it and the D.C.L.I., Suffolks, and K.O.Y.L.I. on the right and the King's Own on the left were in action and under fire all the morning.

The enemy were trying to find the flanks of the British and it is surprising that they did not endeavour to push on around the town of Le Cateau when they saw the D.C.L.I. and Suffolks cut up, and in the case of the latter, surrounded and captured. They must have known that I Corps was at least six miles away; the gap between the two corps, with the flank of II Corps pushed in badly, made a wonderful opportunity for the B.E.F. to be cut in half. But they didn't exploit it.

The German First Army Commander, von Kluck, was marching into battle, if not quite haphazardly, certainly with no over-all plan other than 'finding' the British. He seems to have had little idea as to where they were, and it says little for his tactical ability that having discovered certainly the right flank of II Corps he did not use his discovery. To mount attacks on the centre of the Corps was literally a waste of time because such attacks, although more or less successful late in the day, gained time for the British to get transport and guns away and to make reconnaissances to the rear to ascertain lines of retirement and future positions.

Owing to the bending-back of the outer flanks of the Corps by midday, permission had been given by Corps H.Q. at 3 p.m. to withdraw when necessary, but the G.O.C.'s 3rd and 5th Divisions agreed that each could hold on for a while.

At this time the centre of the line was virtually intact. The enemy had crossed the main Cambrai–Le Cateau road, but could advance no farther. The 9th Brigade (the right-hand brigade of 3rd Division) was perfectly secure, and its Lincolns and Northumberland Fusiliers and the Royal Scots of the next brigade were all apparently immovable, while the Bedfords and Dorsets to the right scarcely fired a shot.

But towards evening the enemy artillery fire increased. The villages in or just behind the line where naturally brigade and battalion headquarters were posted, together with reserve units and services, suffered severely. Both flanks had been turned and by 6 p.m. it was evident that the brigades in the centre, although quite undefeated, couldn't stay much longer without risking being totally surrounded. A complete withdrawal to preserve a line with the retreating flank brigades was inevitable.

By 7 p.m. dusk was falling, as well as a light drizzle. All the officers and men, not only in the battalions but at brigade and divisional headquarters were very tired, and everyone knew, almost for a certainty, that a ghastly night lay ahead of them, with no rest and probably no food, certainly nothing hot.

Brigades, battalions, batteries and companies instinctively remained in their positions until orders to go back reached them. When received they were obeyed—not with alacrity, the men were too tired, but with a wonder as to whether another night out in the open, in the rain, with probable capture might be so much worse than another night-march with no food. The men did not grumble— the British soldier never does grumble when times are really bad— they were just apathetic as to what was happening. There were only two alternatives, they believed; this present hell—or a good sleep, but they knew they wouldn't get the latter.

The order to withdraw in the chaos, failing light and rain failed to reach one unit, the Gordons, as has been seen, and a few individual companies and platoons elsewhere. The dilemma facing a few probably young and certainly very tired officers must have been acute. These young officers heard no firing, they could find no friends on either side of them, each was responsible for a number of men. Obviously he should move back and try to make contact with his own—or at least some—unit. But none had orders to retire and the enemy were not far away. Training forbade them to retreat in the face of the enemy without orders, yet common-sense urged them to do so and seek concentration, and thus shelter, to the rear. The near-crushing responsibility of some of these young officers of the B.E.F. in these few hours in 1914 has not been appreciated or recognised.

II Corps slipped away again in the dark—as at Mons. The weary troops marched all night but they suffered little molestation. Again the enemy had had enough for the time being.

The battle of Mons had been largely a battle of small arms, of both rifles and machine-guns. The enclosed ground on the northern (enemy) side of the canal, and the closely built villages and slag heaps on the southern (British) side had been quite unsuitable for artillery, and small arms on both sides had been the only effective weapons.

The battle of Le Cateau had been, however, an artillery battle. The open, flattish, rolling downs with few woods, little 'dead ground' and wonderful observation was ideal for gunnery. The infantry positions of the British could be seen a long way off and the German gunners had as much of a 'field day' at Le Cateau as the British riflemen and machine-gunners had had at Mons.

The ground at Le Cateau for battalion and company commanders was exasperating. A position selected, occupied and perhaps dug was, in that open country, no better and no worse than the dozens of alternatives all around. All had excellent fields of fire, all were exposed and obvious. The German gunner is an excellent soldier and he took the opportunity to show his skill.

The three British divisions lost nearly 8,000 men from all causes at Le Cateau. Forty per cent came from enemy shellfire on to company and battery positions, while forty-five per cent came from units surrounded with large numbers captured.

The battle of Le Cateau, the last great battle to be fought within the space of a day, achieved its object. It gave many men in the reserve battalions and brigades who were not engaged until late in the day several hours of sleep. It hit the enemy a hard blow from which he recoiled and he did not again closely pursue or harrass the infantry in the great retreat, and it allowed I Corps to get clear away.

Lastly it delayed the programme of the over-all German advance by yet another day. It had been already ten days late at Mons, owing to the resistance of the Belgian forts of Namur and Liége. Mons put it back another day—while Le Cateau added yet another.

For the German Schlieffen Plan to be successful it was essential that its strict time-table was adhered to, so that the Western Allies could be knocked out by a certain date and then the bulk of the German Army transferred to the east to meet the Russians before their mobilisation was complete. Every day lost on this rigid, typically German programme was a day gained for Russia. The resistance shown by II Corps at Le Cateau greatly helped the Eastern Allies.

Nevertheless, despite its satisfactory long-term result, the battle of Le Cateau, wherein an advancing enemy in great strength pushed a British Corps of three divisions off its semi-prepared position, forcing it to retreat through the night can hardly be termed a British victory. Yet the words LE CATEAU appear on the Colours as a battle honour of all the regiments who took part. Quatre Bras, however, where an attacking enemy (also in strength) was repulsed by the British and forced to withdraw into the night, is not considered a victory and its name appears on no Colours.

Krithia–Gallipoli

1915

PRIOR to 1908 the average Turk had little interest in his country. He was far more interested in his God, and Islam represented to him an idea greater than Ottoman nationality. Religion interested him more than patriotism. The Sultan, Abdul Hamid, was the leader of Turkish Muslims rather than the ruler of his country.

But in 1908 a new political, largely nationalistic movement had, in Constantinople, slowly emerged out of nothing—the Young Turks. Animated by a desire to make their country a European power they were aggressive, totally inexperienced, and in a hurry. They were not taken seriously in their own country, but then student movements rarely are.

After the fall of Abdul Hamid in 1909, the Young Turk movement became even more nationalistic. Some of these young hotheads were Jews, most were lax Muslims, and a strong patriotism grew up alongside the waning religious fervour. The morale of Turkey, already high in 1914, was further bolstered by the considerable military support from Germany, in equipment, generals and instructors. Indeed, having visions of their projected Berlin–Baghdad railway and possibly the need of force to establish it, Germany, to woo the Turks, had deliberately encouraged her aggressive attitude and assumed the position of a stronger, more organised and watchful elder brother.

The outbreak of war in 1914, showing several immediate victories for Germany, at Mons, the Great Retreat, and Tannenburg, naturally made the Young Turks believe their German patrons would win, but it seemed early days to jump off the fence. Turkey accordingly remained neutral for several months. However, two modern German battleships, the *Goeben* and the *Breslau* had been cruising in the Mediterranean in August 1914 and, avoiding the Royal Navy, had slipped through the Dardenelles. They anchored off Constantinople and were purchased by Turkey at a knock-down price.

The sight of these two modern warships in the Golden Horn, seen by thousands of workers as they crossed the Galata bridge every morning and evening, did much to raise war fever and in October Turkey declared war against the Western Allies.

By the spring of 1915 Russia was in a bad way. Defeated in several sectors on her Western Front she had been pushed back nearly two hundred miles from her farthest advance. Vast amounts of equipment had been lost in the various retreats, which the Russian arsenals were only able to replace very slowly, and at an insufficient pace to keep up with normal wastage. There were not enough rifles to go round, some men in the trenches were unarmed, while reinforcements arrived from recruiting centres rather than from training centres, ignorant of how to use the rifle that often was not available. The Czar, until now a popular figure believed by many men in the ranks to have spiritual powers in addition to his human qualities, was no longer the father-figure he had been. He did not remove those generals whom the troops knew were inefficient. He did not arrange for arms, clothing or food in sufficient quantities. Morale sank gradually and steadily while the ineffective replacement of arms, artillery, vehicles, clothing and munitions generally caused France and Great Britain gravely to fear Russia's collapse and exit from the war. Something must be done. She must be kept in the field and at all costs her morale raised.

To this end it was decided to force the Dardenelles, capture Constantinople, force Turkey out of the war and so provide a way for freight ships filled with munitions to pass through the Bosphorus into the Black Sea, and there unload at a Russian port. It was felt, probably rightly, that a great and steady stream of munitions would not only take the place of the ineffective Russian arsenals but also cheer the Russian soldiers in the trenches when they saw and received arms made in British and French factories. Having discharged their cargoes these freighters could then be filled for the homeward voyage with Russian grain, of which there was always abundance. The submarine menace had not yet become serious and there was no rationing of food in 1915 in Great Britain, but it was apparent that this situation might not endure for long, that there were difficulties ahead, and that this additional source of food would be welcome.

This strategic conception, the capture of Constantinople, the child of Winston Churchill's brain, (he was at this time First Lord of the Admiralty) was perhaps the most far-sighted and brilliant in our history. If successful it would indeed have been fruitful in results.

As a start the British Fleet was sent to bombard the Turkish forts guarding both sides of the Narrows of the Dardanelles. Several forts were silenced but the mine-sweepers could not get far. Some forts remained in action and enemy field guns were brought down to the coast where the sweepers made perfect targets, never more than eight hundred yards out from the beach. The loss of mine-sweepers was considerable and the morale of their crews became dangerously low. Indeed some civilian fishermen refused to go on and the Navy reported to Whitehall that they could not force the Narrows unless at least one side was in our hands.

Accordingly a military expedition was sent from England and Australia. It consisted of the famous 29th Division, made up of regular British infantry battalions brought home from foreign garrisons, and two divisions, less one brigade, of Australians and New Zealanders. The Commander-in-Chief was Sir Ian Hamilton. (He had been at Majuba in 1881—thirty-four years previously). On his arrival in Cairo, the 42nd (East Lancashire Territorial) Division, then holding the Suez canal, was placed under his command to-gether with a brigade of regular Indian infantry battalions.

The wisdom of employing Mohammedan battalions of the Indian Brigade against their co-religious enemy, and so near Constantinople, created much anxiety. Sir Ian Hamilton finally removed two such units from the Brigade before embarking, replacing them with Hindu regiments, but again anxiety arose as to whether this removal might not be regarded in India as a slight on the fighting qualities of Mohammedan troops in general. This fear was resolved by de-spatching the two units to the two Indian divisions then in France, a move regarded as promotion, or at least a special selection.

On the day of landing two separate operations were carried out, fourteen miles apart. At the extreme southerly tip of the peninsula the 29th Division, covered by the guns, large and small, of the Navy, landed from open boats on four beaches. The division had fearful casualties from the fire from the Turkish trenches just above the beaches, manned by regular Turkish soldiers fanatically defending their homeland. But it got ashore on three of the beaches (the fourth was evacuated twelve hours later).

By mid-day scattered and much disorganised units were ashore and in possession of the cliff tops. After dark they were able to unite and form a line: The Turks withdrew two-and-a-half miles and there dug a trench line across the peninsula. All impetus from the landing had been lost, firing died down, and trench warfare was established.

On 6th May the Turks made their first organised counter-attack, or rather counter-offensive, lasting a week. The men in the front waves had been deprived of ammunition so that they would be forced to go forward into the British trenches and use the bayonet, but their lack of co-ordination and direction was greater than their extreme fanaticism. Coming over in football-crowd formation they suffered heavily, the ten thousand men in the main attack losing nearly half their numbers to the British riflemen and machine gunners. At the end of three days the attack had only secured a few posts in the British line, and had made one advance of two hundred yards on the left flank frontage of half a mile.

On the second day of this counter-offensive the first re-inforcements of the campaign, the 42nd Division (East Lancashire Territorials) arrived. The first Territorial division to go overseas in 1914, it had carried out much training in Egypt, and even had a little battle experience in repelling a Turkish advance against the Suez Canal.

The leading brigade, all Lancashire Fusiliers, went into the line at Cape Helles at once and with two brigades of the original and incomparable 29th Division counter-attacked the Turks.

Successful at first, the attack captured the positions lost and made a few isolated incursions into the old Turkish front line. But no further advance could be made, and the whole of the southern front settled down again into static trench warfare.

The great enemy now was the weather. As it got hotter the dust, flies, dysentery, strictly rationed water and interminable bully beef and biscuits became as omnipresent as they were detested. The soldiers in the trenches in France (whose winter conditions could hardly have been worse) had two ameliorating conditions in their lives. Leave home, although at very long intervals, had started and was something to look forward to. Relief in the trenches by another brigade or division meant, after a march back, civilian billets (although probably only in barns), evenings out in the village café and sometimes a day-out in Hazebrouck, St. Omer or Béthune.

Compared with their life in the trenches these brief spells of rest and relaxation were very nearly heaven.

The troops on Gallipoli had neither of these 'let-ups'. Obviously there was no leave, nor was there any rest billets, except dug-outs in the cliffs by the beaches. These too attracted flies, smells and bully-beef—and were, in addition, under observation from the Asiatic shore and so subject to long-range shellfire. There was, however, bathing, the only form of a bath—but this might well be under shell-fire, too. Life consisted of duty in the trenches, accompanied by danger and acute discomfort—and a 'rest' by the beaches where the danger still existed.

At the same time as the Cape Helles front degenerated into a trench-warfare stalemate, the Australian and New Zealand landings at Anzac—fourteen miles up the western coast from Cape Helles—had also sunk into a static situation, in which neither Colonials nor Turks could manoeuvre, while neither had any intention of withdrawing. Clearly something had to be done. The virtually fresh and reasonably experienced 42nd Division, burning with enthusiasm and of superb quality, was selected to go into the line as a whole and there to be the centre of a great three-and-a-half division attack astride the peninsula. The objective was the village of Krithia, two miles ahead, and the high ground to its right—the lower slopes of Achi Baba, the highest feature on the lower half of the peninsula.

On the extreme right was to be the French Division brought over from the Asiatic shore—where it had made a diversionary and successful landing on the opening day of the campaign. Next was the Royal Naval Division, which was formed after the Antwerp expedition in 1914 from the Royal Naval and Royal Marine reservists called up on mobilisation—and who were surplus to requirements to bring the ships up to full complement. The division remained under Admiralty control. The men remained as sailors and were of the same excellent quality and state of training as the army reservists who rejoined in time for Mons and the Great Retreat. Naturally they were quite unfamiliar with army matters, outlook and training but the standard of the officers and men soon produced good soldiers, and by the time the division reached France in 1916 it was an excellent and reliable division.

Next, in the centre, came the 42nd Division, with the Manchester Brigade (whose fortunes will be followed in greater detail later) on the right. Next to them was the East Lancashire Brigade, while the extreme left was covered by one brigade of the 29th Division.

The 42nd Division attacked on a two-brigade front astride the Krithia—Sed-el-Bahr road, to the left of which and parallel to it ran a deep straight *nullah*, three hundred yards away, leading down from Krithia. Four hundred yards inside the enemy's lines this *nullah* had been joined by a lesser *nullah* from the north-east. In the Manchester Brigade four battalions, 5th, 6th, 7th and 8th Manchesters each had two companies in the first wave, and their other two in the second wave.

The four-hour preliminary bombardment was the heaviest seen in the Gallipoli campaign, and was strengthened by the loan of twenty-four French '75s'. The attack was due to start at noon. At 11 a.m. the bombardment was to be at its fullest and then suddenly cease. The men in the trenches were to cheer and raise their bayonets above the parapet with the object of inducing the Turks to man their front trench. The bombardment then as suddenly reopened, catching many Turks on their fire-steps. This ruse was carried out three times.

Promptly at twelve o'clock the leading wave of the Manchester Brigade went over the top for the first time, and advanced steadily and in good order. They were met by devastating rifle and machine-gun fire, but those who escaped the bullets pressed on in a steady line and by bitter hand-to-hand fighting made good their first objective. In places the wire was untouched by the bombardment, and a number of men died cutting it. The second wave followed at the appointed time. Within five minutes the Turkish first-line trenches had been captured, the second line in half-an-hour, and during the afternoon the fourth line of Turkish trenches had been penetrated. Sappers accompanying the successive waves found and disconnected buried mines, and assisted in the construction of new trenches and the removal of captured ones. On the left the 29th Division had seized their first objective, but their further advance was checked because the barbed wire on their left remained undamaged. The professional soldiers of this division paid generous tribute to the amateurs of the 4th and 5th East Lancashires and 10th Manchesters, who fought with such spirit and determination alongside them.

On the Manchester's right, the Royal Naval Division had also progressed well, but on their right some French Colonial troops were unable to face a small local counter-attack on one of their gains, and came back. The right flank of the Royal Naval Division was now exposed to machine gun fire from the Turks in their newly recaptured positions, and they had to come back. The 7th Manchesters, the right-hand battalion of the 42nd Division, were now exposed, and in a terrible position. The Divisional Commander ordered a partial withdrawal of the brigade back to one of the Turkish lines previously over-run, but the regimental officers up in front had great difficulty in making the men obey the order. C Company of the 6th Manchesters had penetrated to a considerable distance beyond the fork of the big *nullah*, and indeed were within seven hundred yards of Krithia, the nearest any unit got to the village throughout the campaign. All the Manchesters were elated with their success, and the idea of giving up the ground they had so recently and so fairly won was unthinkable. The 7th said they intended to stay and face the enfilade fire they were now experiencing; they would hold on at any cost. But orders had to be obeyed, and the men came back, grumbling, but only after the C.O. had visited the front company commanders and ordered them, in the hearing of the men, to withdraw.

The failure of the French division on the extreme right to get forward, and thereby the exposure of the right flank of the Royal Naval Division, was a great tragedy. Its enforced withdrawal, uncovering the Manchester's flank, caused many casualties, and this brigade lost 1,200 men from all causes. It had captured 600 yards, laterally, of Turkish trenches but the penetration, eventually, was no more than 400 yards. Before they were forced to withdraw the Manchesters had been 1,000 yards beyond their starting line. The two brigades between them captured 217 prisoners, including 11 officers.

Another of the tragedies of this day was the fatal wound suffered by the Brigade Commander of the 127th Manchester Brigade, Brigadier-General Noel Lee. He had been commanding the brigade since 1911, and was the first, and until 1912, the only Territorial officer to be so appointed. He had served through all officer ranks in the 6th Manchesters, and had eventually commanded them. Thus he spent the whole of the twenty-eight years of his military life not only in the same brigade but in the same drill hall, his brigade headquarters being accommodated by the 6th Manchesters in Stretford Road, Manchester.

During the next six weeks, a few hundred yards were gained here and there by small advances on a company scale but no tactical features presented themselves, and the operations were little more than nibbles. By August the line had been carried up to the bifurcation of the big Krithia *nullah*, while astride the road it skirted the southern edge of a large copse, a hundred yards wide, and two hundred yards deep—the Vineyard.

On 6th August the last of the offensive operations in this area of the Gallipoli Peninsula were started. Again the 42nd Division were in the centre with the 29th Division on their left, and the French on their right. The objectives were the enemy trenches beyond the fork of the Krithia *nullah*, here rather deep, and the Vineyard itself. The Manchester Brigade, always a model of what Lord Haldane's Territorials could become, was on the left, and was to cross the eastern arm of the *nullah*, and capture the enemy trenches on the slightly rising ground beyond. Artillery fire on the enemy front line had not been as effective as had been hoped, and the 8th Manchesters, from Ardwick, though able to reach the enemy front line short of the *nullah*, were unable to move down the bank and up the other side.

On the right the Lancashire Fusiliers Brigade attacked the Vineyard. Successful at first, they were counter-attacked and lost a good part of their gains, but held on to their eventual position a hundred and fifty yards inside the old Turkish front line. The 29th Division on the left also had little success, finding the enemy trenches so full of Turks that it seemed they, too, were on the point of attacking. The Essex Regiment did indeed jump down into a trench so crammed with enemy that the bayonet could not be used and fists were the only weapons for a few minutes. On the right the French made little impact.

The trench captured that day by the 8th Manchesters (and on their right the Vineyard captured by the Lancashire Fusiliers) were the last of the enemy front to be captured. They remained the British front line for the rest of the campaign.

Today the Krithia battlefield has three types of country. The vast majority of it is a crude primitive hand-agriculture, and it is not easy to trace trenches and earthworks. However, old trench maps (which were extremely accurate) enable positions to be determined to within ten yards or so, and then a careful look will show either a very slight, almost unnoticeable depression where the filled-in earth has subsided, or a slightly different colour or texture in the grass or crop. The final front line, immediately to the east of the main

Krithia *nullah* and where it overlooks the Turkish position over the
eastern arm, shows no positive sign of its original position, yet the
nullah, and the map make it quite certain that, here, one is within
a yard or two of the old trench. Over the main *nullah*, to the left
and about two hundred yards behind the front line, can be seen in
the soil what was clearly a communication trench. The young corn
shoots are greener, the slight depression is evident, the straggling
winding line is obvious, and it leads directly to where it might be
expected to go—the front line.

The next type of territory is of course the *nullah*, carrying a
definite little stream and filled with boulders, bushes and undergrowth. The sand brought down by the very heavy rain-storms that
occur has buried all debris, and washed away most of the earth-
works, although there are still vague signs of dug-out excavations
on the steep sides, which are eight feet high. However, it cannot
have been much use as a shelter area—as it is entirely at right
angles to the Turkish position, and doubtless snipers fired straight
down it at night, while by day any movement in it must have at
once drawn fire.

Lastly, the Vineyard itself. Largely cut down, it has been under
the plough and traces of trenches are as difficult to see as elsewhere.
However, at its southern end and close to the Redoubt Cemetery, is
still standing an untouched area of trees and bushes fifty yards by
a hundred. Here the trenches are perfectly clear and one stretch,
probably a reserve company area, about two hundred yards behind
the last front line and forty yards long is obviously very much as
it was in 1915. The shell holes around it and its traverses are all
clearly visible.

Four hundred yards back down the road towards Helles can be
seen the front line from which the two companies from each of the
four Manchester battalions advanced on 4th June—the first day of
the battle for Krithia and Achi Baba. The trench is curiously
straight, but with the many shell holes around it is unmistakable.
It lies in an area of scrub which has not been cleared, hence its
present existence. The line of attack is clear and simple; over open
ground, up a barely discernible slope the men could and must have
moved quickly. By June 4th much artillery had been landed in
strength, and in the great depression north of Cape Helles and south
of the Vineyard which the Turks evacuated on 27th and 28th April,
there must have been batteries. Their supporting fire on to the

enemy trenches along the southern edge of the Vineyard must have been very effective, most heartening to the attacking Manchesters and a considerable factor in the successful attack.

In the village of Krithia itself, a thousand yards away, the inhabitants before 1915 were Greeks, as were most of the peasants on the peninsula. After the Greco-Turkish War of 1920–21, they were evicted by the Turkish Government and replaced by Turks from Bulgaria, whose descendants live there today. The village is rather like a village in the Punjab. Low huts made of mud and a few bricks, very little road metal, chickens, goats, dogs, cows, and manure in plenty, while thick dust and smells are everywhere.

In 1962 the author and his interpreter stopped in the village hoping to find some refreshment. Bottled beer, a rickety table and two chairs appeared and were set up in the road; a small crowd of about a dozen villagers collected and the interpreter became very busy. The peasants seemed most interested in the visitor and the object of his visit. After much chatter there were laid on the table by individuals in the little crowd standing behind the chairs listening and gaping, a cap badge of the Lancashire Fusiliers, shoulder titles of Manchesters, Hampshires and K.O.S.B. and a major's crown, all picked up within the past few months.

The shoulder title of the Manchesters was purchased and brought home. It was suitably mounted with the mud of Gallipoli still in the interstices of the lettering. It is placed in front of the Chairman of the 6th Manchesters Annual Re-Union dinner held every year in Manchester, which is still attended by sixty or seventy men who were on the peninsula.

There are only a handful of Bulgarian-Turkish peasants living in the lower half of the peninsula and where the campaign took place. All live in the two villages of Krithia and Sedd-el-Bahr down by the beach where the 29th Division had landed, and many of them are employed as gardeners looking after the 45,000 British graves. Owing to the considerable difficulty of access few visitors ever come to Gallipoli. In the summer months perhaps half a dozen groups of old soldiers come to see the old places and find the graves of old friends. Otherwise the territory is quite deserted and apart from a few peasants in Krithia, the only living things are a few scraggy, semi-wild goats, some lizards, and in the Krithia *nullah* a few small tortoises. Nothing ever happens. Sunshine, silence, and the passing of time only are noticeable.

La Boisselle–The Somme

1916

THE 34th Division, a New Army division, was formed in the spring and summer of 1915. All the individual units however had been raised in the autumn of 1914—as a result of Kitchener's famous call—"Your King and Country needs You".

The Division had two brigades of Northumberland Fusiliers, the Tyneside Scottish, and the Tyneside Irish, and one mixed brigade of two battalions of Royal Scots, one of Lincolns and one of Suffolks.

Many of the units were raised by private enterprise. The Lord Provost of Edinburgh, the Lord Mayor of Newcastle, local rich and influential industrialists, County Committees especially convened for the purpose, the Mayors of Leicester, Norwich, Sunderland, all took not only a personal but also a practical and financial part in raising most units, including the artillery and services. Units raised in this way fared better than those raised by the War Office direct. The raisers were unhampered by the many rules and regulations which control a government department, and the units lacked very little in rations, spare working suits before uniforms arrived, horses, vans, office equipment etc. When direct control was eventually assumed by the War Office, all units agreed that 'private enterprise' had been more effective, and certainly more pleasant.

The men came from every walk of life. There were actors, peers, shop-assistants, miners, school-masters, out-of-works, clergymen, bus conductors, undergraduates, authors, publicans and bank clerks. All were imbued with a spirit of patriotism and adventure. Many of them lied cheerfully and brazenly about their age in order to be accepted. Youth which had hitherto satisfied its natural appetite for adventure in sport, athletics or mountain climbing, was now attracted by the probable danger and certain novelty of war, novelty of a life which the vast majority had not only never experienced in any form but had not even contemplated.

While novelty and adventure were the magnets that drew them it was patriotism that drove them in, and the overriding characteristic in all these hundreds of thousands of enlistments was a sense of mission, a sense of willing sacrifice of jobs, prospects and family comforts for the common good. Never was a body of men so devoted, so dedicated.

They joined often in groups. Cricket clubs, miners from the same pit, men from business houses asked to be in the same unit. 'Pals' battalions, footballers, public schools units were formed, but these groups were in the minority. The vast majority joined as unknown individuals, all strangers to each other. None knew the next man's past, his occupation, his family or his status in society. Occasionally false names were used—for reasons best known to the individual.

The men were immediately formed into groups of 1,000 and a commanding officer appointed. He might be a spare regular major or captain from the parent regiment's reserve battalion, or a commandeered senior officer from the Indian Army home on leave, or most often a retired Regular Army major or lieutenant-colonel brought back to the Active List, the original 'Old Dug-out'. Their first task was to break down the 1,000 men into four companies, and appoint four company commanders from temporary officers immediately commissioned from the universities, public schools and other sources.

A system of selection of N.C.O.s by a month's trial was in force in several units, a system that worked well. In one unit within the author's knowledge 900 men were divided into four groups and sent into the different corners of a field, their to elect their sergeants and corporals. On return each had an outline organisation with which a young officer with no experience could start—the embryo of a company organisation which was to last for four and a half years.

Except for the C.O., whose ideas would usually be out of date, rarely had anyone any previous experience, or real know-how. A good number of the junior officers had a smattering of army drill and tactics from their O.T.C. annual camp, but it did not amount to much. Anyway, the N.C.O.s from the O.T.C. had not commanded men, only their juniors in the school. Apart from the C.O., and if he were lucky one other regular or ex-regular, all ranks were newcomers.

The virility of these new units, not even battalions yet, was outstanding. The 'old dug-outs' were delighted to be in uniform again—to be wanted. Seniors from the reserve battalions were pleased to get a command at last. Indian Army officers were fascinated by the novelty of commanding white men after so many years of leading coloured men. The new captains and subalterns felt it to be glorious adventure, while the men in the ranks realised that they had to reorient totally their whole outlook on life and its living at once abandoned all ideas of the office or over-time, shop-stewards of the five-fifteen train. They became soldiers in spirit overnight, willing to learn and to learn quickly, so that it should be over as soon as possible.

The large majority of Kitchener's New Army were formed into brigades (a month or so after reaching full strength) in the autumn of 1914, and a month later into divisions. By November there were thirty-one new divisions, all newly raised, all composed of Kitchener's Army men, all organised and going concerns—and all lacking training and experience.

The 34th Division, whose units had also been raised by November 1914, was not organised into brigades nor the Division formed as such until the spring and summer of 1915. The author has been unable to discover why this delay in higher formation occurred. It may have been due to the reluctance of the raisers to relinquish their local control, and the War Office, seeing the administrative and financial burden born by someone else, agreed to this 'private army' remaining as such for a while. There is also no indication as to how the groups of battalions were administered by any higher authority. Who convened court-martials?—who allotted training areas?—who granted leave to C.O.'s? It is evident that some form of military control over units must have existed—but no evidence of it can be traced.

In June 1915 the 34th Division came together. By this time all units had nine months experience, each had settled down into its own self-evolved routine. There was no brigade or division *esprit*—but there was a vast, reliable, and greatly varying characteristic individuality in each unit.

The first Divisional Commander, General Ingouville-Williams, was brought home from France where, since the battle of the Aisne in September 1914, he had been commanding the 16th Infantry Brigade of the 6th Regular Division. His first duty, while fostering and encouraging the widely differing individuality of units, was to bring all into line, and instil a Divisional spirit. This he did admirably, and he became a highly respected and very well-known commander. (Tragically he was killed in action at the Battle of the Somme only three weeks after the attack of the Division on La Boisselle.) In January 1916, the Division crossed over to France.

Early in 1916, Sir Douglas Haig, British Commander-in-Chief in France, felt that although the Battle of Loos four months previously had been costly in casualties and had gained little ground, it had provided some useful lessons. The famous Kitchener's Army divisions were now arriving in France and a project of launching a big offensive in the summer seemed both possible and desirable. This project became urgent in the spring of 1916 when the Germans attacked the French at Verdun. The attacks there became stronger and stronger, the French being forced back, some of the impregnable forts fell and our allies were hard pressed. General Joffre, the French Commander-in-Chief, begged General Haig to help him by hurrying on his offensive. Haig complied and it is noteworthy that the Germans ceased altogether their Verdun operations only eleven days after the British attack on the Somme started on 1st July.

As a result of this lessening of pressure the French were able to pass to the offensive in September and by November had regained much of their lost ground.

The greatest battle in British military history in point of numbers and frontage was the opening day of the Battle of the Somme, 1916, the famous '1st July'. On this day, on a frontage of 16 miles, 13 assaulting divisions with six others in close reserve attacked the Germans on their strongly-fortified and excellently-sited positions to the north of the river.

The Battle of the Somme, a campaign within a campaign, lasted four months. Thirty-six square miles of enemy-held territory were gained, and 27 sizeable villages and seven major woods were captured; each of them, strongly fortified and gallantly defended, required a major operation in itself. Indeed, Thiepval, perhaps the most strongly-fortified village on the whole Western Front, was assaulted 11 times by eight divisions or parts of divisions between 20th August and 26th September before it was finally captured by 18th Division, one of the earliest of the Kitchener divisions. The names of some of these villages and woods, Poziers, Combles, Flers, Delville Wood, High Wood, were for several months household words, as well known as Hougomont, Caesar's Camp, the Crecy

Mill, the Valley of Death at Balaclava had been in their time. During the four months' campaign the Germans lost over 600,000 men and their High Command considered that the German Army was never the same again. But by far the greatest operation of all was on the opening day, 1st July.

The 16 mile frontage of attacks ran southward from the village of Gommercourt, between Albert and Arras, for 10 miles to the Albert-Bapaume Road, where it veered slightly south-east for another three miles until it touched the River Somme. Across the river the French co-operated with an attack by five divisions.

The enemy's position was immensely strong, being almost identical with that taken up in October 1914—and so had received almost two years of building, modifying, strengthening and general improving. It was usually down a forward slope and thus close behind it was an area out of sight of the British. Here were the enemy's guns, reserve lines and rest dug-outs.

The front line usually just embraced a village which was heavily fortified. Although an aiming mark for artillery, each village had provided abundant building material for the fortress. The cellars and foundations made excellent fire positions while those at the back of the village made fairly safe bomb-proof shelters. In front of the line and further down the slope much wire had been laid, both tactical and defensive. Lastly, and by no means unimportant, an attacking enemy had to advance up-hill.

Until 1st July, 1916, dug-outs and shelters for the men in the British front line trench did not differ much from those shown in Bruce Bairnsfather's cartoons of 1914. Usually a hole in the trench wall, roofed with corrugated iron and perhaps a double layer of sandbags, they were scarcely any protection against shell-fire and were only moderately weather-proof. Furniture was ammunition boxes, and a sacking curtain or waterproof sheet prevented some of the warmth from a brazier escaping. The smallest man could not stand upright, the floor was trodden mud and they were uncomfortable in the extreme.

But the capture of the German trenches on 1st July showed what trench-comfort could be. The highly industrious, and ingenious, German engineers had tunnelled down into the easily-worked chalk, driving steeply descending staircases often 30 feet deep. These shafts were connected at the bottom where suites of rooms were fitted out. Beds were made of wire-netting stretched on wooden frames, tables, chairs, bits of carpet brought down from the ruined cottages above; in one deep shelter a piano was found. The larger diggings built for battalion or regimental headquarters had electric light installed, fed from little field generators. Cookhouses, telephone exchanges, latrines, rest rooms, stores, all made these excavations self-sufficient and water was the only real shortage. During bombardments infantry were trained to race upstairs with their weapons when the bombardment lifted, and so occupy their fire positions in a few seconds.

These new-found dug-outs were very welcome to the British troops who now occupied them, and the creature comforts and cover from the elements and the enemy shell-fire were much appreciated. Unfortunately the shafts faced the wrong way, and there were a few cases of German shells actually falling down them, detonating at the bottom, causing death as much from concussion in the confined space as from actual impact.

Preparations for the great attack had been going on since December 1915, the artillery bombardment being, up to then, the most skilful, consistent and heavy that had been used in battle. 1,600 guns of all calibres covered the sixteen mile front, one gun per seventeen yards. Tunnelling in the firm chalk soil of the Somme downs was easy, and several mines were laid under the German strong-points, the existence of none of them being suspected by the enemy.

Ten minutes before zero these mines were detonated. When the last of the debris had fallen—it took some seventeen seconds—both British and Germans occupied their rim of the vast new crater. The attackers thus found a yawning gulf in front of them out of which they could not climb if they descended while the enemy greatly appreciated this now impassable piece of No-Man's-Land in front of them.

The shock of the explosions of these mines was, of course, very great and prisoners captured that day in the vicinity of the mines were quite dazed for some hours. Later they explained that many men had been sheltering in the deep dug-outs, waiting for the British barrage to lift and the order to come up and man the fire-steps. The explosion collapsed many of the shafts and it is certain that many hundreds of German soldiers were either killed in their dugouts by the concussion from the nearby mine or buried alive by the collapsing shafts. Sitting in rows, rifles in hand, waiting for the signal to come up, they are entombed there for ever, thirty feet below ground. Two of these great craters were at La Boisselle.

The chief object of the incessant bombardment had been the cutting of the German defensive barbed-wire entanglements, to let the attacking infantry in. This appeared to observers to have been so successful that several brigades of cavalry were brought up in close readiness to exploit a possible breakthrough. However, the objectives of all infantry units were limited. They were rarely as much as a mile and frequently were only a few hundred yards away, usually an enemy support or reserve trench rather than a tactical feature.

Broadly speaking the attack was made all along the line. Special attention was given, however, to the withdrawn flanks of certain salients, in the hope that success there would pinch these salients off. The fronts of these salients were not attacked, although the preliminary bombardment was continued on them to mislead the enemy into believing that they, too, were objectives. The attack started at 7.30 a.m. instead of the usual dawn attack at 5 a.m. and the enemy had broad daylight with the sun behind him in which to see the advance.

To the north of the Albert-Bapaume Road the attack was a failure. The intensity of the enemy machine gun and rifle fire prevented some battalions getting very far beyond their own protective barbed wire; others only just reached the enemy trenches while a few, a very few, were able to cross them and penetrate the enemy's lines. Those that did so, invariably isolated on both flanks, and finding themselves in a salient, were forced to withdraw.

South of the great main road, however, success was partly achieved. One large area, three and a half miles long, and on the average three-quarters of a mile deep was captured, while two smaller ones were also held. The greatest advance of the day was by two Kitchener's Army battalions of the Manchesters, and a regular battalion of the Scots Fusiliers, all from the 30th Division, who captured and held Montauban a mile and a quarter inside the German lines. The success in this part of the front line was due to the bombardment which had so successfully cut the barbed wire that it was virtually non-existent. The German defenders, cowed by the bombardment which had been unceasing for six days (with the result that no ration or water parties could get through to them) were not out of their dug-outs in time to man the front trench and meet the attack. They offered little resistance.

Astride the Albert-Bapaume road, and thus at the centre of the whole line to be attacked, lies the hamlet of La Boisselle, one of the village-fortresses.

At the western end of its few houses, a lesser road running off to the right formed an acute-angled triangle in which the hamlet lay. The German front line trench crossed the main road where the minor road forked off. The British trenches were about 200 yards away to the west of the Germans, although for a distance of three hundred yards they were only seventy-five yards distant. These three hundred yards of trench were known, and marked on the trench maps as the 'Glory Hole'—with good reason.

Being seventy-five yards apart, each side could shell the other's front trench without much fear of 'unders' falling in their own front line. But being only this short distance apart each was very vulnerable to raids, bombing attacks, and indeed major attacks by the other. Consequently the area was heavily shelled well before the 1st July, and had been for many months. The slightest 'jumpiness' in one front line would quickly bring down an S.O.S. defensive barrage on the other, and the ground all around and the trenches themselves were always in a terrible condition, all work being frequently smashed to pieces. For both sides it was a most unhealthy spot and units dreaded being ordered to hold it.

On the north side of the road, the German line bent back sharply owing to configuration of the ground until it was some eight hundred yards away.

As usual in the German positions the ground behind their front line rose back gradually to the east, while behind the British front line the ground too rose slightly to the west. Thus each side was on a slight forward slope facing each other, both front line trenches running alongside the barely perceptible little valley.

On 1st July the 34th Division was allotted the task of assaulting and capturing the hamlet of La Boisselle. The attack was on a two-brigade frontage of a mile and a quarter. On the left the Tyneside Scottish Brigade advanced astride the main road, while to its right the mixed brigade attacked.

Two of the great mines referred to were tunnelled below the German front line at La Boisselle. The left-hand one was just to the north of the main road and its crater was the first objective of the 23rd Northumberland Fusiliers. On their left the 20th Northumberland Fusiliers had an advance of 800 yards in front of them, up a slight rise, and with the enemy's withdrawn flank on their right.

The mine went up two minutes before zero—7.30 a.m., the 23rd reaching its crater with heavy loss after their two hundred-yard advance. The 20th were cut to pieces in their advance although a few individual groups of men succeeded in reaching and crossing the German front line. Here they came under enfilade fire from the left and right. Few were ever seen again.

Meanwhile the 23rd were just holding on to their near-edge of the crater blown in front of them, but by 11 a.m. the few men still surviving had to withdraw. It was from near this crater that they had taken a German officer and thirty-five men from a dug-out. Although dazed, the officer stated that nine dug-outs equally full of men waiting to be called up to the fire-step, must have been closed by the explosion.

To the right of this brigade the 101st Brigade, of the 34th Division, was able to start the first success story of the Battle of the Somme. In front of the 10th Lincolns, the left battalion of this brigade, was the other mine. The battalion succeeded in reaching and holding the near lip of the crater, while on their right, and with a long journey of 800 yards across No Man's Land in front of them, the 15th Royal Scots reached the enemy front line and passing over it, captured an enemy strong-point which had been already named by the battalion prior to the attack as 'Scots Redoubt'. They held this strong-point all day, despite enemy counter-attacks.

Between the Lincolns and their crater and the main road lay the 'Glory Hole', as yet not attacked. The heavy fighting at each end of this line, and the partial success at the right-hand end, prompted the G.O.C. to put his reserve brigade in through this temporarily quiescent part of the enemy's line. Accordingly the Tyneside Irish Brigade advanced down the gradual slope, crossed the old British line, and passing on either side of the Lincoln's crater advanced a long way into the enemy position. Heavy casualties were suffered but a section of the German trenches, four hundred yards long, and eight hundred yards inside their lines, was captured and held. Two parties of the 24th and 27th Northumberland Fusiliers from this brigade in fact reached the village of Contalmaison (which had been the second objective for the 34th Division on the 1st July) a mile-and-a-half inside the German lines but owing to their isolation so far forward had to leave the village, which they could barely hold, and rejoin their own battalions—or what was left of them—in the newly-won enemy trenches.

The 16th Royal Scots, following the 15th, started to consolidate not only their Scots Redoubt but also the enemy reserve trenches to its right and left.

The 11th Suffolks had followed the Lincolns after the latter's occupation of their crater, but moving round the right flank, came under heavy fire and suffered severely. But many men pushed on and a few in fact passed beyond Scots Redoubt.

The situation map of this area at about mid-day shows utter chaos—with units, and parts of units, both large and small, badly mixed up. The 24th and 27th Northumberland Fusiliers are shewn as either being in Contalmaison or returning from there. The two battalions of Royal Scots are in and around Scots Redoubt, and the vicinity parties of the 24th and 27th Northumberlands are on both sides of them. A joint party of Lincolns and Suffolks, despite their heavy casualties, are shewn at 11.30 a.m. as out in front of Scots Redoubt, although the majority of these two battalions were either pinned down at the Lincoln's crater, or badly shot up moving to the east over the open ground.

In this area, a thousand yards square, with units mixed up, casualties to C.O.s, dust, smoke and noise predominant everywhere and sense of direction lost, chaos ruled supreme. Many German prisoners had been taken, most of whom were only too glad to be sent back to the British lines, but many German soldiers remained in little pockets in the smashed trenches and dug-outs, fighting bravely. Bombing parties were busy all the afternoon and it was nightfall before the area captured could be said to be in firm possession.

These Kitchener's Army soldiers of the 34th Division had done extremely well. Totally inexperienced in battle only six months before, nine of the battalions in the Division crossed over the enemy's front positions, capturing many prisoners who, until capture, fought well. Opposition had been very strong, yet despite very severe casualties in their battalions, men of the Suffolks and Lincolns were found a mile beyond their original front line trench. Parties of 24th and 27th Northumberland Fusiliers penetrated a mile-and-a-half to Contalmaison. C Company of the 15th Royal Scots took only an hour and a quarter to move forward one mile against heavy opposition, where it stayed for over two hours before withdrawing into its Scots Redoubt.

The vitality of these new battalions was striking. The enthusiasm of August and September 1914 when they had rushed to join 'their' Kitchener's Army had not abated, and they felt that this was for what they had joined.

But the 34th Division payed a terrible price for its success. Altogether fifty officers and four thousand five hundred other ranks became casualties either killed or wounded. The Suffolks lost 15 officers and over 500 men. Five commanding officers were killed and two wounded.

On the evening of 1st July, the left brigade of the 34th Division which had suffered very heavy casualties was withdrawn. Two brigades of the 19th Division relieved it and attacked La Boiselle early on 4th July. They eventually captured the hamlet except for a few ruined cottages at its easterly end.

To the right of the successful brigade of the 34th Division, the 21st, 7th, 18th and 30th Divisions all penetrated the enemy's lines on a wide frontage and in some depth. (The extreme right division in the great attack, the 30th, was holding on firmly, a mile and a quarter beyond its starting line). During the three days following 1st July these 'bites' into the enemy's position were linked up and with the capture of La Boisselle itself on the 4th enclosed seven and a half square miles of enemy-held territory. The bag included four villages, three woods and, very importantly, a good deal of higher ground.

Today there is still much to be seen in and around La Boisselle. The two great craters are still there, very clearly defined. The right-hand one, the lip of which the Lincolns had seized and held is sixty yards across and forty feet deep. It is believed to be the greatest hole in the world ever caused by explosion, engineered and set off by man. Its sides are very steep and being in chalk are so slippery as to be dangerous after rain. An adventurous tourist would be very foolish to descend without a rope around his waist and a companion at the top to hold it. The sides are to a certain extent covered by turf but the steepness prevents anything more than clumps of grass from growing. At the bottom are still a few scraps of war-debris. The crater at the north side of the Bapaume Road is similar but smaller.

The 'Glory Hole' is easily found. An area of about fifty yards long and eighty yards wide, the 'Hole' has not been levelled by the villagers and the numberless shell-holes, of every calibre and from both sides, allow of no level ground at all. Every hole adjoins others, many over-lapping, and the area merits the words tortured, tangled and torn. All is now covered in a thin layer of turf but little or no digging is needed to uncover bits of steel shell, bullets, nose-caps, pieces of barbed-wire, and angle-irons.

To the left of the 'Glory Hole' and at the junction of the lesser road running down from Contalmaison and the main Albert-Bapaume road, is the War Memorial to the Tyneside Scottish and Irish, whose attack, astride the road, started from where the junction had been. The memorial is in the form of a semi-circular seat, facing westwards into the sun, within the angle made by the two roads. In front of it are a few square yards of turfed lawn, while along the back of the seat are engraved the names of the units of the two brigades taking part in the great attack.

The whole hamlet and the two roads were, of course, utterly pulverised by the bombardment prior to the 1st July and then in the next few days, while the hamlet was being captured and unsuccessfully counter-attacked, it virtually disappeared.

All was rebuilt in 1919—and the thrifty villagers, many of whom rebuilt their own houses themselves, used a large amount of the remains of trench material lying about. Many pigsties were made of trench revetting wood, fences today are of salvaged barbed-wire, scraps of 'duck-boards' are now firmly trodden down into garden paths, many bricks built into the walls were picked from the ruins and the rubble.

In the corners of several cottage gardens are little dumps of war-metal, turned up by the plough and later brought into the village by the finder. Twice a year scrap-metal merchants from Paris come up and buy all the 'finds' available, lead in particular being much sought after. For a week or two prior to the half-yearly visit it pays the farmer, his sons, and labourers to knock off farming and become metal scavengers. (In 1964 the author and his wife, helping an elderly couple in their task of metal-finding in a ploughed field by Trones Wood, about two miles inside the 1916 German front line on 1st July and captured on 16th July, filled an old basket with scraps of metal for them. After twenty minutes of admittedly back-breaking work, they had almost filled the basket which by now took two hands to lift).

By means of the July 1916 trench maps, it is possible today to pin-point very accurately the two opposing front-line trenches of 1916. Prima facie there is no trace of the trench at all, all debris has been moved, the trench and surrounding shell holes have long since been filled in and smoothed over. But if the observer goes back a couple of hundred yards or more and looks back along the line of the 1916 trench he will see unmistakably a vague white smear of chalk several yards wide. It marks where the original chalk soil was dug into and thrown up onto the darker clayey top-soil. The smear was widened by the big shell holes whence further chalk was thrown up. These smears, after the autumn ploughing, will be visible for many years yet.

It is interesting to stand exactly where the British front line trench ran, and, looking eastward and slightly up-hill, see exactly what the British soldiers saw as they climbed out of their trench on 1st July and advanced across No Man's Land.

In 1956, forty years after the battle of La Boisselle, an old soldier, paying his first return visit to the Front since 1916, walked up and across the No Man's Land to where the German trench had been. It was a raw cold November morning, with a close mist. The grey mud so well remembered was everywhere, there was not a breath of wind, there was dead silence. The old soldier was entirely carried back to 1916 by the atmosphere he so well remembered. Suddenly he heard 'Pop, pop, pop'—so like an enemy machine-gun opening up. The atmosphere of 1916 was complete. Instinctively he ducked, from habits of long ago but never forgotten. Then, feeling rather foolish, he stood erect again and looked in the direction of 'firing'. Through the mist appeared a line of about six farmers carrying guns. It was a Sunday morning and they were out shooting partridges.

Standing on the main road at La Boiselle near the northern, lesser, crater and looking due north, the remains of the village-fortress of Thiepval can be seen, a little more than two miles away. Thiepval was never rebuilt except for one house, and the Church. All the devastated tangled results of bombardments have been untouched by man and not greatly by nature. The village-battlefield is now covered by turf, bushes, stinging nettles, under-growth, saplings, a few young trees. But the results of the almost four months shelling are quite clear in the exceptional uneveness, extremely difficult to walk over.

The village is entirely overshadowed by the 'Memorial to the Missing on the Somme'. This gigantic edifice, designed by Sir Edward Lutyens, stands a little to the west of Thiepval, on the highest point of the ridge and just about where the German front-line trench ran. It carries the names of fifty-five thousand officers and men who were missing between 1st July, and the end of October 1916. It can be seen from all over the Somme battlefield, making a superb landmark for many miles around. Coming in the train from Amiens, it first comes into view eight miles away.

Between Thiepval and La Boiselle, and just inside the enemy's line on 1st July, lies the village of Ovillers—whence came so much of the enfilading fire that decimated the 20th Northumberland Fusiliers on 1st July. To the battalion's right the enemy front-line trench, bent back sharply to conform to the ground, was on higher ground. It had a superb view over the shallow valley up which the Fusiliers tried to advance, and the battalion thus enfiladed on both flanks only eight hundred yards apart can be seen to have been in a cruel trap. There is not an inch of cover, and perhaps the greatest surprise to be felt during the whole visit to the battlefield of La Boiselle is the fact that quite a few men of the 20th Northumberland Fusiliers were not hit in the double enfilading fire through which they passed and did in fact reach the German front line.

Passchendaele

31st July, 1917

FROM after the end of the Second Battle of Ypres in May 1915, all major operations on the Western Front had been British or French offensives. Loos, Somme, Ancre, the German retreat to the Hindenburg Line, Arras, Messines had all in greater or lesser degree pushed the Germans back from their forward positions, causing considerable casualties. Lessons in the technique of attack had been learnt.

In the British Army a sense of aggression and possession of the initiative was increasing. Growing numbers, both of men and of formed divisions, in themselves suggested attack. By the autumn of 1917 there were 3,000,000 British soldiers on the Western Front, trained, experienced, and of good morale.

During the first half of 1917, the German U-boat campaign against shipping around the British Isles had become extremely effective and was causing great hardship in the U.K. (800,000 tons of British shipping were sunk in April alone). The need to deny the enemy the use of the ports of Dunkirk, Ostend, Zeebrugge, from which so many German submarines operated was becoming acute. Obviously a great offensive from around Ypres would, if directed north-eastward, close these ports and ease the food situation in Great Britain. The idea took shape in the minds of the Cabinet in London and that of Sir Douglas Haig in France.

The need for an offensive so far north was greatly enhanced by the ghastly failure of the latest French offensive, under General Nivelle in April. Nivelle had replaced Joffre as the French Commander-in-Chief and a much younger man was expected to bring new life and new tactics into the French Army. He promised great things and the belief of the French *poilu* in their new young 'military messiah' was great. All felt that with new methods, a new leader and a new offensive spirit, their famed élan could at last find an opening. Perhaps the new attack would open the door into

Germany. Perhaps the end of the war was not far off, enthusiasm was high.

The attack on a seven-mile frontage with twenty divisions was a fearful failure. A copy of the orders for the attack had been circulated to front-line officers as low as company commanders. Inevitably a raid must lead to the capture of one copy somewhere and the one the Germans got merely confirmed their observation of the ground and what preparations for a French attack were being made in front of them. They now knew for certain where, when, how and by how many divisions they would be attacked.

In twenty-four hours Nivelle's twenty divisions had lost 120,000 men, yet had only nibbled into the enemy position. Along the main front 600 yards only had been gained. The soldiers had been told it would be six miles.

Their sweeping enthusiasm and confidence evaporated in twenty-four hours. In their place, almost over-night, there appeared depression, defeatism, more than apathy—resentment deep and bitter.

Resentment gave way to contempt for, and resistance to, authority. A fortnight later a division out at rest refused to do normal parades or duties. It was sent back into the trenches and there unexpectedly decimated in action. Revolt spread and mutiny, with the murder of a few officers, gripped fifty-four divisions—over 20,000 men deserted.

The immediate removal of Nivelle and his replacement by Pétain, the victor of Verdun, only just averted a complete collapse. Pétain visited many divisions, giving talks which, with his cold, efficient 'unflappable' manner, greatly impressed them, and gradually won them back into discipline and patriotism, though there was no possibility of active operations by the French for a long time. It was felt that not only must all pressure be taken off the French (for tactical reasons) by an offensive elsewhere, as had been necessary at Verdun the previous year, but also that a great moral victory somewhere else would persuade the French troops to go on trying, to give them fresh hope, to show that victory was possible.

The news of this serious situation reached Haig early in May, although miraculously it was kept from the knowledge of the B.E.F. Clearly an offensive as far away as possible from the mutinous French Fifth Army in Champagne was highly desirable, in order to distract the strength of the enemy from its new and tempting target. Strategically and tactically, Ypres, far to the north, was indicated.

But was the area for the new British offensive the best one? Certainly it would, it was hoped, deny the three French and Belgian ports to the German U-boats, and would attract the enemy from the danger spot. But it was known that this part of Europe, only a few square miles, had the heaviest average annual rainfall of anywhere on the Continent. It was also known that from the beginning of August continuous rain might be expected—for three months. It would start with the regulariy of the Indian south-west monsoon, whose annual advent can be gauged to within a week or ten days. What were the alternative areas?

A continuation of the Somme battle when the summer came was, prima facie, attractive. Its long, rolling downs were suitable for tanks, maybe even cavalry. But in front lay the Hindenburg Line, behind which the enemy had deliberately retreated and there barricaded himself in. Additionally, all lines of supply must pass over the devastated battlefield of 1916—whose roads were still meagre. Its railways had not yet been relaid.

Out beyond Arras lay the beginnings of the heavily built-up industrial district of North-East France. It extended eastward for twenty miles, and north-east for forty miles, and included the city of Lille. All built-up areas are avoided by soldiers as fighting areas, whenever and wherever possible.

Farther north the industrial area of Loos, La Bassée and Armentières was already part of the line, and there the army was already bogged down among coal-mines, slag heaps, canals and small towns. Lille was still in front.

Far away on the right of the B.E.F.'s area lay the Somme valley, low-lying and criss-crossed with a mass of small streams and canals, each one an obstacle. (During the retreat to the Hindenburg Line in March 1917, the 48th Divisional Engineers had to build six temporary bridges over these waterways before it could occupy Peronne.)

All these areas for an offensive thus had a sound tactical objection to them, each different. But all had one common disadvantage. Success would not release the three channel ports from the U-boats. Ypres was decided upon.

Until July 1917, the greatest battle in history had been the Battle of the Somme. On its opening day, the famous '1st July' 1916, thirteen British divisions had attacked the strongly fortified German positions on a sixteen-mile frontage. The battle was to last four months.

On 31st July 1917 a similar great battle was to start, the battle for Passchendaele, the 3rd Battle of Ypres. On its opening day again thirteen divisions advanced on a fifteen-mile frontage. Again the battle would last three and a half months. Here the similarity between the two great opening days ceases.

On the Somme on the 1st July, only four and a half divisions succeeded in penetrating the enemy front line and remaining on captured ground behind it. Eight and a half divisions were utterly repulsed and were back in their own front line in the evening. 57,000 total casualties were suffered.

At Passchendaele all the attacking divisions penetrated the enemy front line defences and remained therein. In several cases they were twelve hundred yards inside his lines. The 8th Division penetrated for over a mile, and remained in their position. 20,000 casualties were suffered.

Another dissimilarity between the two great battles was the weather. On the Somme for the first six weeks, there was hot, dry weather with its inevitable accompaniment of flies, dust, and revolting smells in the smashed trenches. At Passchendaele rain started to fall on the already heavy, muddy ground twelve hours after the attack started. There were no flies or dust but in their place was mud such as man had never seen before.

The plan was not complicated. On the right of the attack, and south of Ypres, three corps of Plumer's Second Army were to push on from the Messines Ridge captured six weeks previously and to capture a strongly built, and held, German defensive position a mile inside their lines. It was intended to give the enemy the impression that Lille was an objective and so contain some of his reserves to the south. In fact it was little more than a feint attack, certainly only a holding attack.

The main assault, from around Ypres itself, was to be carried out by Gough's Fifth Army consisting of four corps of ten divisions. Its immediate task was to secure the higher ground to the north-east of the town, about six miles out. From there it would move almost due north and threaten from the rear the three small channel ports—the U-boat bases.

Among the ten divisions were some famous names. On the

extreme left was the Guards Division, whose late commander, the Earl of Cavan, was now the Corps Commander. He was later to be Commander-in-Chief in Italy and finally C.I.G.S. The Division had been formed two years previously by assembling all the Guards battalions then serving in France in various divisions. It was still two short of the required twelve and two entirely new battalions, 4th Grenadiers and 2nd Irish, were raised in France by transfers from existing Guards battalions and the use of quite a number of picked officers and men from the ordinary line regiments. The Division never lost the standards of the Guards, and its discipline, training and dedication to duty made it, in the eyes of German soldiers, the most respected division in the B.E.F.

On the 31st July it advanced to and captured, not only its final objective, a mile and a half inside the enemy lines, but reached and held a position another quarter of a mile on. It suffered only 1,200 casualties from all causes among all ranks.

The next division but one on its right was the famous 51st Division. All kilted, all from the Highlands, it was, by 1917, perhaps the best not only among the Territorial divisions in France, but in the whole Army. Very strong in numbers before mobilization, it went to France in May 1915. At Loos, in September 1915, it started its prestige-earning career. Success and enhanced reputation at the Somme (twice) and Arras, had built up for it such a reputation for skill and dash that the Germans feared it perhaps more than any other division, indeed, as much as the Guards. It was the last Territorial division to go to France in 1915 and thus had a full eight months' training in England before embarkation, a fact that must partly explain its excellence. Re-formed in 1920 its spirit lived on between the wars, still largely with the original units of 1914. From 1939 it was always in the news. Cut to bits, surrounded and made prisoner (including its G.O.C.) at St Valéry in June 1940, it was yet again re-formed, and fought at El Alamein, Italy, D-Day and it was the first division to cross the Rhine. It existed until the break-up of the Territorials in 1967. It, too, captured all the objectives set for it on the 31st July and on the left advanced to, and remained in, an enemy minor trench 400 yards farther on.

Next was the 39th Division whose fortunes on the 1st July will be followed in more detail later.

Then came the renowned 55th West Lancashire Territorial Division, the Red Rose Division. With a brigade and a half of King's

Liverpools, two King's Own, two Loyals, and two South Lancs battalions, it was a typical north-country division.

In north-west England the Volunteer, later Territorial, 'Movement' had always been strong, popular, well-supported and intensely local. With its next-door neighbour in Lancashire, the 42nd East Lancashire Division, it was able to keep up to full strength comfortably in peace time, and most battalions had a waiting list not only of officers but for the men in the ranks. As a result the Regular Adjutants could be selective in accepting recruits, and the standard of these Lancashire units was very high. Attendance at drills, parades, and annual camp showed few men on leave because of their business. Most knew that non-attendance might easily result in the next man on the waiting list taking their place.

A story runs in the 7th Manchesters, in the 42nd Division, that in 1913 a battalion parade was held on a Sunday afternoon for a Memorial Service in the local church, in memory of the Regular soldiers of the Manchester Regiment killed at Ladysmith in the Boer War. Of a full strength of 650 men only 450 turned up. The Colonel was so furious that he refused to march such a paltry body through the streets of Manchester, and ordered the second-in-command to take the parade. On the 31st July the 55th Division advanced a mile and a quarter and captured over 600 prisoners.

Next came the 15th Highland (Kitchener's Army) Division. One of the best of the early Kitchener's Army divisions, it had been put into the battle of Loos in September 1915—together with its sister Highland Division, the 9th. There both had suffered terrible casualties, largely on account of the inexperience of junior officers and men. 6,600 men of the 15th were killed or severely wounded. The Division and the battalions were not old enough to take the shock of these heavy casualties and morale sank badly. For almost two years this division remained not of the best, until, on the 31st July, it refound itself. On this day it captured its first two objectives, advanced a mile and a quarter, and played its part as well as any of the divisions that day.

The 8th Division was a Regular division made up from individual Regular units brought home in August 1914 from Malta, Egypt, South Africa and the West Indies. It was good—no more—and had taken part in most of the minor engagements through the two years in France until the battle of the Somme. Here on the opening day,

14. A photograph taken in 1962 showing the trench dug and held by the Lancashire Fusiliers in the vineyard at Krithia.

15. La Boisselle. The 'Glory Hole' in 1970.

16. La Boisselle. The inside of the great crater as it is today.

17. Passchendaele. A view of Mousetrap Farm taken in 1970.

18. One winter's ploughing on the Somme in 1960.

the 1st July, it had a terrible task. It had to attack across 600 yards with no cover or features of any sort, and to find, half-way across, enfilade fire coming into both its flanks from the enemy trenches which on both sides receded from the general line to conform to the ground. The battalions walked not into a trap (they could see the enemy trenches bent back) but into a square three sides of which were firing at them. The division lost over 5,000 officers and men, and was never the same again.

On the 31st July, it fared better. Advancing on a 1,200-yard front-age, it reached the first objective a mile and a half inside the Ger-man lines, taking over 600 prisoners. 3,000 men became casualties, however, including two C.O.'s killed, and six wounded.

Other divisions taking part in the 5th Army attack were the 38th, 30th, 24th—while in the 2nd Army in its holding attack on the right were the 41st, 19th, 37th, 3rd Australian and the new Zealand Divisions. All played their part well, all were effective—none failed. Their omission from this chapter is solely due to the fact that, com-pared with the divisions that have been mentioned, they lacked notoriety, personality, reputation—but not ability.

Mention must be made, however, of the 18th (Kitchener's Army) Division. It did not 'go over the top' at zero hour on the 31st July, being in close support of the 30th Division. During the morning, however, when the 30th were in trouble it was put through them and directed on to the third objective. But as it advanced it found that the left brigade of the 30th had now got forward again. Con-sequently the two leading brigades of the 18th became mixed up with the reserve brigade of the 30th. But worse was to follow. The 18th had been told that Glencorse Wood had been captured and a battalion of the Royal Berks went gaily forward to gain its shelter. But suddenly intense machine-gun fire opened on the battalion from three sides. Immediately the two following battalions had to fan out to search all features in front and on either flank. Doubtless the 30th had unknowingly passed them by. Chaos reigned.

The excellent quality and training of the 18th Division now showed itself and a broad convex line—to include Glencorse Wood —was secured and consolidated, to be held permanently. It was a great feat of arms that this division, barely under fire and expecting an easy passage for a while, should so suddenly and effectively deal with a totally unexpected and dangerous situation.

The 18th was perhaps the best of all the thirty Kitchener's Army divisions. It consisted entirely of early Kitchener battalions raised in the Home Counties and East Anglia. With one exception all its original units remained with the Division throughout the war, and that exception was the introduction of a neighbouring Bedfordshire battalion in place of a Royal Fusilier unit. On the 1st July 1916, the 18th was one of the only four divisions that captured any considerable portion of the enemy front line and rearward areas. On that day, attacking on a one-mile front, it advanced one and a quarter miles at its deepest penetration and captured almost 700 prisoners and some one and a quarter square miles of enemy-held ground, trenches, redoubts and strong-points.

It suffered 3,700 casualties on the 1st July, exactly one-quarter of its total for the whole war. A fortnight later it captured Trones Wood, and two months after that completed the capture of Thiepval, the strongest fortified village in the whole Somme battlefield and which had held out against attack by seven divisions in the nine weeks since the 1st July.

The fortunes of the 39th Division to be now followed are of interest. They were very ordinary, successful, and entirely typical of all the divisions that day.

The Division was one of the later Kitchener divisions, many of the units not being formed until early 1915. It did not arrive in France until March 1916.

It was mostly a South-of-England division and had three battalions of Royal Sussex, one Hampshire, one 60th and one Rifle Brigade. Its third brigade had been transferred to another division in 1916—and in its place came a brigade of the Cheshire Regiment, and three territorial battalions, the Black Watch, and the Cambridgeshire and Hertfordshire Regiments—a mixed bag.

Generally speaking the men were not in the first flush of their youth nor had they the glamour or enthusiasm of the early Kitchener's Army enlistments. Nevertheless, it was a good steady division and in the three territorial battalions of the newly joined brigade, the men were of very good quality.

On arrival in France it had spent from March 1916 until November holding the line around Beaumont Hamel, Hebuterne and Gommecourt. It took no part in the battle of the Somme, but played a satisfactory part in the battle of the Ancre in November 1916.

During the first six months of 1917 it was a 'line-holding' division, either being in the trenches—'Peace Time Trenches'—or out at rest. It gained good 'know-how' of active service conditions but not much battle experience.

In mid-June 1917 the division was put into the line to the north-east of Ypres—where it held a line of trenches 1,500 yards long. Its right rested on the Ypres—Wieltje—Poelcappelle Road. On its left was the famous 51st Highland Division and both divisions were periodically relieved by the two other divisions in the XVIII Corps, the 11th and the 48th. The 39th and 51st were to be the assaulting divisions on the 31st July.

The British line from which the 39th Division was to attack was about half-way down an almost imperceptible slope, at the top of which was Hill Top Farm. It certainly was on a hill-top, being on ground perhaps seven feet higher than any other ground in the vicinity. A farm it was not, the buildings having long since been reduced to rubble. Being on a slight rise, and therefore its ground-floor never water-logged, cellars had been inserted by the original builder, and later much extended by the R.E. These cellars provided extensive shelter for brigade and battalion headquarters. It was about 600 yards back from the front line.

At the bottom of the 'slope' ran a good cart-track along and just in front of the line of the British front trenches, Admiral's Road. No-man's-land was about three hundred yards wide and where the ground began to 'rise' again, the German front line had been sited.

On the German side of the lines were a number of farms and small, clearly defined woods. One, Mousetrap Farm, was an extensive homestead, with several barns, farm-implement sheds, and cattle-stalls. It stood up clearly, and although completely in ruins, was an obvious objective for a battalion to assault.

The 39th Division was to advance down the slight but lengthy slope, cross Admiral's Road running through no-man's-land, parallel to the two front lines, and then ascend the slope to Mousetrap Farm, passing over the German front line half-way up the slope. Passing the farm, it was to reach, capture and hold the large village of St. Julien, nearly two miles beyond the German front line.

The preparatory bombardment, lasting several weeks and followed by the preliminary bombardment, the greatest ever made, had entirely pulverised the enemy front and support lines, Mousetrap Farm, and to its left Kultur Farm. The leading infantry battalions of 39th Division, the Royal Sussex and the Hertfordshires on the right, and the Sherwood Foresters with the Rifle Brigade on the left, had little difficulty in crossing the road, the enemy's front lines, and then in reaching Mousetrap and Kultur Farms, both of which fell easily.

St. Julien lay in low ground, and from the British line, and its highest point, Hill Top Farm, only the tip of the village church could be seen. It was believed that as the highish ground around Mousetrap Farm was captured, the enemy from the houses in St. Julien would have a superb view of any further advance from the Farm. Being out of sight from anywhere except the Farm the Germans would be well covered and able to do great execution amongst the advancing British infantry. The only opposition against them would be the unobserved British artillery fire.

To neutralise partly this German advantage, the 145th Machine Gun Company from the 48th Division, was attached to the right brigade of the 39th Division in its advance to Mousetrap Farm. Here from just short of the higher ground to the left of the farm, it was to maintain for three hours continuous permanent fire of never less than one of its sections on to St. Julien. It was hoped that an unceasing stream of machine-gun bullets, from only 1,600 yards away and from an unseen battery, would seriously impede and probably knock off-balance the enemy defensive fire against further British advances from Mousetrap Farm.

The amount of ammunition required for this extremely heavy fire programme was far in advance of that usually carried into action. The number of filled belt-boxes accordingly was trebled and four infantrymen from the 48th Division were attached to each gun team as carriers of these additional boxes. This machine-gun company, in which the author was a subaltern, spent the night in the cellars of Hill Top Farm, and ten minutes after zero at 3.50 a.m. followed the reserve companies of the Hertfordshires up the steps, down the slope, and across Admiral's Road. The company suffered its first casualty before leaving the cellar. One of the infantrymen attached for carrying the belt-boxes, trying to move through the very congested cellar-passage, with his load and full personal equipment and rifle, unable to stand upright, had a heart attack and died immediately, his load of boxes having to be redistributed.

There was little opposition except unaimed 'overs' from Mouse-trap Farm directed against the forward companies. The Hertford-shires had comfortably captured the Farm with the Royal Sussex off to their left in and around Kultur Farm. Between the two the so-called higher ground flattened out and the leading companies of both battalions had apparently nothing in front of them.

The 145 M.G. Company found a piece of ground most suitable for its task and got the four sections, each of four guns, into the bigger shell-holes and were quickly able to open fire. All range tables, angles of fire and deflection, compass-bearings etc. had been worked out beforehand, and St. Julien, the tip of whose church could just be seen, was now receiving the constant stream of bullets ordered.

The reserve battalions, the Black Watch and Cambridgeshires passed through the machine-gun positions and the Hertfordshires, and moved on to St. Julien, which fell. This exultant brigade, flushed with success, then did a foolish thing. It had been ordered to advance and capture the village only and to go no farther, the wire behind it not having yet been cut. However, in its enthusiasm it did go on and of course was held up by the uncut wire, suffering heavily. It had to come back, but at least the 39th Division was on its final objective for the day.

When its three hours of constant fire was over, the 145 Company hoped to be recalled. It had received quite a lot of shellfire, as doubtless it had been spotted by a German O.P. in the St. Julien church spire, although few casualties were suffered. It felt its task was done. However, it was ordered to remain, presumably to resist any big counter-attack, and stayed in its shell-holes with nothing to do. Fire could not be opened again for fear of hitting the Cambridgeshires in St. Julien, and there were no targets to be seen. After the excitement of the morning, the afternoon became very dull. Then the rain came.

The discomforts of the troops in the forward areas were severe but were slightly ameliorated by the many captured 'pillboxes' behind the German original front and support lines and now occupied by the British soldiers. About forty yards in circumference, immensely strong and shell-proof, they provided cover from fire and, almost as important to the men, cover from the weather.

A large one near by accommodated the M.G. Company—which it shared with battalion headquarters of the Hertfordshires, now in reserve and preparing a defensive line to meet the expected counter-attack. The sentries on the guns outside spent a wretched night. Inside the pillbox there was enough warmth, light, dryness (and smell) for everyone. Any German shell that might arrive from the east and explode near the entrance of the pillbox would, by its blast, usually blow out the candles and there would be much cursing while matches were sought.

The 39th stayed in the line until the 6th August, when it was relieved by its partner, the 48th Division. The 145 M.G. Company remained in the line until the relief by the 48th when it had the consolation of being with the reserve brigade.

On the whole, the first day's advance along the whole front to be attacked must be counted as a success. Although results were not as had been hoped for, nevertheless the sweeping advance all along the line was at striking variance with the first day's results on the 1st July 1916, on the Somme. The British Staffs were by now very experienced. Artillery barrages were now highly scientific. Aerial observation—on the first day certainly—was more used. Tactical employment of tanks had been studied and practised behind the lines, and they were well handled on the 31st July. The casualties occasioned on the Somme had been replaced and the men in question had now been in their units for nine weeks, settling down. All these factors explain why twelve divisions out of thirteen successfully captured, and in most cases passed on beyond, the enemy front line. The average advance was a mile and a half—some sixteen square miles of enemy-held ground was captured on the opening day. 6,000 prisoners, including 130 officers, were taken, together with twenty-five field guns. In addition the enemy's observation posts on the Gheluvelt plateau and along the ridge between Bellewaarde and Pilckem were captured. Nine enemy divisions were badly mauled and had to be replaced within a few days. The quick availability of these new divisions implies that they were in close support. They and the men they relieved would not be available to go south and attack the French, still slowly recovering from the mutiny of May.

After further massive bombardments, refilling with ammunition and stores, and the relief of two or three divisions, the Army could have attacked again after a few days and secured an even greater success. But this possibility of achieving another great advance and success was entirely ruled out by one factor—rain.

In the evening of the 31st it started, and rained all night and all the next day—and for several days and nights. In six hours the whole area became a bog—largely caused by the complete breaking-up of the ground by the heavy and incessant shellfire of several days. All ditches and field drains had been smashed or filled with debris. The water could not get away, shell-holes filled with water and twenty-four hours after zero on the 31st, both sides could barely move. Life for the German troops must have been as acutely uncomfortable as for the British, but at least they knew that they could not be attacked, no infantrymen, and certainly no tanks, could move except to climb into or over shell-holes, holding on to and frequently slithering down into dirty, muddy, soon to become smelly, water.

Never have the elements so drastically affected military operations as did the rain at Passchendaele on the 31st July. It prevented a minor turn in history, certainly it prevented a great turning-point in the 1914–1918 War.

During the War and on after 1918 Ypres bore and still bears a notoriety comparable with Mons and Verdun. It became a Mecca for visitors immediately after the Armistice of 1918, and still has a considerable tourist trade. Having been so extensively damaged it was entirely rebuilt and is today a bright, smiling, prosperous town. All the streets, buildings, drains, electricity, even the famous Cloth Hall and Cathedral are new, and the people seem to have kept up with the 20th Century, and are far more sophisticated and up-to-date than those in similar towns in the district like Haze-brouck, Poperinghe, or Armentières. Most of the shopkeepers, hoteliers, and taxi-drivers speak English, and it is obviously a semi-English town, having a record of fifty years of countless visitors.

Visits to the Salient could hardly be easier. There are several adequate two-star hotels in Ypres and to hire a taxi from the *place* in the centre of the town will invariably result in finding a driver who not only knows the whole area very well but whose English is 80 per cent perfect. His job of being a taxi-driver-guide has become a profession handed down from father to son. All the visitor has to do is to give his driver a list of half a dozen names of woods, or villages, which he wishes to visit, and he will quickly start on a circular tour adequately, interestingly, and correctly described by his chauffeur, who probably drives this, or a very similar tour, seven days a week from April to October.

Out in the Salient, Hill Top Farm, Admiral's Road and Mouse-trap Farm, the starting point and steps on the advance for 39th Division, are easily found. Hill Top Farm was completely rebuilt on

the same plan and it is again a large and imposing cluster of buildings. The cellars, though not in use, are still in existence. Admiral's
Road was, in July 1971, barely recognisable on account of its line
through 'No-Man's-Land' and its unceasing reception of 'overs'
and 'unders' from both British and German guns. Today it is re-
made on the same line and is a good, well-made second class road
with ditches on both sides. Mousetrap Farm, which was so pulverised before 31st July, had several natural ponds on two of its
sides. The shelling broke these up, and as a result the area around
the farm was always damp and boggy, even before the rain came.
After the rain started the farm site became almost impassable, and
in 1919 the new Mousetrap Farm was built two hundred yards
further to the south, on slightly higher ground. Today it is a large
enclosure with farm house, barns, vehicle sheds, cattle stalls (and
an enormous wire cage, eight feet square, in which a ferocious
Alsatian dog is kept. He barks loudly, angrily and frighteningly at
any movement, except that of the farmer or his wife. He is never
allowed out for excercise, his temper has been irretrievably ruined
and yet he seems to be in very good condition). In the farm yard is
the usual dump of broken rifles, tin helmets, and fragments, big and
small, of exploded shells (and some unexploded) still being turned
up by the plough and brought in for the periodic collection by a
Paris firm whose business makes it worth while to salvage and use
this metal. Walking along the ridge to the site of the original farmstead, its foundations can be traced. From its forward edge its perfect position as an observation post is apparent, as is also the glaring
aiming mark it made for British artillery. During a good summer
recently and after a rainless fortnight the ground was still heavy
and the fields still water-logged, although the farm is now some
distance from the shattered ponds. Life here today in this damp area,
is not very comfortable in the best weather, and in the winter must
be cold and raw in the extreme.

One of the most 'unhealthy' spots in the Salient, and there were
many, was 'Hell-fire Corner' where the Zillebeke-Potijze road met
the Ypres-Menin road, and where a light railway track also crossed
the road. Hereabouts the ground is largely pasture, and of course
all debris has been overgrown by grass and sucked in to the Salient
soil as well. Yet this pasture seems suspiciously and needlessly
uneven—and the many indentations around the cross-roads are
silent witnesses that the shell holes are still there and that many

years must have passed before Nature finally levelled them out. In 1968 an empty cartridge case, flattened almost beyond recognition, was picked up beside the little railway track, having survived there for fifty years. It was from near this cross-roads that the reserve brigade of the 8th Division advanced on 31st July.

A little further down the Menin Road, Maple Avenue runs off to the right, specially planted to lead to Maple Copse, where the great Canadian cemetery lies. Just beyond the cemetery is preserved a small area about 100 yards by 50 yards, much grown over by young trees. Within the enclosure is the German front line exactly as it was prior to 31st July, 1917. Somehow it escaped the obliteration of the following years. The trenches with softening outlines are quite clear. The siting and fields of fire show that they are genuine and professional, while the debris and relics in the undergrowth are clearly 'right'. If a few bigger relics are negligently and rather obviously placed to catch the visitor's eye and unfortunately suggesting a slight air of commercialism, their presence is a small price to pay for being carried back fifty years. At the entrance to this preservation area are two large huts housing a good collection of battlefield relics. The curator-caretaker-guide is proud of his collection, and of his English.

Apart from the killed and wounded in the Salient during the four years, some fifty thousand officers and men were missing. The Belgian Government, like the French at Thiepval on the Somme, gave an area for a memorial of these men and it has been incorporated with the famous rebuilt Menin Gate, where the Menin Road passes through the ramparts and out over the moat to the south-east. About forty yards long, the Memorial straddles the main road with a long, continuous arch. Off both sides ceremonial entrances lead up on to the top of the ramparts, and around these two entrances, as well as on the walls of the main arch itself, are inscribed the names of the missing. At the outer end of the arch and over what must have been the drawbridge, many years ago, sits a lion, its head erect, its great paws well to the front, its gaze fixed out across the Salient.

Although the Ypres-Menin Road, leading on to Courtrai and Brussels, is a busy thoroughfare every night an impressive ceremony takes place here. At 8.58 p.m. two gendarmes appear, one at each end of the long arch. They face inward and, extending an arm, hold up all traffic behind them. Carrying silver bugles two men wearing mackintoshes and berets with a silver badge of the Ypres Fire

Brigade appear from among the passers-by and take post in the middle of the now empty roadway. All traffic movement and noise stops, silence is everywhere. At nine o'clock the two buglers sound 'Last Post'. Everyone is silent, all men standing to attention with hats off, and as the notes die away the silence is almost audible. The buglers, then the gendarmes, break off and mingle with the spectators. Traffic flows again. Life goes on.

Facts, Figures and Trends

FROM a study of the fifteen battles described in this book, together with those from its companion—*Famous Engagements* Volume I—several facts, figures and trends emerge that are not without interest.

Firstly, so many battles in the world's history have been fought in four very clearly defined areas. North-east France and south-west Belgium, the 'Cock-pit of Europe', includes within the quadrilateral of Calais, Abbeville, Sedan, and Ostend, the names of Crécy, Agincourt, Tournai, Ramillies, Oudenarde, Malplaquet, Quatre Bras, Waterloo, Sedan, Mons, Le Cateau, Ypres, Arras, Somme, Passchendaele, Dunkirk, covering eight wars. Within sixty miles of Helpmakaar in Natal lie the battlefields of three wars—Isandhlwana, Rorke's Drift, Ulundi, Ingogo, Laing's Nek, Majuba, Talana Hill, Elandslaagte, Colenso, Caesar's Camp, Spion Kop, Vaal Krantz and Railway Hill. In Northern Italy are Pavia, Castiglione, Vittorio Veneto, Rivoli, Lodi, Marengo, Lonato, Solferinto, Magenta, Asiago, Capporetto, all within two hundred and forty miles. Challons, Verdun, Valmy, Mars-la-Tour, Gravelotte, St. Privat, Chateau Thierry, Woerth and Spicheren, about one hundred and thirty miles east of Paris, form another group.

Not all these actions were astride a major line of invasion whereon a defender attempted to halt an aggressor. Only Crecy, Agincourt and Dunkirk are alike where an army, trying to escape to the coast for re-embarkation, had to fight its way through. Sedan, Waterloo, Dunkirk and Verdun were desperate defensive actions, with so much depending on the result, yet totally disimilar in every other way.

Mons, Le Cateau, Ypres and Quatre Bras were again desperate defensive actions yet less strategically important. Colenso, Magersfontein, Spion Kop, Vaal Krantz all bear the same imprint of bad generalship. In each the enemy was attacked and the British heavily

185

repulsed, the loss being due to faulty tactics and in the plan. In each the enemy was good but no more.

Ramilies, Oudenarde, Malplaquet, were straight-forward attacks against a well-found enemy who not only expected attack but welcomed it.

All these famous engagements are part of history, yet each differs from the other.

Many battlefields are found in these four areas because these areas lie near frontiers, either physical or political, of two neighbouring but differing antagonistic races or nations. Differences in blood and national characteristics and outlook breed dislike, suspicion, fear. Conflicts between them seem to have been inevitable through history on aesthetic as well as on material grounds. France and Prussia, France and England, England and Germany, Italy and Austria, British and Dutch Boers, have all in the past experienced this apathy, and a common frontier of sea or river or mountain as a barrier to invasion, has not always been the bone of contention.

Indeed the differing personalities of either side has as often been the *casus belli* as the material dispute.

Another trend that emerges is that British generalship in the past nine hundred years has passed through three distinct phases. There was firstly a steady rise in leadership, command, and tactical skill from 1066 until Waterloo. Harold's choice of his defensive position at Battle was excellent though he made a mistake in leaving it to go forward before he was certain that William's army was wavering. As a result he was caught in the open, charged by cavalry and, in his turn beaten. Edward III's position at Crecy is the finest in all the mediaeval defensive battles, while the plan for Capitan de Buch's ride round the left flank of the French army at Poitiers, to co-ordinate with the Black Prince's advance in the centre, was a masterpiece. Henry V's skill at Agincourt in choosing a position where he was protected by thick woods on each flank—is very apparent. Marlborough's skill and deception at Ramillies in bringing the unsuccessful Orkney from his right flank to the left centre and victory stamp him the master tactician, while his handling at Malplaquet and Blenheim was masterly. Wellington's position and situation at Waterloo was very similar to that of Harold at Hastings. Wellington, however, more experienced and much more skilled, held his hand until he could see that the attack of the Old Guard up the ridge had been halted by the flanking fire of the

Oxford and Bucks Light Infantry. Realising that it was probably the last effort of the French and that momentarily they were at his mercy, he advanced to victory. In the Peninsula both his strategy and tactics were successful.

After Waterloo, the standard goes down for ninety-nine years. In the Crimean War Raglan, with his head-on attack across the Alma and then up the steeply-stepped hill in front was lucky in that the Russians ran. Had they been of better quality the British and French must have been repulsed and the Alma would have been a defeat. His own position at Balaclava, with his staff, on high ground six hundred feet above the valley from where he could see the whole battle taking place below him as if from the dress circle at the theatre, rendered him completely out of touch with his subordinate generals. His only communications were mounted Staff Officers, who could only ride very slowly picking their way down the cliff front. They took far too long, and frequently a situation had entirely changed by the time a message dealing with it had been delivered. Lord Cardigan's famous charge of the Light Brigade at Balaclava against well-sited enemy guns, and down a valley between two lines of both infantry and guns only twelve hundred yards apart could hardly have been more gallant or more foolish or impractical.

Colley's performance at Majuba, though well-intentioned, was quite absurd, while Buller at Colenso, Methuen's plan for Magersfontein, and Warren at Spion Kop all touch rock bottom in fatuous ineptitude.

Colonel Long who led his twelve guns across the open Colenso in front of the infantry he was supposed to support was badly wounded when the Boers opened fire. Would he have been retained as C.R.A. had he not been a casualty? By the standards and outlook of those days it seemed probable that he would.

In 1914 a slow and slight upward curve in ability appears. Sir John French was adequate for a while, Smith-Dorrien and Plumer were good, while Allenby was excellent. Haig, the 'Master of the Field', commanded 3,000,000 men in France in 1917, led the army with its 'Backs to the Wall' in March 1918—and finally to victory in November 1918. He was Commander-in-Chief for nearly three years and might well have gone down in history as one of the great British generals had his professional reputation not been scarred by his policy at Passchendaele in 1917.

At the end of the Second World War, Great Britain had been

served by Wavell, perhaps our greatest 'thinking' soldier in this century, Brooke, the greatest C.I.G.S. in our history, Alexander, who touched success though not necessarily victory wherever he went, and Montgomery, the pure professional. These four restored the prestige of their profession to the high level of the Black Prince, Marlborough and Wellington.

One curious little feature appears in many British battles in the 19th century. After the Crimea and until 1914 all the campaigns were colonial and the engagements therein so frequently were fought by conglomerate forces made up of companies from different regiments or by incomplete units. At Majuba the assault was made by two companies of Northamptons, two from 60th Rifles and three from the Gordons. Only five out of the eight companies of the Devons took part in the charge at Wagon Hill; Ingogo was fought by five companies of the 60th Rifles, with four Horse Artillery guns under command, a curious combination. Only six companies of the Royal Lancasters climbed Spion Kop. The 2nd Battalion of the South Wales Borderers left one company behind in the camp at Isandhlwana, which was alread garrisoned by the other battalion of the Regiment.

How were these odd groups of companies commanded? Did the C.O. with his adjutant take them leaving the 2nd-in-Command with the remainder? If so, did the latter have some command organisation, any signal communications, any Quarter-Masters Department? What was the rank of the officer of the Northamptons who commanded their four companies at Laing's Nek and how did he organise his command? Was he the senior of the four company commanders, was he the Second-in-Command? If the C.O. led them, who commanded, and where, the other four companies? Would it not have been better at Majuba for one battalion at full strength to have been used? It would have been roughly equal in numbers to the three scratch-sub-units that did go up and would have had all the advantages of a 'going-concern'.

The occasions on which the commander of an independent operation has been killed in action are naturally rare. In the eight hundred years from 1066 to 1881 only four such soldiers had fallen in action, Harold, Richard III, Sir John Moore and Nicholson at the Kashmir Gate. In the next nineteen years Colley at Majuba, Penn-Symons at Talana Hill, Wauchope at Magersfontein, and Woodgate at Spion Kop—all major generals—fell in action in the front line. It would have been better—certainly more practical—if Colley had sent one battalion under its own C.O. up Majuba, instead of commanding the small scratch force himself. Had Wauchope at Magersfontein been in a reasonable position in rear of his Brigade when the Boers opened fire, might have taken some tactical action to outflank the enemy position or at least been able to extricate more of his men. Woodgate, had he not been the nearest man in his 'red hat' to the enemy might have survived and so obviated the appalling muddle on Spion Kop. Penn-Symons at Talana Hill can only be regarded as culpable in riding on his horse through the plantation up to the front line, and, there dismounting, using his field glasses, in general's kit, in full view of the most skilful marksmen in the world. Although technically Penn-Symons, Wauchope and Woodgate had a Commander-in-Chief behind them, they were in supreme command on the spot. Penn-Symons's chief, Sir George White, was forty miles away in Ladysmith, Sir Charles Warren, Woodgate's superior officer, was not only fifteen hundred feet below the battle but made no effort to come up, assess the situation, or help or direct in any way. Lord Methuen was five miles behind Wauchope at Magersfontein; he did not intervene or take any action until well into the day and long after the disaster had occurred. It is noteworthy that these four deaths of major-generals in action leading forces of only Brigade strength or less, all occurred during the poor period of British Generalship. Clearly bravery had nothing to do with the then low standard of command or tactics.

Frontages occupied by armies both in attack and defence have largely reflected the weapons and tactics in use. In the 'Mediaeval Triangle', where disciplined cohesion was the only formation known, and where the range of the bow and arrow was so limited, men were packed close to each other and close behind each other. At Crecy 30,000 Englishmen covered only two thousand yards, at Agincourt the 30,000 Frenchmen attacked on a frontage of two thousand five hundred. At Ramillies, Marlborough's army of 55,000, spreading out somewhat, had a frontage of four thousand yards, while at Waterloo Wellington's 65,000 covered four and a half miles. Rorke's Drift and Isandhlwana, both freak actions, took little space, and cannot be included in this broad survey, but the relationship of numbers, employed to yards occupied applies markedly to Modder River, Magersfontein, Colenso and Spion Kop. It is only when the period from 1914 onwards is considered that an entirely new situation arises. Deployment—'Extended Orders'—has replaced 'Shoulder-to-Shoulder'. Co-hesion by massed discipline is replaced by intelligent use of ground by lance-corporals and privates, forced on them by modern rifle fire and machine guns. As a result, units are much 'thinner' on the ground presenting a more dispersed target in order to get forward under fire and numbers to yards or even miles has greatly decreased.

The adoption of these broad frontages started at Mons, where General Smith-Dorrien's 11 Corps of 3rd and 5th Divisions—about 30,000 men had to hold twenty-one miles of the Mons-Condé Canal, while three days later this same Corps, now joined by 4th Division from England, covered thirteen miles at Le Cateau, one of the classic rearguard actions of military history. Including reserve companies, battalions and brigades not in direct contact with the enemy infantry, but belonging to Divisions holding the line, and the artillery, this works out at three men per yard. At Crecy there were fifteen to the yard, and at Ramillies fourteen. Wellington had nine to the yard at Waterloo. On the first day of the Battle of the Somme, 1st July 1916—fourteen Divisions advanced on a frontage of eighteen miles at five men per yard. El Alamein took ten miles for seven divisions, three men per yard.

A most important conclusion to be drawn from these surveys of battlefields and their appearance today is the least expected. It is the 'unwisdom' of ever writing an account of a battlefield and its battle unless the site has been actually visited.

Recently the author met and chatted to perhaps the most eminent living British historian. He was amazed to learn that this great man had not visited several of the sites of famous battles about which he has so graphically and absorbingly written. When asked whether he believed it was possible to see the French advance from a certain point in the English line at Crecy he confessed he did not know, having never been there. Yet Crecy is the second nearest battlefield to Great Britain on the Continent of Europe being only sixty-five miles from Dungeness. (Dunkirk is fifty miles from Dover).

Of a well-known battle there are so many descriptions and plans of the ground. All seem to differ from each other in minor details yet so many of these apparently unimportant details did, in fact, effect the tactics.

The Official History (nearly always accurate in recent years), the

Times History, 'eye witness' accounts, the well-written and documented book for which much research has been done years after, are all good and usually reliable, but many differ in minor points. But the fanciful flowery 'story' usually written soon after the action, often creates quite a different impression of the facts and the ground. Having read them all, the reader is confused not as to what happened so much as what the ground was, in fact, like. He does not feel certain that some of the writers have not perhaps grossly exaggerated, or failed to stress, some physical feature that vitally effected the action. He can only be sure by visiting the site, and thereby satisfying himself as to what in fact was and is, there, how much was visible from some point. If he has an 'eye-for-country', he will bring back a mental photograph that is precise, and, of course, correct.

The ridge at Waterloo is merely a very gradual slope the top of which provides a good—no more—position for infantry. It is no obstacle for cavalry at all and only very slightly hindered the Old Guard on foot. Yet historians make much of it. The same applies to the ridge at Poitiers, and its existence would not be noticed by the visitor had not the historians in the past laid stress on it. Even Fortescue in his monumental classic, *The History of the British Army*, refers to the very slight depression in front of Maupertuis as a 'ravine', and it appears from his sketch map that the advancing French infantry must have climbed down and up its sides. The slight rise does not cause even a cyclist to change gear, and any ravine that had been there in 1356 would today, if not deeper, still be very obvious. There is no sign of one. He also says that the Black Prince took up a position facing north-east whereas, of course, it was north-west.

The slopes down to the brook Nebel, and then up to the stockade around the village of Blenheim, are barely noticeable. The Nebel can easily be jumped with a run, yet it appears as a feature worth mentioning by several historians. Conversely the gradient of the slope up to Ramillies is not only considerable but the slope is very much longer than that at Waterloo, yet the advance of the British troops up it is rarely mentioned as having been in any way retarded.

There are many other examples of where the true shape of the ground, its features, and their effect on the battle should be seen at first-hand for an accurate appraisal to be made. The forming of such an appraisal in this way is the object of this book.

INDEX